Jane-Frances Kelly was Cities Prog
from 2009 to 2014. She has led strategy work for the United Kingdom, Queensland, Victorian and Commonwealth governments. Prior to moving to Australia in 2004, she spent three years in the British Prime Minister's Strategy Unit.

Paul Donegan is Fellow, Cities at the Grattan Institute. He has helped governments tackle some of Australia's biggest social and economic challenges, as a Commonwealth and state public servant, ministerial adviser and at the Grattan Institute.

CITY LIMITS

Why Australia's cities are broken and how we can fix them

Jane-Frances Kelly and Paul Donegan

MELBOURNE UNIVERSITY PRESS
An imprint of Melbourne University Publishing Limited
11–15 Argyle Place South, Carlton, Victoria 3053, Australia
mup-info@unimelb.edu.au
www.mup.com.au

First published 2015
Text © Grattan Institute, 2015
Design and typography © Melbourne University Publishing Limited, 2015

Cover design by Nada Backovic
Typeset by Typeskill
Printed in Australia by McPherson's Printing Group

National Library of Australia Cataloguing-in-Publication entry

Kelly, Jane-Frances, author.
City limits: why Australia's cities are broken and how we
   can fix them/Jane-Frances Kelly and
   Paul Donegan.
9780522868005 (paperback)
9780522868012 (ebook)

Includes index.

Urbanization—Australia.
Sociology, Urban—Australia.
City planning—Australia.
Cities and towns—Australia—Growth.
Community development, Urban—Australia.

Donegan, Paul, author.

307.760994

CONTENTS

Introduction

Australia is a nation of city-dwellers. Many of the joys of Australian life—its energy, optimism, cultural diversity, good food, green space and passion for sport and the outdoors—are found in cities. Many of its problems are as well.

Home ownership among younger people is declining, while renters, who make up one in four households, face insecurity and instability. As more people live further from city centres, traffic congestion is getting worse. For many, commuting is becoming intolerable. Social isolation is deepening, while polarisation between rich and poor, young and old, the inner city and suburbs, continues to grow. Failure to manage our cities well is hurting our economy.

This is a book about these problems, and how to solve them. Over the next eight chapters, we will explore what life is like today in Australia's cities. We will meet individuals, couples and families all struggling with situations our cities have imposed on them. In a few cases names have been changed at a person's request, but all case studies are of real people in real situations.

Across the world, leaders, policymakers and experts are paying increasing attention to cities and the benefits they bring. Developing countries know that rapid urbanisation is good for the living standards of their population. Australians are lucky that so many of us already live in cities. But we barely recognise our luck, and we're in danger of wasting it.

Partly this happens because we're complacent about our cities. They aren't central to our national identity. Australian cities rank highly on international 'liveability' league tables, giving us an excuse to ignore their problems. But many Australians' lived experience of cities is quite different from what international rankings designed for globetrotting executives suggest.

Chapter 1 asks why we live in cities, and looks at their evolving role in Australian history. It looks at how cities work, the trade-offs and hard decisions they confront us with, and what we need from them.

Chapter 2 looks at how we depend on cities for jobs and good living standards in the evolving global economy. We see how the greatest concentrations of economic activity in Australia are not in the Pilbara and other mining regions, but in the centres of our largest cities. To be productive, businesses need a choice of potential employees, while employees likewise benefit from as wide a choice of potential employers as possible. The chapter asks whether Australian cities do a good job of connecting people and jobs—a critical task in an economy where we increasingly rely on our brains to earn a living.

Chapter 3 looks at how cities affect the opportunities available to us—the 'fair go'. Being able to get to a good choice of jobs in a reasonable commute time is vital to individuals. If people have no choice but to live far from jobs and transport, they will have fewer jobs they can get to, making it harder to build their skills, and making them more vulnerable if they lose their job. Difficult and expensive commutes can also take a considerable toll on family life, leaving many women in particular to face very hard choices.

Of course, we are not just workers and employees. Chapter 4 looks at social connection, perhaps our most important psychological need, and how our cities can help or hinder it. At a time when single-person and single-parent households are growing fast, we look at how limited housing choices and inadequate transport leave many at risk of isolation and loneliness.

Chapter 5 looks at how the current housing market often works against the interests of the economy, the fair go and social connection, particularly in preventing people from living in the kinds of dwellings and neighbourhoods they would choose if they could. Myths about housing—that everyone wants to live in a detached house on a quarter-acre block, for example—are among some of the most embedded in Australian culture. In fact, Australians want a mixture of housing options, but the market isn't supplying them. Australia confronts an increasing divide between older home owners and a younger generation that is either locked out of home ownership or pushed to the fringes of cities, far from jobs and good transport.

Chapter 6 looks at how we get around our cities. More and more Australians face longer commutes over longer distances. Roads are congested, while public transport is not a realistic alternative to driving on congested roads in many areas, especially outside the inner city.

Chapter 7 looks at why we are not only failing to fix these urgent problems, but are barely recognising them. Cities are caught between the three tiers of Australian government, hardly registering on the agenda of many politicians. Yet their leadership is also poor because many residents are unwilling to consider the possibility that cities could get better. And so we get short-termism and failure: easy answers that don't work, plans that never happen, and more of the same things we've been doing, even when these make matters worse.

Yet there are reasons to be hopeful. Cities have been turned around before. Some overseas cities are models of change and decision-making that have involved all residents in shaping the future. The final chapter outlines the kinds of changes that would fix our cities, and build a richer, fairer, better Australia. The ideas exist. We only need the courage to adopt them.

Chapter 1

A nation of cities

IN AUSTRALIA WE BELIEVE many myths about our country. We think we are laid-back, but we work some of the longest hours in the world. In the spirit of Ned Kelly, we think of ourselves as anti-authoritarian, yet we comply with seatbelt and bicycle helmet regulations, and nearly all of us vote in elections, as the law requires.

When we Australians portrayed ourselves to the world in the opening ceremony of the 2000 Sydney Olympics, we chose 120 stockmen and women dressed in bush clothing and riding horses to the movie sound-track of *The Man From Snowy River*. Similarly, all but one of the thirty-nine drawings in the Australian passport depict flora, fauna and outdoor recreation, while the thirty-ninth is an outback pub. Citizens of one of the most urbanised nations on the planet carry an identity document that does not depict a single feature of any Australian city or town.

A greater proportion of Australians live in cities than nearly any other country. Sydney, Melbourne, Brisbane, Perth and Adelaide all have populations of more than a million. Together they house more than three in five Australians. Three-quarters of Australians live in cities with a population above 100 000, compared to 68 per cent of Americans, 71 per cent of Canadians and 62 per cent of people in the United Kingdom.

Australia's cities date from European settlement: the first settlers landed at Sydney Cove in 1788. Subsequent permanent colonial settlements included Hobart and Newcastle in 1804, Moreton Bay (now Brisbane) in 1824, Swan River (now Perth) in 1829, Adelaide and Port Phillip (now Melbourne) in 1836.

The discovery of gold in the mid-nineteenth century transformed the Australian economy. In just twenty years the population grew from 430 000 to 1.7 million. Aside from this first—and biggest—mining boom, agriculture dominated the early Australian economy. Shortly after Federation, in 1906, almost half of Australia's four million-strong population lived on rural properties or in small towns of fewer than 3000 people. Many were market towns serving the agricultural economy. Only about one in three Australians lived in a city of at least 100 000 people.

The legacy of our historical dependence on the bush is powerful. In 1901 a third of Australian workers were employed in agriculture, forestry, fishing or mining. Australian ingenuity—including inventions such as the stump-jump plough—made our farmers some of the most productive in the world. Until well into the twentieth century we depended on wool as our main export. The men who produced it came to epitomise what it was to be Australian.

But we are no longer a nation of farmers, graziers, shearers and drovers. The days of the economy riding on the sheep's back are long gone. Wool is now much less important as an export, even if the phrase still evokes the importance the agricultural industry had to the country's wealth. The volume of agricultural production continues to increase, in no small part through the increasing role of machines, and the sector is still a big exporter. But today agriculture employs only 3 per cent of the Australian workforce and contributes about 2 per cent of our national income.

After World War II came the rise of manufacturing as Australia's dominant industry. Around 1960, more than a quarter of all working Australians worked in manufacturing. The industry generated almost a third of our income.

With the rise of manufacturing, Australia's prosperity shifted to big cities, and often to their suburbs. Many people migrated there from rural areas, drawn by the prospect of jobs in manufacturing. By the end of Robert Menzies' record term as prime minister in 1966, more than three in five Australians lived in cities of more than 100 000 people.

The manufacturing industry greatly influenced the layout of cities. Many manufacturers, needing large amounts of land, located their factories where it was plentiful and affordable. Suburbs away from city centres had far lower rents and less congestion. Western Sydney became Australia's largest manufacturing region. The outer suburbs of Melbourne and Adelaide became home to many industrial plants, including car manufacturers such as Ford and General Motors Holden.

Postwar growth in car ownership made possible the shift to a manufacturing economy with a strong suburban presence. 'It is easy to forget just how liberating the car was,' write city planning and economics experts Marcus Spiller and Terry Rawnsley. It delivered an enormous boost to productivity by giving people access to a wider selection of jobs. 'Skills were better matched to industry needs and workers acquired new skills more rapidly, simply because of the mobility offered by the car.'

Car ownership and dispersed employment opportunities enabled many people to build houses in what were then outer suburbs of Australia's cities—places such as Altona in Melbourne, Silverwater in Sydney and Acacia Ridge in Brisbane. Owning a detached house on a quarter-acre block came to be known as 'the great Australian dream'.

Growth in the manufacturing industry eventually began to decline as a proportion of the economy. In the last twenty years the number of people employed in manufacturing has broadly stood still as the nation's economy and population have grown. Manufacturing now employs less than 10 per cent of working Australians.

More recently, the mining boom has been pivotal to Australia's economic growth. Yet it is worth putting mining's importance to the economy into context. Since Federation in 1901, mining has never produced more than 10 per cent of gross domestic product (GDP). Today the industry employs 2 per cent of working Australians, while the Reserve Bank of Australia estimates that the Australian mining sector is 80 per cent overseas-owned. It is much less important to the economy now than manufacturing was in the 1960s.

While Australia's natural resource deposits are typically in remote areas, many mining-related jobs are not located in the Pilbara, the Hunter Valley or the Bowen Basin. In Western Australia, where the most productive mining regions are located, more than a third of people employed in mining actually work in Perth. These include geologists who assess mineral deposits, engineers who design mining equipment and programmers who develop mining software. All these highly skilled workers have enabled the Australian mining industry to be one of the most productive in the world.

Today, when more than three-quarters of Australians live in cities, the economy is no longer driven by what we make—the extraction and production of physical goods—but rather by what we know and do. Some of the highest recent employment growth has come from professional services such as engineering, law, accountancy and architecture, from construction—whether of housing, offices, mines or roads—and from health care to support an increasingly affluent and long-lived population. Today Australia's fourth largest export sector is educating international students—something we barely did thirty years ago. Like other advanced economies, our economy is becoming more knowledge-intensive, specialised and globally connected. We have limited control over these trends, but they present us with many opportunities. And as with other periods in our economic evolution, this kind of economy has implications for what happens where.

Yet old notions die hard. Legacies and myths about the Australian economy keep a powerful hold on the popular imagination. The reality is that cities, knowledge and services are the engines of the Australian economy today, even if the bush and primary production still carry a certain romance. It's probably more glamorous and exciting to think of ourselves as a nation of jackaroos or mine supervisors than desk-bound office-dwellers, sales assistants or nursing-home attendants. But the facts don't lie.

Cities generate most of our national income: 77 per cent. Big cities are especially important. Sydney, Melbourne, Brisbane, Perth and Adelaide together generate two-thirds of Australia's income. Sydney alone produces around the same amount as the combined economic output of every city and town of less than 100 000 people, and all rural and remote areas, across every state and territory. To make this contribution, Sydney requires a tiny 0.16 per cent of Australia's land mass.

Australia's cities

Australia's biggest cities are large even by international standards. For example, the Netherlands has a population of seventeen million, roughly similar to Australia's twenty-three million. But its largest city, Amsterdam, is a quarter of the size of Sydney.

Australia's five largest cities are all home to more than a million residents. Together, Sydney and Melbourne are home to about two in five Australians. This has many advantages. As we will see, large cities provide more opportunities for their residents and larger markets for the businesses operating in them.

The concentration of people in a handful of cities has deep historical roots. Unlike most countries, in Australia towns were created first, and rural populations followed. Instead of emerging slowly from farming communities, our cities began as administrative bases for the colonies.

Although they have similar beginnings, Australian cities differ on many dimensions, from size and shape to demography and climate. Sydney has almost three times the population of Perth. The typical family in Canberra earns roughly 60 per cent more than the equivalent family in Hobart. Sixteen per cent of Adelaide's population is over sixty-five, compared to 6 per cent in Darwin.

In the thirty years to 2013, Australia's population grew by almost eight million people. Population growth comes from the number of children people have. It also comes from immigration. Natural increase (births minus deaths) and net migration (people arriving in Australia minus people departing) both contributed about four million new residents to Australia across this period.

Most of Australia's population growth happens in cities, with their greater opportunities for employment and for connecting with other people. Figure 1.1 shows how the size of Australia's five largest cities has grown between 1981 and 2011.

Figure 1.1: Population of Australia's five largest cities, 1981–2011

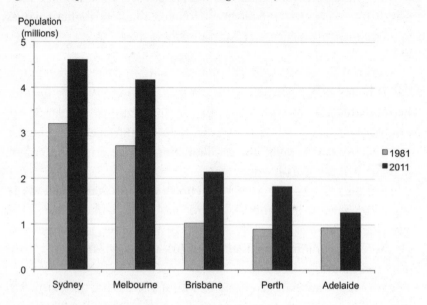

Australia's large cities also have diverse populations. One in four residents speaks a language other than English at home. One in three was born overseas.

Why people live in cities

Living in a city with many other people has many benefits. One of them is scale. The more people who come together, the more that businesses and employees can specialise. Pooling lots of people's needs and wants creates many opportunities to specialise in meeting common needs. The large populations of cities offer more sellers and buyers, looking to buy and sell more things.

When lots of people own cars, for example, different mechanics spring up. All compete with each other to earn income from customers. Some might expand to offer services across the city, offering consistency wherever customers live. Repco boasts about thirty authorised service centres in Brisbane, and KMart Tyre and Auto Service around the same. Others run more boutique businesses, providing customised services. Memory Lane Classic Auto Restorations in Perth specialises in repairing classic automobiles and vintage cars. Still other mechanics might make convenience their point of difference. Lube Mobile has offered services at their customers' homes since 1982.

A critical mass of mechanics means that suppliers of equipment such as hoists and car parts are more likely to do business in that city. The mechanics themselves benefit from more choice and lower prices as suppliers compete for their business. In cities with large populations, these kinds of benefits snowball across the economy.

Competition between mechanics drives prices down and gives customers more choice. People who want jobs as mechanics also benefit, as they can specialise in the kind of work that fits best with their own skills and interests.

Cities also make it possible to specialise in meeting more niche needs. For example, there is enough demand among chess-playing Melburnians to sustain a dedicated chess supply shop. Chess World is the kind of niche business that wouldn't be viable somewhere with a small population.

The diversity of needs and wants across cities' large populations makes it more likely that individuals can find work that makes the most of their abilities and experience. For example, the job market in Sydney, our biggest city, is extremely diverse. Cleaners, plumbers, manicurists, scientific researchers and senior executives of multinational companies can all find plenty of job opportunities. The Australian Bureau of Statistics divides the Australian job market into 474 kinds of role, encompassing everything from outdoor education guides to sales assistants, truck drivers and nurses. There are people doing 473 of these kinds of jobs in Sydney. The only group missing is aquaculture workers. So if it's possible to do something for a living in Australia, there's a very good chance you'll be able to do it in Sydney. Cities give people more choices.

Sydney's job market is also very deep. Its two million workers span many employers: sole traders; small, medium and large businesses; charities and government agencies. Not all of them will be hiring at any particular time. But the depth of the job market increases the likelihood of there being at least one employer looking to hire someone with any given set of skills.

Almost all migrants to Australia—85 per cent—settle in a city of more than 100 000. Half of them settle in Sydney or Melbourne. One of the reasons they do so is to maximise their chances of finding a job that makes the most of their skills and experience.

The number and range of needs and wants in cities—especially large ones—give people an incentive to train and develop their skills. Becoming an engineer requires four years of full-time study. Students are unlikely to undergo the long years of training—paying considerable fees and forgoing income they could otherwise be earning—unless they are reasonably confident there will be a demand for their engineering skills when they finish their degree. A large city is more likely than a small town to have enough demand for engineering services to justify students learning these skills. This is even more the case in specialised fields such as software, electronic or hydrological engineering.

In turn, universities, TAFEs and colleges are needed to enable people to develop their expertise. These institutions are more likely to flourish in places with sufficiently large populations to create the demand for the skills they teach, and from which they can recruit experts to provide the training they offer.

As a result, many people stay in cities and move to cities. They provide opportunities: to get a job, to get a better job, to start a business or to build skills.

After finishing school in Ballarat, Cameron Harrison completed an economics degree down the road in Geelong, but there was little local demand for the specialised economic modelling and analysis skills he had learned. He moved to Melbourne and found a job in the public service, helping to provide economic advice to the Treasurer.

Cameron's experience of moving to a large city to make the most of his skills is not unusual. Nor is moving to a larger city to develop those skills in the first place. In Ballarat, fewer than one in five people have a university degree, and the average income is about $50 000 a year. Melbourne's larger population creates much more demand and reward for more specialised skills. The financial pay-off from making the most of your skills in a big city can be substantial: the average income in Melbourne is almost a third higher than in Ballarat.

Cities also make it easier for households in which both partners want to work. They make it possible for each partner to get to jobs that best utilise their skills. There are simply more jobs and a broader range of jobs available.

The breadth and depth of city job markets also make it easier for people to bounce back if they lose their job. Cities also offer more opportunities for a person to find a better job than their current one. In rural areas, with smaller numbers of employers and ranges of jobs available, it can be much harder for people to find another job if work in their own industry is drying up.

At the start of 2014, SPC Ardmona's parent company, Coca-Cola Amatil, foreshadowed that SPC might close its fruit-canning operations near Shepparton, a regional centre of around 30 000 people in northern Victoria. Closure would have led to about 750 SPC employees losing their jobs, and wiped out a major source of income for local farmers, other SPC suppliers and the town as a whole. Shepparton's mayor, Jenny Houlihan, said the closure would leave 'an irreversible gap' in the local economy, causing the unemployment rate to jump by a third—to 10 per cent. In response to the potential damage SPC's closure would cause to the Shepparton community, the state government committed $22 million to enable SPC to continue its operations.

In context, the greater diversity of jobs available in large cities means someone losing their job will typically have a better chance to find a new job with a reasonably close fit for their skills and experience.

Mat Beyer worked for a Melbourne restaurant, serving customers and maintaining the restaurant's website and social media presence. The restaurant abruptly went out of business in early 2014, and Mat lost his job. But he was not unemployed for long. A small business specialising in developing websites for restaurants and helping them market themselves using social media employed him, and he was again using the skills he had built up at the restaurant.

The way cities help people to bounce back if they lose their job also makes it easier for people to take risks and start businesses of their own. If the business fails they have a good chance of finding another job in their field. By improving people's economic security, cities can also stimulate entrepreneurship.

Of course, people have other priorities beyond material needs. Social connection and health are among the most important. The reasons permanent migrants to Australia mainly settle in Sydney and Melbourne are not just economic, though these cities offer diverse economic opportunities to make the most of migrants' skills. Even more importantly for many, these cities are more likely than other places to have communities from the migrant's home country. These support networks can be vital for someone adapting to a new country and often a new language and way of life. They explain why many immigrants from Vietnam, for example, have settled in Springvale and Footscray in Melbourne, and Bankstown and Cabramatta in Sydney.

Wanting to connect with people with similar experiences and perspectives to our own is a human phenomenon, not just an immigrant one. Social connection is integral to wellbeing. Relationships with family and friends are among the most important things in our lives.

Cities offer more chances to connect with like-minded people than small communities. Just as cities give car-owners a wider choice of mechanics, they provide people with a wider choice of non-work activities and a wider range of possible social connections, including a wider choice of potential partners and friends. Throughout history people have moved to cities not just for economic opportunities, but also to connect with other people. While some people see cities as anonymous, uncaring places, others appreciate that in cities, if you want to live your life in a particular, even unusual, way you can.

The scale of cities permits specialisation, which means you are much more likely to come across people with similar interests, no matter how obscure. Cities that are big enough can support everything from amplified ukulele collectives to competitive dog grooming. Their populations make a critical mass—it's no surprise that major international bands touring Australia rarely venture beyond our big cities.

People living in cities live longer, on average, than people living in rural and regional Australia, and also typically enjoy better health. For example, a higher proportion of Australians living outside cities suffer from type 2 diabetes than do people within cities.

Higher incomes and better job prospects help to make city-dwellers more healthy than people in smaller communities. Better access to health care is also a factor. Specialised care such as cancer treatment and heart surgery is expensive, and since only small numbers of people have the skills to provide this care, it is almost inevitable that the small number of hospitals offering it will be located in the nation's biggest population centres.

The link between geography and health is reflected in people's own perspectives. Social research among New South Wales residents found that people in regional New South Wales are much more concerned about health care than are Sydney residents. In 2014, Rural Doctors Association president Dr Ian Kamerman was reported as saying that some rural residents have to wait up to six weeks just to see their GP, then face a wait of up to a month for tests such as ultrasounds, MRIs or CAT scans. City residents do not typically face such long waits.

The downsides of cities can be managed

Cities have polarised people throughout history. The eighteenth-century philosopher Jean-Jacques Rousseau called them 'the abyss of the human species'. In nineteenth-century novels, newly growing cities were often portrayed as 'antisocial'. Disconnected from tradition and nature, city-dwellers were depicted as culturally rootless and morally adrift. The desolate city found its opposite in idealised accounts of village life, where residents were still grounded in the seasonal rhythms of agriculture that bound them as a community.

As with most things in life, polarised positions are a poor guide to real experience. But there is no doubt that many people coming together in cities create challenges that must be managed. Our own choices often affect the choices other people can make, or they impose costs on others. When multiplied by thousands or millions of residents, these small individual choices can compound to have major effects. One person choosing to dispose of leaves and rubbish by burning them in a backyard incinerator is unlikely to have much impact on others. But if hundreds of thousands of city households did so, it could lead to significant air pollution and increases in breathing problems. Indeed, burning rubbish and garden waste used to be commonplace, but is now banned in many parts of Australia precisely because the airborne particles it created harmed residents.

Concentrating large numbers of people in cities has been associated with opportunity, freedom, material prosperity and social connection. But cities have also been associated with infectious disease, pollution, crime, traffic congestion and high housing costs.

Thankfully, we have largely learned how to manage infectious disease. Before the introduction of public sanitation, Australian cities were incubators for disease. In nineteenth-century Melbourne, most sewage and waste from houses emptied into open drains that flowed into street channels, to mix with waste from stables and industrial activity. Bad smells and rampant typhoid were endemic, inspiring one wit to name the city 'Smellbourne'. But from the 1890s these problems were progressively eradicated as the Melbourne Metropolitan Board of Works built an underground sewerage system.

Cities still carry health risks. If you're close enough to repair a person's car, exchange a chess set or play amplified ukulele together, you're probably close enough to pass on an illness. Yet our capacity to manage public health risks in our cities and elsewhere has improved dramatically. Measles is one of the most severe and highly infectious diseases of childhood. In 1925, a bad year for measles infections, there were 2742 cases per 100 000 of the population. A measles vaccine became widely available in Australia in 1970. In 2007 there were only 0.33 cases per 100 000 people.

Australia has also done well in controlling air pollution. State environment protection authorities restrict emissions that harm air and water quality from industrial emissions and burning waste in backyard incinerators. Australia has had road vehicle emission standards for new vehicles since the early 1970s and these have been progressively tightened over the subsequent decades. Fuel quality standards have increased, and leaded petrol was phased out at the end of 2001. As a result of these and other regulations, Australian cities have some of the cleanest and safest air in the world. In a World Health Organization survey of 1100 cities, only Canada rivalled Australia for having the world's least polluted air.

Cities are frequently associated with crime. Books and films routinely depict them as shadowy places of criminal activity. And it is true that in large cities a person is more likely to be a victim of property crime, yet he or she is less likely to be a victim of violent crime. While radio shock-jocks and television current affairs programs seem eager to convince us that crime is out of control, the reality is that crime rates have declined since 2005, and have declined fastest in big cities.

Yet other costs or downsides of living in cities endure, and some are increasing. There is a gulf in housing costs between Australia's big cities and the rest of the country. The typical monthly mortgage repayment across Australia's five biggest cities (Sydney, Melbourne, Brisbane, Perth and Adelaide) is $1989, much higher than outside those cities, where the typical repayment is $1572. Rents are also much higher in our big cities: typically $320 a week, compared to $225 across the rest of Australia.

Serious traffic congestion also only happens in cities. Big city roads are increasingly congested, as anyone stuck in the 4-hour morning peak on Sydney's M4 motorway can attest.

These downsides of living in cities can be managed, but we're not doing a good job of it. Later chapters will show how large cities' housing markets and transport systems are letting Australians down, and set out ways they can be made to work better.

Ultimately, whether you consider living in a city to be good or bad depends on your values and preferences, and even your stage of life. The pace of life is faster in cities than in regional areas or the bush. Within cities, inner-city areas may be louder and busier than suburbs further out. Some people find this exciting and stimulating, others find it unpleasant, even harrowing.

Some people find that the choices and relative anonymity of big cities gives them the freedom to be themselves, while many small town residents like knowing most of the people around them. An Australian phenomenon of the last fifteen years or so has been the 'sea changers' and 'tree changers' who leave big cities to escape the fast pace of life, to bring up children or to retire. Proximity to friends, family and social networks are important to both—it's a matter of taste and preference. In a liberal democracy, people get to choose.

But Australia is a nation of city-dwellers, and this is only intensifying. Cities of more than 100 000 people have grown by about a third since 1991, twice the growth experienced in rural areas and in cities of fewer than 100 000 people.

The Victorian Government has put a considerable amount of money and effort into promoting the benefits of living in regional Victoria. This has encompassed a television advertising campaign and an annual Regional Victoria Living Expo, established in 2012. Yet a 'Melbourne Living Expo' would be unnecessary, even implausible. Plenty of people are willing to move to or stay in Melbourne without any official prodding.

Living in cities involves trade-offs

People living in cities face many choices, including where to live, the kind of housing to live in, where to work and how to get there. Scarce land makes these choices more complicated. Land in the centre of a city or in desirable suburbs can't be increased or moved around. Nor can we build infinitely high buildings. Consequently there are unusually strong trade-offs in how we use land. If a person builds a house on a plot of land, it can't then be used for another house, a shop, or a road. Inevitably, some people end up unable to live in the suburb or location they would prefer.

So while we rely on markets to give us choices and get us what we want at a reasonable price, markets for housing in cities are very different from the market for mechanics.

The same goes for traffic. Far more people need or want to drive to inner-city employment centres, major sporting events or shopping centres in the lead-up to Christmas than there is space on the road. Congestion is inevitable. Only so many cars can travel down Parramatta Road or over the West Gate Bridge every hour. Much as drivers stuck in traffic might wish otherwise, the laws of physics are immutable.

The inevitable scarcity of land, especially land in desirable locations, means we face strong constraints in making choices that involve place: where to live, the kind of home we live in, how to get around and how close we live to family, friends, schools, transport and work. It means we are less likely to get everything we want. As in other markets, how much money we have to spend also restricts what we can get.

In addition, the choices on offer tend to come bundled together. The number of bedrooms in a home is often bundled with the type of home available. Most inner-city flats have one or two bedrooms. Of course, it is possible to build flats with more than two. But because the type of home and the number of bedrooms usually come bundled together, if a family requires a three-bedroom home, in practice the only viable option may be a detached house.

Housing is also often bundled with particular location and transport options. For example, lower-priced detached houses tend to be located in outer suburbs. Many have limited access to public transport or to services such as hospitals. Detached houses can of course be located near public transport or hospitals, but in practice this is not the bundle on offer to many first home buyers at a price they can afford. If a family requires a large home to bring up children, the parents may have to endure a long commute to work by car. They're not choosing the latter, they're putting up with it.

It isn't just the physical characteristics of a dwelling that get bundled up. Proximity to certain features, such as an ocean view or a good school, in effect gets bundled with the housing in that area and shapes its price. The limits on land close to the good school or ocean view exacerbates this effect.

Another reason that the housing market differs from the market for mechanics is that the former is very slow to change. Many people move house only infrequently: about once a decade on average across the Australian population. More than a quarter of all adults stay in the same home for fifteen years or more. Therefore the range of housing choices available to us may not reflect what we want very well. In the market for mechanics, changes in customer preferences lead an enterprising mechanic to provide fast services, to specialise in servicing particular kinds of car or to fix customers' cars at their homes. All these new practices can be introduced relatively quickly.

Mechanics can also quickly remove from the market products and services that no longer meet customers' needs. Housing, by contrast, endures for a very long time once it is built. Inner suburbs, such as Surry Hills or Fitzroy, are expensive and desirable for their proximity to city centres and the lifestyle they offer. This is in spite of the often cramped and deteriorating housing in those areas, built in response to the preferences of people many years ago.

The amount of new housing constructed every year is a tiny proportion of the total number of homes in a city. Of course, the new housing that gets built today in turn further constrains what tomorrow's buyers will be able to afford and live in. Moreover, the needs of people building and buying new housing are probably not representative of the housing needs of the city as a whole.

Housing markets are notorious for not responding quickly to what people want. Developing land and building homes takes time. More fundamentally, the restrictions and regulations governing housing— what can be built where and who gets a say in it—are far more onerous than the rules governing how mechanics operate. These constraints, which this book will consider further, shape how much housing gets built, what kinds of homes get built and therefore the range of choices on offer.

Our cities are the results of decisions made by the people who governed, worked and lived in them in the past. We cannot wipe cities clean and start again. Nor would we necessarily want to. For example, train lines built in the nineteenth century continue to move people to work, school and leisure activities today.

Often, though, the way we live and work has changed enough to make it hard to live with yesterday's needs and decisions. Over time, the results of individual decisions in turn can constrain the decisions other people are able to make. When multiplied by thousands or millions of residents living in a city, small individual choices can add up to major effects, and can create big problems.

This book seeks to cast more light on how these trade-offs work, who they affect, and how we can improve the choices available to all our cities' residents.

What we need from our cities

There are different ways of thinking about what matters most in cities. Because we love to compare ourselves with others, international rankings are one method of measuring cities that always makes the news.

Two well-known rankings are *The Economist*'s Liveability Index, and Mercer Consulting's Quality of Living Rankings. They rate cities according to the quality of infrastructure, cost of living, cultural opportunities, crime rates and so on. Australian cities usually do well in these rankings, but they tend to take a narrow perspective—that of globally mobile, highly educated professionals. Indeed, Mercer describes its index as a product designed to 'Compare cities and set hardship allowances for your internationally mobile workforce'. The rankings say much less about whether a city is liveable from the perspective of ordinary residents of those cities. (Quality of life is a real and important phenomenon, and the term 'liveable' often comes to mind when we are asked to describe our cities' identity. But it is also one of those terms that can seem to have as many definitions as users, so its explanatory power is limited. It's no accident that this is the last time the word will appear in this book.)

So what matters? What should we care about most?

Cities are where most people live their lives. We should judge our cities according to how well they meet the needs of all residents, insofar as cities can shape those needs. Basic needs such as having somewhere safe to live; a job that provides a decent income, and grows our skills so we can keep earning income in the future; healthy relationships with family and friends who care about us. Also essential is a degree of control over our lives, including scope to make meaningful choices about how and where we live, our social and family life, our education and that of our children, our job, how we balance work with the rest of our lives, and how we might have a comfortable retirement.

Cities have a more partial effect on other human needs. They undoubtedly influence the health of their residents. Today we take for granted regular garbage collection and sewerage systems that help prevent disease. Also important are the location and accessibility of health services, the degree to which cities enable walking and cycling and whether residents can access parks and sports grounds. These elements can either promote or discourage healthy lives. But cities are far less influential on our health than are other factors, such as our genes, or whether we smoke.

We live in cities because they offer the best chance to earn income, use our skills and connect with other people. They are the engines of the economy, and contain diverse mixes of people. This book therefore concentrates on how well Australian cities support the economy, provide access to opportunity and promote social connection for all their residents.

Being a nation of city-dwellers has helped Australia become one of the world's most prosperous countries. Cities generate most of our income. They provide the setting for us to connect with others—whether family, partners, friends, neighbours, workmates or strangers.

As the global economy grows ever more connected, specialised and knowledge-intensive, it turns out to be a stroke of luck that most Australians live in cities. But if our cities don't work, if we fail to manage the downsides of living in them—expressed in limited housing choices, poor access to jobs, traffic congestion and loneliness—then we squander our luck. The future of our cities will shape everything from national prosperity to the quality of everyday life. Yet there is little appreciation of the hard choices we face. The fate of cities barely registers on the agenda of our politicians. This book seeks to change that, in order to give cities their rightful place in the Australian story.

Chapter 2

Cities and the economy

Since European settlement, the driving force behind the Australian economy has constantly evolved—from agriculture and primary production, to manufacturing in the twentieth century, to today's knowledge-intensive economy. Similar shifts have occurred across the developed world.

Each of these kinds of economic activity has a geographic dimension. Agriculture and primary production almost exclusively occur in rural and regional Australia. The suburbs of many Australian cities grew hand-in-hand with manufacturing. Knowledge-intensive businesses—which are the most productive today—tend to cluster and thrive in the centres of large cities.

In contrast to the days when Australia's economy relied on gold and fleece, today's economy is extremely concentrated. In fact, 80 per cent of economic activity takes place on just 0.2 per cent of Australia's land mass. The vast majority of economic activity takes place in Australia's large cities—they are the backbone of our economy. Within these cities, economic activity is heavily concentrated, making central business districts and inner-city areas critically important to the nation's prosperity.

* * *

When the Boston Consulting Group's (BCG) 10-year lease in Sydney's CBD expired in 2013, the business faced a difficult decision. There was no doubt the business had outgrown its home in the 53-storey Chifley Tower. There was also no doubting the high costs of staying in the city centre. Sydney's punishing rents were some of the world's highest. They seemed to jump, with unnerving reliability, by up to 4 per cent each year.

A number of options were proposed, including shifting the business's headquarters to suburbs such as Bondi or Chatswood. Managing partner Ross Love swiftly rejected these scenarios. The proximity to clients, the easy road and rail access to the airport, and shorter commute times for staff, were obvious advantages to remaining in the city centre. Love was not even convinced by an attractive alternative in an historic warehouse at The Rocks, on the CBD fringe. It offered more space for roughly half the cost, but he sensed the new location would be deeply unpopular with staff. It was an extra 10-minute walk from the train station and near a more subdued retail environment.

The central city location was vital for finding and keeping the best employees, for winning what is sometimes called the war for talent, whether the talent comes from Sydney's suburbs, the rest of Australia or overseas. So Love and his senior colleagues agreed that the benefits outweighed the costs, and reaffirmed BCG's commitment to the CBD.

BCG ended up shifting to a new $800 million office development in Pitt Street Mall in the middle of the CBD. They leased three of the building's forty-three floors, and secured ample growing room for the future.

The engineering business Sinclair Knight Merz (SKM) faced a similar choice when it needed to renovate its ageing Melbourne office in the suburb of Armadale, about seven kilometres from the CBD. It was close to a train station and two tram routes, had good access to main roads and offered lots of parking. The CBD alternative was on congested Flinders Street, had no car parking and cost 75 per cent more per square metre than the company's suburban home. Yet SKM decided not to renovate but to move its 850 staff into the heart of town.

In the end, the decision paid off, despite the far higher cost. The prospect of cross-city travel had in the past put off some skilled workers and top graduates from the west and north of Melbourne. Being in the city has allowed SKM to hire from a deeper talent pool. It makes coordination on projects with other businesses and with government easier. Clients are far more likely to come to SKM at its new address, and staff are better able to connect with potential clients or with colleagues in their industry. Offsite meetings are usually a short walk or tram trip away. For SKM workers the city is a rich, supportive ecosystem. Being there is not just good, but essential to success in their high-knowledge line of work.

* * *

BCG and SKM are far from alone. Across Australia and the world, knowledge-intensive work that generates high levels of wealth is concentrating in major cities. More than that, it is clustering in very small areas within those cities—usually in or near CBDs. Figure 2.1 is a map of where goods and services are produced in Sydney by their dollar value.

The map shows that the Sydney CBD, including Haymarket and The Rocks, produces much more than any other small area in Greater Sydney: almost a quarter of the metropolitan area's economy, with only 13 per cent of the two million-strong workforce.

The area with the next highest level of economic activity is North Sydney, which produces around $10 billion of goods and services, compared to $64 billion in the CBD. As with the CBD, the North Sydney commercial area is dominated by professional and financial services. A number of large insurance and financial services companies such as MLC and AMP built their headquarters or large offices in North Sydney in the mid-twentieth century, combining the benefits of then relatively affordable land with proximity to the CBD.

Macquarie Park, Ryde, Pyrmont, Ultimo and around Mascot airport are also more productive than most parts of Sydney, though far less than the CBD. The same goes for Parramatta and nearby Homebush Bay, further west from the city centre.

Figure 2.1: Where goods and services are produced in Sydney

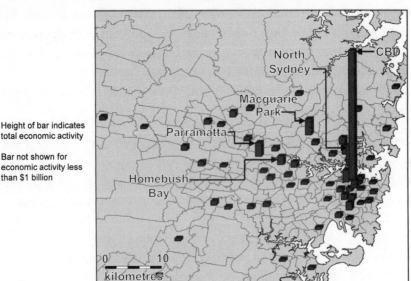

The same phenomenon can be observed in Melbourne, Brisbane, Perth and Adelaide. The central business districts of Sydney and Melbourne—around 10 square kilometres in total—produce $118 billion worth of goods and services, almost 10 per cent of the whole Australian economy. This is more than three times the contribution of the entire agricultural sector.

Central business districts have by far the biggest concentration of highly skilled and productive work. But other areas, where businesses doing this kind of work cluster together, are also important. These include Ryde in Sydney, where pharmaceutical and other businesses are concentrated; Clayton in Melbourne, home to advanced manufacturing activity and Monash University; and Fortitude Valley, where advertising and media businesses cluster just north-east of the Brisbane CBD. Nonetheless, the gulf in economic activity between city centres and other parts of our cities is vast. For example Parramatta, often said to be Sydney's second CBD, produces just a tenth of the value of goods and services generated in the CBD.

Knowledge-intensive businesses are clustering together in the age of the Internet, when technology was supposed to decentralise workplaces, allowing businesses to locate in the cheapest places, connected to the rest of the economy by high-speed broadband.

It seems strange. Surely being located close to other businesses and having skilled employees near each other should matter less in the time of the telephone, email, webinars and Skype? Surely technology would enable us to work from home or anywhere? Wouldn't the computer industry, above any other, be the best at videoconferencing and collaborating remotely?

The evidence says otherwise. Silicon Valley is the world's most famous example of clustering in one area. Finance is another of the world's most digitised industries, yet the head offices of Australia's major banks are concentrated in just a couple of streets in Sydney and Melbourne, even though CBD rents are the highest in the city, parking is prohibitively expensive and the traffic is terrible.

Knowledge-intensive jobs cluster together

The way that businesses cluster together is critical to the modern, high-value workforce. The more knowledge-intensive a job is, the more important it is to find the best person to fill that role. This is vital for professional services businesses such as SKM and BCG that sell nothing other than their knowledge and expertise. But finding staff who best fit the job is very important for any business where the work involves knowledge, expertise, judgement and learning. These jobs represent an increasingly large proportion of the Australian economy, and an increasingly large number of jobs.

Locating in the centre of cities gives businesses access to the largest possible number of potential employees. This makes good job matching—the fit between the skills required for a particular role and the worker who fills it—more likely. With knowledge-intensive jobs in particular, the better the match, the more productive the employee, and the business, will be.

Having lots of similar jobs located near each other works for employees too. People get more experience and skills when they are surrounded by experienced people working in the same field. A wider choice of jobs gives people the best chance of finding a role that makes the most of their skills. These jobs will also tend to be more fulfilling and better paid. Further, being around other businesses like themselves allows businesses to work with and learn from each other as well as to compete.

This is not a story predominantly about some industries rising while others fall. Work in every sector of the economy is becoming increasingly knowledge-intensive. Even as their share of the Australian economy declines, agriculture and manufacturing are becoming more and more sophisticated.

Jim Gardner (name has been changed) runs a second-generation family business, based in Spotswood in Melbourne, specialising in air compressor technology. Years ago the business mainly made compressors for industrial uses in other factories. While the business still makes compressors, over time they have increasingly made money from their knowledge. Patent revenues and research partnerships with companies in India, China and Belgium are now an important source of income.

Working with other organisations to grow the business's knowledge has been essential to staying competitive. Jim's business has also collaborated with the University of Melbourne's engineering department for many years, taking in engineering students for internships, and sponsoring masters and PhD students. Jim values working with them: 'I get updated by them about the new software and processes they're studying, and they bring fresh energy and enthusiasm that I feed off. But while they're fantastic, they're simultaneously hopeless because they have no experience of the real world. So it's a constant cross-fertilisation'.

Modern work is increasingly specialised. But this does not mean people pursuing their various specialisations can be isolated from each other. When different businesses work together on complex projects, they need to be close.

A construction project such as building a freeway or a train line is not simply a matter of pouring cement or laying sleepers. Such a project requires finance to get it off the ground—often a consortium of banks, fund managers and other investors. Engineering expertise is essential. Urban design, architecture and landscaping will probably also be required. Sophisticated electronics and information technology may be incorporated into signalling, tolling or traffic management systems.

And construction companies and a small army of subcontractors are needed to get the project built. All these different businesses need to work closely together if they are to navigate the complexities of delivering such a project, drawing on many different sources of expertise. Being located near each other makes this easier.

Being close to suppliers, customers and rivals also helps businesses generate new business opportunities, new ideas and better ways of working. The phenomenon is not new. The economist Alfred Marshall explained the great productivity of cotton mills in Lancashire in the mid-nineteenth century. Different mills learned from each other simply by being clustered together and observing what others were doing— Marshall described the knowledge as being 'in the air'. Clustering allowed Lancashire to compete successfully with the rest of Britain while paying wages that were almost a third higher than the rest of the country, and even to compete with the rest of the world while paying wages that were six times the Japanese and nine times the Chinese level. It produced lots of suppliers, skilled workers, technological breakthroughs and cheap, high quality cotton.

Face-to-face still matters

Internet company Yahoo made headlines in 2013 by banning its employees from working from home. The memo that the company sent to its employees read:

> To become the absolute best place to work, communication and collaboration will be important, so we need to be working side-by-side. That is why it is critical that we are all present in our offices ... Some of the best decisions and insights come from hallway and cafeteria discussions, meeting new people, and impromptu team meetings ... We need to be one Yahoo, and that starts with physically being together.

Google agrees. Its chief financial officer, Patrick Pichette, has said that 'as few as possible' employees work from home because it is harder for them to collaborate and come up with new ideas.

Workplaces are centres of face-to-face contact. Offices, far from being a dying breed, are thriving. Why are so many people stuck in traffic, or travelling on trains and buses, commuting to the busiest parts of the city, where jobs and production are most intensely concentrated? Why is face-to-face interaction still so important? Part of the answer is that we are human.

New ideas often emerge from combining and recombining knowledge to come up with new products and ways of doing things. Workers build on each other's thoughts, solve problems, break through impasses. These complex conversations are best had in person. Face-to-face talk allows a depth and speed of feedback that is impossible in other forms of communication. You can interrupt, re-explain, see whether people look like they understand you and, if not, adjust how you are explaining midstream. These feedback cycles are so quick they are virtually instantaneous.

Face-to-face interaction also matters because of the kind of animal we are. Humans are quick to sense non-verbal messages about emotions, cooperation and trustworthiness. Personal contact gives us so much more to go on, from the warmth of a handshake to the sincerity of a look. We can more easily judge whether people are genuine, or uncertain, or even lying. In crime dramas, no detective ever interrogates a suspect on Skype.

Because of this, the more business is connected to the rest of the world, the more important local contact becomes. Even as the cost of connecting across distance falls, the value of being close to others rises. Globalisation and close physical proximity turn out to be joined at the hip.

Jim Gardner confirms this. The first time we called him to ask for an interview, we woke him up in the middle of the night in Belgium, where he was spending a few weeks working with researchers in a partner's factory. He says that spending time with business partners in person remains critical: 'the face-to-face is about building the relationship and the trust to where working apart is possible, and then about regularly reinforcing those bonds. Business is a fundamentally human activity, it always has been and always will be'.

Jim's company is far from alone. Many businesses are involved in complex long-distance supply chains. Often these span continents, time zones and languages. The depth and richness of face-to-face communication helps enable businesses in these global supply chains to work together despite language, cultural, legal and other differences.

The role of caffeine

Melbourne's CBD has transformed since the early 1990s. Twenty-five years ago people used to joke that tumbleweeds would roll down the city's streets by 6 p.m. on weekdays. Now there are hundreds of restaurants and cafes, all full of people, day and night.

Almost three times as many people live in the CBD as in 1991, but this isn't just an evening or weekend phenomenon. Stand on any street corner during a working day, and you can sense the buzz. People walking in groups, bumping into each other, watching each other, on pavements and trams, in cafes and restaurants.

New ideas often come from interacting with other people. Cafes provide a neutral space for workers to share news and information, a process crucial to the innovation and deal-making essential to the modern economy. It's no surprise there are lots of cafes near knowledge-intensive economic activity. Businesses need access to places where people meet informally, and cafes are perfect for that. On any working day, many meetings take place in cafes. Certainly the nearest cafe to a city workplace sometimes seems like an extra meeting room—some weeks employees see their barista more often than they do some of their colleagues.

In one sense, caffeine fuels modern capitalism. Indeed, the link between capitalism and coffee goes back a long way. The ideas of the Enlightenment that underpinned the birth of modern capitalism were hotly debated in London coffee houses in the seventeenth and eighteenth centuries. The London Stock Exchange, one of the world's oldest, started life when a list of stock and commodity prices was issued at Jonathan's Coffee House in London in 1698.

Centuries later, and on the other side of the planet, cafes and restaurants are still places where financiers, professionals and others meet to share ideas, gossip about who is doing what where, and do deals.

The professional services business Deloitte is located in Sydney's city centre so it can be close to its clients. Deloitte also highly values the proximity of its staff to allied professionals such as lawyers, bankers and insurers. This allows for the exchange of ideas and expertise in the city's cafes and restaurants, as well as in their own offices.

For example, when a Deloitte's employee suggests to a client that they meet at a nearby cafe or restaurant that's 'halfway' between their respective workplaces, it is not just convenient but it also sets the right dynamic for the encounter.

'In-between' places such as streets and cafes also result in unplanned contact with others. This kind of contact helps to build networks of familiarity and trust, making it more likely that employees from different firms might collaborate on new projects, or create a new product in partnership. SKM staff say they often bump into professionals from other firms in the centre of Melbourne. The encounters build personal networks and share knowledge.

Technological advances such as email and videoconferencing will undoubtedly continue to change the way we work. They will make more flexibility possible, enabling some workers to telecommute part of the time. They will also help us to prolong and deepen relationships through more frequent opportunities for interaction. But because of how we create and exchange ideas—because we are human—technology will not erase the need for us to see each other in person.

More knowledge everywhere

So far we've mostly talked about the businesses and jobs clustered close to the centre of cities. We've seen how important they are to generating wealth. But while there are proportionally more jobs in city centres than any other part of cities, most jobs in major cities are not in CBDs. Many—such as teaching, running a medical practice or cutting hair—provide services directly to people, so they have to be located close to where people live.

Other businesses have higher priorities than having access to the widest possible number of potential employees. Trucking and warehousing businesses still benefit from getting the best worker for the job. But because cheap, plentiful land and avoiding traffic congestion are even more important, these businesses tend to locate in outer suburbs where land is cheaper, often close to freeways and with good links to ports and airports.

Across all industries, getting the right person for the job matters more than in the past. An employer with a large choice of potential employees is more likely to find a suitable person for the job than an employer with only a limited choice of potential employees. When they work well, cities play a vital role in making this possible by enabling large numbers of potential employees to live near a wide range of employers, and enabling them to get to those employers in reasonable commute times.

While the jobs in the inner city might typically be the highest skilled and highest paid, the trend towards skill exists right across the economy, not just in high-tech sectors or among highly paid consultants working in skyscrapers.

There are three related reasons for the increasing importance of skill that together are making it all the more crucial for employers to find the best person for the job. The first is the complexity of what we do at work. The second is growing levels of specialisation in our jobs that make it possible to handle the complexity of our work. The third is the increasing role that technology plays in just about every workplace.

In our jobs we're solving more complex problems than ever before. Figure 2.2 shows that the number of knowledge-intensive jobs among managers, professionals, technicians and skilled tradespeople has grown substantially in recent years. The number of lower-skilled jobs among salespeople, labourers, and clerical and administrative workers has grown much more slowly.

In order to deal with this complexity at work, we are better educated than ever. Many more people finish high school than they did twenty years ago, and many more of us go on to do post-secondary

Figure 2.2: Employment growth by job category, 1997–2012

education. In 2002, one in five Australians aged twenty-five to sixty-four had a bachelor degree or higher qualification from a university. Just ten years later, this proportion had risen above one in four. The proportion of people with no post-school qualifications dropped sharply over the same period.

We are also specialising in narrower fields of expertise so we can solve these increasingly complex problems at work. Thirty years ago universities produced 'engineers'. Now there are many different kinds: chemical, mechanical, electrical, materials, biomolecular and many others. There is now such a large body of knowledge in each engineering specialisation that nobody can be expected to develop a deep understanding of more than one field, given the amount of study involved.

Specialisation has been part of the way advanced economies work since it was first described by the father of economics, Adam Smith, in eighteenth-century Scotland. Today it is accelerating at an unprecedented rate. The phenomenon is most pronounced in knowledge-intensive jobs. But increasing levels of skill and specialisation can be seen right across the economy.

The use of technology as part of our work has grown exponentially in recent years. Technology has enabled all kinds of businesses to become more productive. Self-checkout machines in supermarkets reduce costs. Robots play an increasing role in the manufacturing sector. Forklift truck drivers in warehouses now depend on sophisticated logistics management systems. We do our banking online when and where it is convenient rather than having to queue up in business hours on a weekday to be served at a branch.

Of course, this more technology-intensive economy has downsides, too. Introducing online banking leaves banks with less need for tellers, and self-checkout machines reduce supermarkets' need for checkout workers. Some people who lose their jobs may struggle to find new ones. But few of us want to give up online banking in favour of queuing at a branch at a time most convenient for the bank. Banks would be even less eager to increase their costs in this way.

Like it or not, increasing levels of technology are a fact of life in the modern workplace. So businesses need employees who have the skills to harness its benefits.

Increasing levels of technology mean that more businesses need employees with higher and more specialised skills. Being able to access the widest choice of potential employees will make any kind of business more productive.

An increasingly skilled economy heightens the importance of cities to Australia's future prosperity. Their large populations and diverse economies create enough demand for highly skilled tasks and roles. For example, Sydney, Melbourne, Brisbane, Perth and Adelaide together account for less than two-thirds of Australia's population. But they account for almost three in four people with a university degree.

Connecting people and jobs

The forces shaping Australia's economy today all have a geographic dimension. Increasingly knowledge-intensive businesses place a premium on locating near each other. Their employees benefit from face-to-face contact, also requiring close proximity. The growing importance of skilled, and often highly specialised, employees makes it more important than ever for employers everywhere to have the largest number of potential employees to choose from.

These trends all contribute to intense concentrations of economic activity closer to the centre of cities. In all our major cities there are proportionally more jobs closer to the CBD than in suburbs far from the city centre. There are almost eight jobs for every ten residents of the suburbs within 10 kilometres of the Sydney city centre. The suburbs 10 to 20 kilometres from the city centre have less than half that employment density. And the parts of Sydney more than 20 kilometres from the CBD have only about three jobs for every ten residents. Half of Sydney's population live in these suburbs furthest from the city, but only about a third of the city's jobs are in these suburbs.

Jobs in Melbourne are similarly distributed relative to the city's population. In Brisbane and Perth jobs are even more heavily concentrated in the 10 kilometres closest to the city centre, partly because these cities have smaller populations than Sydney and Melbourne.

Cities that work well, that are doing their job as a city, have lots of jobs that can be reached by lots of workers within a reasonable commuting time. Connecting the most people to the most job opportunities is important in CBDs and suburbs alike.

Of course, all jobs are accessible if you are willing to commute for long enough. Yet few people want to spend more time commuting than they have to. Given current travel patterns in Australian cities, we defined a reasonable commute as forty-five minutes by car, and sixty minutes by public transport.

In the map of Sydney in Figure 2.3, the darkest areas are those in which residents can get to more than half of all the jobs in the city with a one-way driving time of forty-five minutes. The map shows how the amount of jobs that can be reached falls away markedly with distance from the CBD. Central parts of the city are where opportunity is located—the areas with the greatest concentrations of jobs and economic activity. But, for people living in much of western Sydney, along with other outer suburbs, large parts of the city are very difficult to commute to by car.

The situation is not quite as bad in Melbourne, as the map in Figure 2.4 shows. Nonetheless, people living in some outer suburban areas of

Figure 2.3: Access to jobs in Sydney in a 45-minute car trip

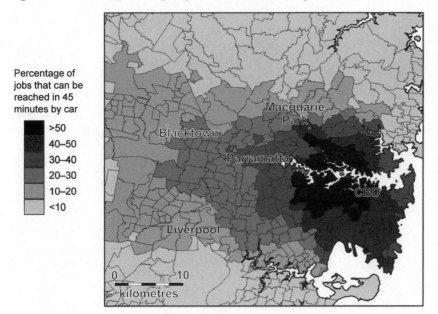

Percentage of jobs that can be reached in 45 minutes by car

- >50
- 40–50
- 30–40
- 20–30
- 10–20
- <10

Melbourne—for example Epping North or Point Cook—can reach just a tenth of all the city's jobs in a 45-minute drive.

Brisbane has a similar level of access to jobs by car as Melbourne. Access to jobs is better in Perth. Except for a few suburbs to the far north, south and east, it is possible to reach more than half the jobs in Perth from just about any home in the city within a forty-five minute drive.

For people commuting on public transport, the advantage of being close to the city centre is even more marked than it is for drivers. In the map of Sydney in Figure 2.5, the darkest areas are those in which residents can get to more than half of all the jobs in the city with a one-way public transport trip of sixty minutes. The map shows that access to jobs by public transport is patchy at best in most areas, and very poor in Sydney's west and south-west.

Similarly, large swathes of Melbourne, where most of the city's population lives, give poor access to jobs by public transport. The map in Figure 2.6 shows good public transport access to jobs rapidly diminishes beyond the inner suburbs.

Figure 2.4: Access to jobs in Melbourne in a 45-minute car trip

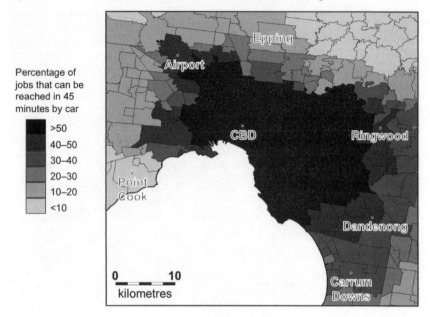

Figure 2.5: Access to jobs in Sydney in 60 minutes on public transport

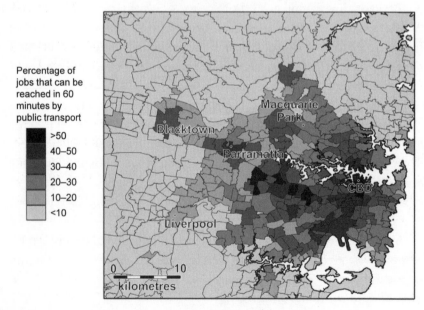

Figure 2.6: Access to jobs in Melbourne in 60 minutes on public transport

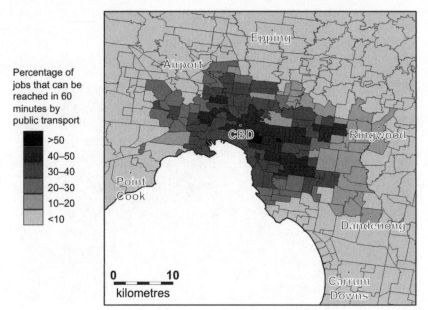

In most of Brisbane, the situation is worse. Fewer than one in ten jobs can be reached in a public transport journey of an hour (see Figure 2.7).

In all of Australia's big cities, there is a clear advantage to living close to the centre. A resident of central Melbourne can access 90 per cent of all the city's jobs by car within forty-five minutes, and just under half the jobs with a 1-hour public transport journey.

Outside the centre, by contrast, workers have access to a far smaller proportion of jobs. In parts of Sydney, only 14 per cent of jobs can be accessed by car and only one in ten by public transport. Our maps show sizeable areas of Australia's largest cities where less than 10, 20 or 30 per cent of jobs can be accessed within a reasonable commute time. At the extreme, there are suburbs in Melbourne, Brisbane and Perth where the share of jobs that can be accessed in under an hour by public transport falls below one in a hundred.

Their distance from most jobs makes residents of outer suburbs far more vulnerable if their industry declines or their employer goes out of

Figure 2.7: Access to jobs in Brisbane in 60 minutes on public transport

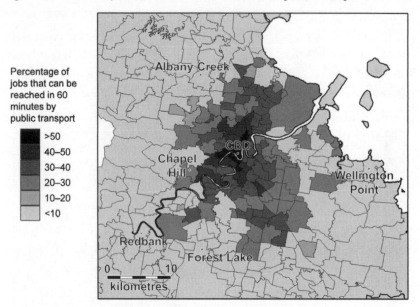

business, since they are able to easily reach far fewer alternative jobs than people who live closer to the centre.

Distance matters for employers, too. Employers in the centre of Australian cities can draw on the largest proportion of workers, although this varies widely by city and transport mode. Businesses in Melbourne's CBD can access just under half of the city's workers by car, and around a third by public transport. Sydney can offer its CBD employers access to less than a quarter of the city's workers by a 45-minute car trip, and 37 per cent by a 60-minute trip on public transport. In fact there are two Sydneys: a Sydney to the west where the labour market is thin—meaning the connections between jobs and people are poor—and a well-connected Sydney to the east.

Outside CBDs, there is also wide variation. Businesses located in Brisbane suburbs such as Chapel Hill can draw on almost half of Brisbane workers commuting for forty-five minutes by car, but only 6 per cent commuting for sixty minutes by public transport. Businesses in Melbourne suburbs such as Point Cook and Carrum Downs can draw on a third or almost a half of workers commuting by car respectively, but less than one in a hundred commuting by public transport.

It's hard to draw a direct link between people having more job choices and being better at their job. Most people won't change jobs at the drop of a hat to go and work for an employer where they can use their skills more productively. But in any given year, some people will, if given the opportunity.

International academic research has confirmed these phenomena. Studies in overseas cities show how increasing people's access to jobs within a reasonable commute time benefits both employees and employers. For instance, in the United States, making more jobs accessible in a reasonable commute time for people in a particular area has been shown to lead to higher wages for workers in that area. Doubling the number of jobs people in major cities could access within a 20-minute commute was associated with up to a 7 per cent boost to their wage.

Studies have shown that having a wider choice of potential employees is beneficial to employers too. In South Korea, increasing the number of jobs people could access in a reasonable commute time by 10 per cent meant that, on average, they were 2.4 per cent more productive. A 2.4 per cent boost may not sound like much. But by way of comparison, a 2.4 per cent boost to the Australian economy would involve the nation producing an extra $37 billion of goods and services—not a trivial figure.

Being able to get to more jobs didn't somehow make people better employees in their current role. But over time it meant people were more likely to end up working for an employer that was able to make better use of their skills.

Why this matters

The capacity of people and businesses doing knowledge-intensive work to come up with new ideas and better ways of doing things makes them vital for economic growth, and therefore the living standards of the whole country.

Knowledge-intensive jobs typically generate more wealth than other kinds of job. For example, a typical manager will earn $73 000 a year, while a typical salesperson will earn $45 000 a year. The wealth generated in knowledge-intensive jobs also benefits the community. According to the Australian Tax Office, people in managerial jobs pay an average of $25 000 a year in taxes, while salespeople pay an average of $5000.

Knowledge-intensive work doesn't only benefit the people who do it. Having a lot of this work in a city seems to benefit lower-skilled workers in that city as well. Recent US research found that as these kinds of jobs increase in a local economy, so do wages, not just for the skilled workers but also for less-skilled jobs. The research found that wages were higher for waiters, hairdressers and cleaners—not just software engineers and marketing executives.

New ideas coming from knowledge-intensive work are not just about technological progress. They might be as simple as getting people buying furniture to assemble it themselves, an idea that has enabled Ikea to sell furniture at much lower prices than it otherwise could have. Knowledge-intensive work is also the reason the clunky, brick-like and incredibly expensive mobile phones of the early 1990s have evolved into the much more powerful—yet much cheaper—smartphones of today.

Indeed, new ideas come in many guises. New ideas might involve developing new products that better meet customers' needs, or managing people better within an organisation, so that they are more fulfilled and able to do their jobs more effectively.

Irrespective of the kind of new idea, cities offer the most fertile ground for them to flourish in. The skilled workers across different specialisations needed to generate and refine new ideas are most likely to be found in cities, as are the various business partners and professional service providers needed to turn the idea into reality. Cities also typically offer the largest number of potential local customers, and best links with international markets.

Without using new ideas to improve what they do, businesses eventually fall prey to competitors who step in and do it better or more cheaply. One way this happens is when competitors in countries with lower wages and lower living standards do the same work at lower cost.

Isolation from this kind of global competition might sound appealing. Global integration means competing with businesses in the United States and Japan with many highly skilled employees, and businesses in China where wages are much lower than in Australia. This is genuinely tough.

For example, the bookseller Angus and Robertson was established in Sydney in 1886. Less than a decade later it moved its premises to Castlereagh Street, and the store became known as 'the biggest book-shop in the world'. Over the next century it grew and thrived, developing a presence across Australia. But the twenty-first century proved difficult. Competition from overseas online giants such as Amazon and The Book Depository was fierce. By 2011 Angus and Robertson had gone into administration.

These kinds of changes can be very hard for people. Manufacturing has declined as a proportion of the Australian economy as local manufacturers have found it ever more difficult to compete with low-wage producers in China and elsewhere. Factories have closed down or moved their operations overseas. But it is difficult to hold back the tide of globalisation, any more than we can hold back advances in technology.

One reason for this is that people like mobile communications, cheaper consumer goods, overseas travel and the other material and lifestyle benefits that global integration has brought us. For example, in 2013 Benjamin Carle, a young French journalist, tried living for a year only using things that had been made in France. He was shocked to find that less than 5 per cent of the contents of his flat were made in his home country. The removalists left his home almost bare. To use only French-made goods meant far more expensive underpants, socks, polo shirts and espadrille shoes, and no jeans at all because none are made in France.

He had to give up his Chinese-made smartphone, television and refrigerator, his Italian spectacles, Moroccan underpants and Guatemalan coffee. No more listening to David Bowie on his sound system, which itself probably wasn't made in France. He had to store his milk outside the window to keep it cool, and he struggled to find the last French-made toothbrush. 'It was a full-time job', he said. Anyone trying this in Australia would have a similar experience.

People also value the new jobs and opportunities to earn income that increasing global integration has generated. Australia's fourth largest international export industry is education. Unlike the kinds of exports that are put in containers and shipped around the world, international students come to us. The industry barely existed thirty years ago, yet in 2014 around 300 000 students started courses at Australian universities and TAFEs. International students earn Australia $15 billion in export income each year—more than wheat, beef or natural gas exports.

The growth in international students studying in Australia has created many jobs, not only at universities and TAFEs. Retailers, hairdressers, cafes and restaurants all benefit from having more people to sell to. Construction companies build all kinds of accommodation. New forms of business have emerged: Student Housing Australia is a company established just to provide property management services for purpose-built international student accommodation. It now manages more than 2500 apartments.

Our economy has always been changing. Increasing integration with the global economy is just another dimension of this constant change. Ultimately global integration is a fact of life in today's Australia. We can either adapt and make the most of the opportunities that it presents or be left behind.

Knowledge-intensive jobs are more protected from global competition. Because they require expertise and judgement, they are less at risk of being outsourced to a low-wage country, or performed by a machine or a computer instead of a human. The only viable future in a globally competitive environment is one in which we continue to increase skill levels and specialisation right across the economy. And this is only achievable if our cities are connecting people and jobs.

Australia is well placed for the future in many ways. Having most of our population living in cities equips us to navigate a future in which knowledge, skills and expertise are more important than ever before. So does our skilled workforce, highly educated by world standards. But for both employers and employees, our cities do a very patchy job of connecting workers with jobs. Worse, we're actually headed in the wrong direction. The locations of our jobs and people are growing ever further apart.

This makes the economy much less productive than it could be. Many employers have access to much smaller pools of potential employees than cities should be offering. In our increasingly knowledge-intensive economy, this is a big problem. If our cities don't work, our economy won't work. This is bad for the whole community. And it's especially bad for people with limited access to jobs. People living in areas with poor access to jobs are cut off from opportunity, which harms their material standard of living. Many also have little alternative but to commute for long distances to areas with more jobs, which drives up their cost of living and can harm family life.

Chapter 3

Cities, opportunity and fairness

IN HER TWENTIES, ALICE Jaques lived in pokey little student flats in inner-Melbourne suburbs such as Kensington and North Carlton while she finished her doctoral research in public health at Melbourne University. Most days she walked to work.

In 2005 she married Jason Osborne, an IT professional who worked in a city bank, and they began planning a future with children and their own home. They didn't even bother looking in the inner city. Alice's friends told her 'it would be six, seven [hundred thousand dollars]-plus for anything decent'.

At the time, Alice's sister lived in Point Cook, a new suburb 25 kilometres south-west of the CBD. It was growing fast, with new shops, schools and childcare centres. The couple liked what they saw. They bought off the plan and in a couple of years moved into their 4-bedroom home. They caught the Werribee line train together to work, and life was good.

Then Alice had their first child, William, and took nine months off. When she went back to work two days a week, Jason took three months paternity leave. After he returned to work, they enrolled William in the new childcare centre at nearby Sanctuary Lakes while Alice continued her part-time job.

The two days Alice worked were hectic. She woke at 5 a.m. so she could get to work at the Murdoch Childrens Research Institute at the

Royal Children's Hospital by 7 a.m. (Jason dropped William at child care about 8 a.m. on his way to work). This allowed Alice to leave for home at 3.30 p.m. She was anxious to keep William's days in child care as short as possible.

Naturally, sometimes problems occurred. On one particular day, Alice left around her usual finish time to get back to Point Cook and pick William up. But at North Melbourne station she heard announcements that trains were suspended indefinitely on the Werribee line. There were replacement buses, but she was already imagining the crush to get on board. By now it was at least 4.30 p.m. The childcare centre closed at 6.30 sharp. Alice 'began freaking out'. She called Jason at his CBD office. They made a snap decision to brave the traffic in a taxi. The fare cost $90.

Yet even that day wasn't the final straw. With the birth of their second child, Lucy, Alice again took nine months maternity leave, then returned to work while Jason again took paternity leave for three months. During that time they decided that their carefully calibrated, 'tag-in, tag-out' arrangement with work and parenting was unsustainable.

They assessed options, laid out spreadsheets on the dining room table, pored over the weekly budget. Could they afford to live on one salary, and keep up the mortgage? If Alice continued to work as before, Jason would have to get two kids off to child care during peak hour. He'd probably get to work even later than 10 a.m. As well as it taking longer to get two kids out of the house, Point Cook's growing population and increasing traffic congestion had by that point doubled the time it took Jason to drive to the train station. He also had to park further away from the station. Would it hurt his career?

There was also the high cost of child care, which would eat into Alice's salary. But it was the logistics—the traffic, the limited public transport, the exhausting distances—that proved the clincher. Remembering that day at North Melbourne station, the frantic taxi ride, Alice gave notice to her employers. For the foreseeable future, her career in public health was over.

She tried to keep her hand in with some university teaching, tutoring in genetics a couple of times a year. But she found it too hard to keep abreast of developments in her field of prenatal screening for birth defects. On the other hand, she was over-qualified for most jobs that came up around Point Cook.

The family lives more frugally since Alice stopped working in public health. Their last proper family holiday was three years ago, though sometimes they go camping. Two days a week Alice works at William's primary school. She collects a half-day's salary for teaching sewing classes, and dabbles in a sewing business from home. Perhaps once Lucy starts school, she'll consider getting a teaching qualification herself, so she can work part time while staying close for school pick-up.

One thing they won't do is move from Point Cook. The community spirit is strong, and Alice loves the place. But for all its positives, she is clear that if she lived closer to the city she would not have been forced into the trade-off that cut short her career.

The Osbornes are typical of millions caught on the far side of a new urban divide, one that is changing Australia and challenging long-held ideals of economic opportunity and fairness. It is the growing gap between people who live near the centre of our cities and those who live near the outer fringes. These groups experience our cities very differently. For those on the wrong side of the divide, poorer access to jobs affects their ability to maintain and build a career over time, and long commutes are expensive and exhausting. In some cases, commutes can make juggling the responsibilities of home and work so difficult that some—usually women—have to give up work altogether.

Cities are dividing

In Australia's five biggest cities, people who live in outer suburbs are more likely to have lower incomes (that is, lower wages from work or a business), to be less wealthy (have fewer assets such as housing and shares) and to have less control over their employment situation than people who live close to the centre of their city.

Looking at income first, employees living furthest from the city centre get paid less. The average yearly individual income among employees living within 10 kilometres of Australia's five largest cities is 25 per cent higher than that of employees living more than 20 kilometres from city centres.

In Sydney, people between twenty-five and sixty-four years of age on the highest individual incomes are clustered around the inner suburbs, Sydney Harbour and the North Shore. Typical incomes in Bondi, by the sea, and St Ives, in the north, are also comparatively high, above $60 000. Incomes in western suburbs such as Bankstown and Wetherill Park are typically below $40 000. In Brisbane, typical individual incomes are highest—above $60 000 a year—among people living near the centre in places such as Bulimba or Ashgrove, and in well-located riverside suburbs such as Graceville. Incomes in more distant suburbs, such as around Sunnybank Hills, are typically below $40 000.

The income gap between inner and outer suburbs is growing. Since the mid-1990s, income growth among people living in suburbs close to city centres—such as Alexandria in Sydney, Albert Park in Melbourne and Morningside in Brisbane—has been 3 or 4 per cent a year (adjusted for inflation). Income growth in the west and south-west of Sydney, the far south-east and north-west of Melbourne and south Brisbane suburbs, such as Acacia Ridge, has been almost zero over the same period.

The changes are reshaping our cities, the opportunities they offer and their very identity. Living north or south of the Yarra River used to be Melbourne's biggest class marker. The working class lived in the north, and the well-heeled in the east and the south. But people on high incomes have increasingly clustered in inner suburbs on both banks of the river. Similarly, in Brisbane the economic and cultural divide between people living north and south of the Brisbane River is eroding, with proximity to the city centre more and more desirable. Today, how close you live to the Melbourne or Brisbane CBD matters more than what side of the Yarra or the Brisbane River you're on.

The pattern is less pronounced in Perth, where incomes have grown strongly across the metropolitan region, a legacy of the recent mining boom. Also, Perth's smaller manufacturing base means the decline of manufacturing has not hit the city as hard. Nevertheless, income growth is still highest close to the city centre. Suburbs where typical incomes are highest, such as Dalkeith and Cottesloe, are close to the centre or the beach. Incomes in more distant suburbs far from the coast, such as Gosnells and Armadale, are much lower.

Part of the reason outer suburban residents earn lower incomes is they are more likely to be employed on a casual basis. Casual employment is most common in lower-skilled roles, which represent a higher proportion of jobs in poorly connected outer suburbs. For example, almost half of all sales workers and labourers are employed on a casual basis. Fewer than 10 per cent of managers and professionals—higher-skilled jobs with higher wages that are concentrated in city centres—work as casuals. While more flexible, casual jobs offer less certain hours, lower wages and less job security. The average weekly wage of casual workers Australia-wide is $538 per week, less than half the average weekly full-time wage of $1276. Almost a third of casual employees are under-employed and want to work more hours.

Differences in wealth, or assets, could give a more meaningful indication of people's material living standards than differences in income. For example, a retiree may have a low annual income despite having accumulated extensive assets during a long career. It is difficult to get an accurate geographic breakdown of wealth in Australia. However, house prices provide a rough proxy for distribution of wealth in Australia's big cities. Housing is easily the most valuable asset that most home-owner households own.

The highest property prices are increasingly found in suburbs close to the CBD. Households with the greatest levels of wealth congregate in the parts of cities with the best access to jobs and transport. The further you go from city centres, the more house prices fall. The declines in house prices as you get further from the CBD are steepest in Sydney and Melbourne. These two cities have the greatest concentrations of knowledge-intensive jobs in the inner city. They also have outer suburbs that are furthest away and, of all Australian cities, offer the worst access to jobs.

Of course, access to jobs and transport are just two factors in creating a person's wealth. Education and skill levels are also vital—people with higher skill levels tend to have higher incomes. There is now a strong link between skill levels and where people live. Figure 3.1 shows how university graduates are concentrated in Melbourne's inner suburbs, and some middle suburbs east of the city centre. Outer suburbs have lower shares of university graduates.

Figure 3.1: Melbourne residents with a university degree, by suburb

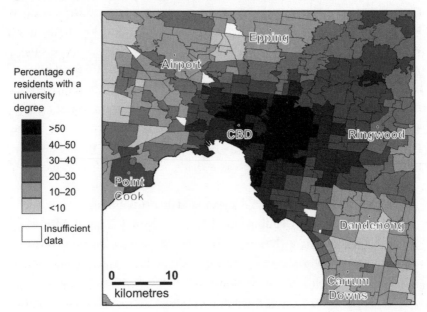

The closer residents live to city centres, the greater the number and range of high-skilled jobs they can reach by car, bicycle, foot or public transport, which better services the inner city. By contrast, the opportunities to do higher-paying, knowledge-intensive jobs get fewer and harder to access the further out you go. But many people can't afford to live further in.

A *new divide*

This divide is rarely discussed by politicians and opinion leaders, yet is reshaping our economic, political and cultural life.

'A metropolitan economy, if it's working well, is constantly transforming many poor people into middle-class people, many illiterates into skilled people, many greenhorns into competent citizens. Cities don't lure the middle class. They create it.' The words of American journalist Jane Jacobs, written in 1969, encapsulate the great dream of American and Australian cities in the boom years after World War II.

Dennis Glover's family, migrants from Northern Ireland, shared in that dream. As a boy in Doveton, a working-class suburb about 30 kilometres south-east of the Melbourne CBD, he and his mates never worried about trouble when they hit a cricket ball into someone's back-yard because 'everyone's dad was at work'. It was the 1970s and the car manufacturing plants near Doveton helped to produce 'a relative pros-perity unknown to ordinary Australians, and perhaps ordinary people anywhere in the world until then', Glover, a speechwriter and former political adviser, wrote in *The Age* in early 2014. From his street cricket pitch, Glover looked onto a secure world:

> On the off-side, number 28's dad is at Perkins Engines, number 30's dad (mine, a leading hand) is at GMH [General Motors Holden]; so is 32's (he's a GMH line manager, and one of my dad's bosses, who caused a minor street-wide sensation when he brought home a Leyland P-76). From memory, 34 and 36 were in vehicle production too, probably making trucks at International Harvester.
>
> On the on-side, 23 worked for Ford (it must have been in retail, as the Ford plants were far away), 25 was a self-employed car mechanic and 27 was an engineer called Boothroyd, the only person in our street with a degree.
>
> ... Cars—their design, manufacture, repair and sale—gave us our bread and butter, our political direction and our social structure. They were the art we created, and the delight of our little community, which centred on the primary school and neat strip shopping centre at the end of the street, with its kindergarten and its stop for the bus that would take our mothers to Dandenong for the weekly shopping.

Doveton was not alone. Many outer suburbs, especially in Sydney, Melbourne and Adelaide, depended on mass production in big factories for their comfort and prosperity. In the 1960s, one in four Australians worked in manufacturing, and the sector offered well-paid, full-time work to hundreds of thousands of people, including those with lim-ited education and the young. Our rising living standards rolled off the production line. And it didn't matter where you lived, because there was usually a factory nearby, needing workers.

Yet from the 1980s, life changed in Doveton. Glover writes:

> Like many similar factories, Doveton's biggest source of employ-ment—the GMH plant in Dandenong—closed its gates in the mid-1990s after a long decline. Dad had been laid off a little earlier, in the 'recession we had to have', and got another job the very next week—cleaning vehicles in a used car yard for lower pay, prestige and respect. My mother lost her job too, when Heinz [a food cannery] downsized, and she never worked full-time again.

Mr and Mrs Glover's unhappy fate was common in those years. There were many human consequences of the shift from a more sub-urban economy driven by manufacturing to one that became increasingly knowledge-intensive.

Meanwhile, big cities kept expanding further outwards as their populations grew. They continued patterns of population settlement suitable for Australia's manufacturing era even as opportunity and pros-perity concentrated more intensely near city centres. The result has been a big and growing divide between two of the things we need most from our cities—jobs and housing.

Widening gap between people and jobs

More than two million people live in western Sydney, a vast urban region encompassing areas including Parramatta, Blacktown, Penrith, Liverpool and Campbelltown. Once it was the country's industrial cap-ital, home to the factories that made King Gee overalls, Hush Puppies shoes and Rosella tomato sauce. Migrants came from all over the world to join Australian-born workers in factories that were located close to shopping centres and homes.

Western Sydney remains Australia's largest manufacturing region, but the sector's broader decline has not helped the area. Between 2006 and 2011 alone western Sydney shed nearly 8000 manufacturing jobs.

It wasn't only factories that closed. In those five years, net private sector employment growth in western Sydney has been very low. The only recent significant jobs growth has been in public sector jobs such as nursing, social work and policing.

Yet the population has grown, even as jobs have not. In 1996, about 1.8 million people lived in western Sydney. By 2011, that number had reached 2.1 million people, a larger population than Perth or Adelaide, and close to half of greater Sydney. Yet there were only a third that number of jobs in the area, about 646 000.

Western Sydney has a poor match of people and jobs, but it is not alone. Since 2006, the ten fastest growing areas across Australia were on the outer edges of Melbourne, Brisbane and Perth, and in the Melbourne CBD. The populations of places such as Wyndham Vale, Berwick, Cranbourne and Whittlesea in Melbourne, Rockingham and Wanneroo in Perth and Redbank and East Ipswich to the west of Brisbane have boomed. Indeed, Figure 3.2 shows that outer suburbs more than 20 kilometres from city centres absorbed more than half the population growth in Australia's five biggest cities across the same period. But the jobs aren't following. The shift to a more knowledge-intensive economy is reflected in strong inner-city employment growth.

Figure 3.2: Location of changes in employment and population between 2006 and 2011 in Sydney, Melbourne, Brisbane, Perth and Adelaide

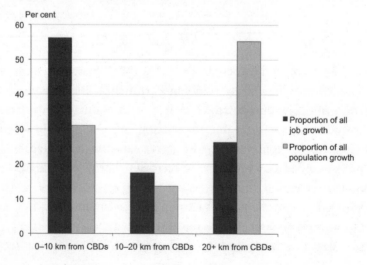

The graph also shows that more than half of the employment growth in Australia's five biggest cities between 2006 and 2011 occurred less than 10 kilometres from city centres.

As a result, job opportunities in many outer suburbs are thin. There are 5.9 million residents of Australia's five largest cities living 20 kilometres or more from the centre, but less than one local job for every three local residents. Not only is this bad, it's getting worse. The ratio of jobs to working-age residents in the outer suburbs of Australia's big cities is getting lower over time.

Jobs far from city centres also tend not to be as well paid as those in city centres. The average full-time job located 20 kilometres or more from large city centres pays $56 000 a year. Within 10 kilometres of city centres, the average full-time job pays more than a third more, around $77 000 a year. And opportunities to do higher-paying, knowledge-intensive jobs are more limited in poorly connected areas. Managerial and professional jobs represent less than a third of the jobs located in suburbs further than 20 kilometres from city centres. In contrast, these higher skilled and better paid jobs represent almost half the jobs located within 10 kilometres of city centres. So the growing income gap between people living in inner and outer suburbs is no surprise.

Increasing vulnerability

People living in suburbs poorly connected to jobs and transport are not just at a disadvantage when it comes to improving their incomes and living standards in the short-term. They also experience lower levels of job security.

Even if they have a job now, someone whose housing and transport situation gives them limited access to other jobs is very vulnerable should the industry they work in decline or their employer go out of business. Many people are well placed for the manufacturing economy of yesteryear. But they are not well placed for the shift to a higher skilled, more specialised services economy where opportunities are greatest in the inner city.

As manufacturing has declined, governments have sometimes tried to create new jobs in areas hit by factory closures. In 2013, Ford announced that its Australian car plants in Broadmeadows in outer Melbourne and in Geelong would close in 2016, shedding 1200 jobs. The Commonwealth and Victorian governments promised to help the two areas by pledging $39 million for intensive employment assistance and new local job opportunities. The two governments and South Australia promised similar support when Holden announced in 2013 it would cease manufacturing in Elizabeth in outer Adelaide and Port Melbourne, and Toyota announced in early 2014 the closure of its plant in Altona in Melbourne.

By contrast, governments feel no need to provide assistance packages when people lose jobs in areas rich in employment. Implicitly, they are saying that people with good access to large concentrations of jobs are well equipped to bounce back when they lose their job. Around the time of Ford's announcement, Optus announced 290 job losses, bringing the company total in just one year to nearly 1200, the same number as at Ford. IBM retrenched several hundred employees and ended up retrenching 1500 people across 2013. At the ANZ Bank, about 820 people had lost their jobs over the previous year, Telstra announced 648 job losses from its struggling Sensis division, and Origin Energy announced it would cut 350 jobs on top of 500 already flagged.

Why did governments support retrenched car industry employees in particular? The political sensitivity of the car industry as an iconic symbol of Australian manufacturing was undoubtedly a factor; likewise, the long periods that many employees had been working in car manufacturing, possibly making it harder for them to adapt to new roles. But importantly, the industry is shedding jobs in suburbs that have limited access to large concentrations of alternative employment. Employees living near Ford factories can reach a narrow range of new jobs, and the competition for these jobs will be fierce once Ford closes and many of its former employees compete for them. The local jobs that are not in manufacturing are fewer in number and not as well paid. Across Australia's outer suburbs, high population growth and stagnant employment growth are a toxic mix.

In a recession, larger numbers of industries discard jobs. Decline is not confined to a single sector such as car manufacturing. Some employers are able to take people back on again as economic conditions improve, but some cannot. Others go out of business entirely. In Australia it has been a very long time since a recession—according to most measures the last one finished in 1991. But history would suggest the current period of economic growth can't last forever. Should another recession occur, people living in areas poorly connected to jobs and transport will be much more vulnerable than people in better-connected areas. People who can access lots of jobs will typically be better placed to bounce back and find new work.

Long commutes

Almost all of western Sydney is more than 20 kilometres from the Sydney CBD. Some parts of the region—suburbs near Parramatta, for example—give residents access to a fair choice of jobs within a reasonable commute time. But more areas in the west—the populous suburbs west of Blacktown or north and west of Liverpool—do not. Many western Sydney commuters travel for a long time to get to work in distant parts of Sydney where there are more jobs. In 2014, western Sydney director of the Sydney Business Chamber David Borger outlined the toll long commutes took on families: 'People are travelling up to three hours a day to get to work and that can have a catastrophic impact on family life and community life'.

* * *

The problem is the same in the outer suburbs of Melbourne, presenting huge challenges for the many families like the Suratwalas of Epping North, a new suburb around 25 kilometres from the CBD. Meera Suratwala gets up at 6 a.m. every weekday morning. The 33-year-old dresses fast so she'll have time to help her husband, Hiren, get the kids ready. He works as a chef at the Grand Hyatt in the city and sometimes gets home as late as 4.30 a.m. to the Aurora estate where they live.

'I know, it is crazy,' he laughs, and Meera laughs with him. 'Crazy' is their catch-all word to describe the logistics and lengthy commutes required to earn a living and raise a family on Melbourne's fringe. Meera leaves home at seven. On a good day the drive to her accountant's job in Blackburn, in the city's east, takes fifty minutes, on a bad day an hour and twenty minutes or more. She has tried to find a part-time job closer to home. She pursued without success an opening at the nearby Northern Hospital, even though it would have meant a 30 per cent drop in salary. She applied to an accounting business ten minutes down the road, and was even prepared to volunteer one day a week in the hope it might lead to something stable. But they never replied.

Still, Mondays, Tuesdays and Wednesdays are bearable. On the first two, Hiren doesn't work, having worked on the weekend. He takes care of their toddler, Aryan, and picks up 5-year-old Nandini from school. Wednesdays are okay after Meera decided to give up half a day's work and stay home to save the family's sanity. Thursday and Friday are the days that demand quasi-military logistics. Meera goes to work as usual, but again only for a half day. She leaves Blackburn at 12.25 p.m. sharp, hoping there'll be no roadworks or disruptions, and drives for about thirty-five minutes to Reservoir in the city's north. When she pulls into a Coles car park, Hiren is waiting in their second car, Aryan in the back. With brisk efficiency and scarcely a word, Hiren and Meera change cars.

'The time frame we have is 1 to 1.10,' Hiren explains. 'The only chat is: "Was your day good?" "Okay." "What did Aryan have for lunch?"'

It's easier to change cars than disturb a child, and it's better they use Meera's small and fuel-efficient Mazda for the long drives to work. Even so, Hiren estimates the couple's fuel bill at about $600 a month. Nothing they can do about it, though. Or about Hiren's parking costs: $300 or so a month, even with the Hyatt's $14 discount rate for staff. Meera wants to go on a family holiday to India so that her children can get to know their grandparents, but it has been four years and she's still saving.

After the car switch, Meera returns home with her son, shovels in lunch and leaves no later than 2.30 p.m. to collect Nandini from school in Mill Park, nearly ten kilometres away. Hiren finishes his hour-and-a-half drive to work. Most weeks the couple spends a total of twenty hours in a car.

Hiren only sees his daughter on two weeknights and two weekend mornings. His precious time with Nandini is further squeezed because he must leave for work hours before his shift. After six years in Australia they are citizens and glad to be here, but life is not easy. As Meera says, with an edge in her voice, the days when the family can be together without commitments number 'just five days a year'.

Modern Australia has many stories like the Suratwalas—people who have to commute for a long time to earn a living, putting pressure on family life. More than a quarter of all commuters in Australia's big cities spend more time commuting than with their children. People with very long commute times have the worst reported work–life balance of any group in Australia.

Women face hard choices

There are many stories like Meera Suratwala's, who had to reduce her hours because long commutes were making family life unmanageable, while local work was impossible to find. There are also many stories like Alice Osborne's, who for similar reasons had to leave her job as a genetics researcher in the city centre and instead earn half a day a week's pay teaching sewing classes at the local primary school. These and many other people living far from city centres aren't reaping the full material benefits that living in a city should bring them, benefits that previous generations of Australian city residents have enjoyed.

Poor access to jobs is a particular problem for mothers. Because women still do most of the work looking after children or frail older family members in Australian households, they are more likely than men to reduce their work hours from full time to part time or casual. They are also more likely to be constrained in how long they can spend commuting to work.

Many find it difficult to obtain suitable work. A 2014 newspaper article quoted two mothers in this position. Anne Sasulu, a single mother from the western Sydney suburb of Bankstown, stated she was looking for part-time work in office administration but struggled to find opportunities near her home. 'Most of the jobs that I see online or in the paper are always out in the city, North Sydney, Surry Hills [or] Ryde,' she said. A long commute from Penrith forced Melinda Leyshon to give up her job in publishing after her first child was born: 'To keep doing that and to lose, on average, four hours a day in travel time just wasn't feasible for me'.

The map in Figure 3.3 compares the extent to which women and men in Melbourne are in the workforce. Men and women in lightly shaded inner and middle suburbs such as Yarraville, Preston and Bentleigh are participating in the workforce at relatively similar levels. But in outer suburbs to the west, north and south-east of Melbourne, women's workforce participation falls more than 20 per cent below that of men. The patterns are similar in Brisbane, Sydney and Perth.

Many mothers living far from city centres would like to work, or to work more hours. But distance from a good choice of job opportunities cuts them off from choices that families in suburbs with better connections to jobs and transport take for granted. What should be a boon of city living—both members of a couple being able to work in jobs that make the most of their skills—is a mirage for many Australians. Yet studies show that increasing women's workforce participation is one of the best ways to both increase household wealth and grow the economy.

Figure 3.3: Differences in male and female workforce participation by suburb, Melbourne, 2011

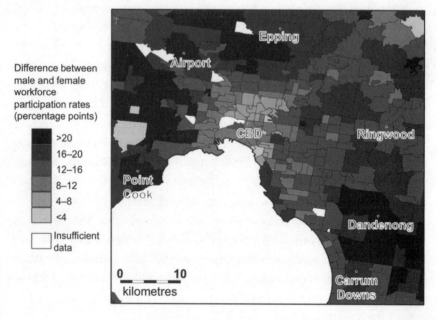

People who live in inner suburbs tend not to have to make such punishing trade-offs between job opportunities and family life. It may still be hard to decide whether to work more, knowing that this will cost more in child care. Access to good child care is difficult in many parts of Australia. But when it comes to travel times and the range of job options available to them, residents closer to the city centre have a much easier life. And in terms of travel costs, a cheaper one.

Travel costs are a big part of household budgets—exceeded only by housing and food—and cars represent by far the largest part of travel costs. The further from the city centre a household lives, the more cars the household is likely to own, since often there is no other easy way to get around. Car dependence caused by limited access to jobs and transport puts extra costs of sometimes thousands of dollars a year on many households, and makes them particularly vulnerable to increases in petrol prices. People who commute by car to inner Sydney from outer western suburbs such as Shalvey or Plumpton can spend as much as or even more than the Suratwalas' $900 a month on petrol and parking, then pay $600 a month more on motorway tolls. A monthly train ticket in Sydney costs far less than commuting by car, around $189, but it is not much use to someone whose home or destination is poorly served by public transport.

Geography is now destiny

The entrenching of opportunity in inner and middle suburbs is relatively new. In the 1970s, the edges of our cities were closer to the centre than they are today. Traffic congestion was less of a barrier to getting to jobs. And the manufacturing economy of the outer suburbs offered a clear route to prosperity.

Because today's knowledge-intensive economy is most concentrated around the inner city, households buying their first home far from city centres face much higher barriers to opportunity, job security and material prosperity than their parents ever experienced. Where someone lives also increasingly influences the likelihood of their having a job at all.

Between 1976 and 1991, the spatial distribution of employment changed dramatically. Economists Bob Gregory and Boyd Hunter showed that in 1976 there was little difference in levels of employment between different suburbs. People in places like Doveton were just as likely to have a job as people in places like Hawthorn. While some suburbs were richer than others, it was not the proportions of the population that were employed that drove the difference.

But by 1991, the picture was very different. A significant fall in male employment, linked to the impact of the early 1990s recession, was not equally distributed within large cities. Instead, unemployment was much higher in more disadvantaged suburbs, often with poor access to jobs and transport. Between 1991 and 2011, overall employment rates went back up as the national economy grew across nearly all of this period. But the gap between well-off and disadvantaged suburbs remained, and in some cases increased, especially among women.

Over time, this polarisation of suburbs could increase the number of disadvantaged areas while further concentrating wealth in other suburbs. People in disadvantaged areas can experience additional consequences that are often described as 'area effects', where the immediate environment can influence their lives, in part by shaping their outlook and attitudes. For example, a young person growing up in an area of entrenched unemployment may come to regard living on government benefits and not working as normal. Social scientists have found that some people growing up in areas where people typically have shorter lives and where there are higher rates of drug use, crime and violence may come to see such a life as the best they can hope for.

Increasingly, geography is destiny. Recent US research compared the experience of children growing up in poor families across 221 cities. Children who grew up in cities with better connections between jobs and housing were much more likely to be able to escape poverty and become high-income earners by age thirty than those growing up in cities with bad connections between jobs and housing.

Similarly, no matter how hard Australians in suburbs with poor access to jobs and transport work, and how much they sacrifice to secure their economic future, over time their income, wealth and job options will not grow as rapidly as those of people living in better-connected areas. Without change, their children will not grow up with the opportunities that children living in areas with good access to jobs and transport take for granted.

Both sides of politics think that all Australians should have the chance to better their material circumstances through hard work. Former Liberal prime minister John Howard's speechwriter John Kunkel wrote of how Howard and his office sought to 'make the moral case for economic growth and social mobility—ensuring a bright kid from a disadvantaged background could get ahead—as being just as relevant as ever'. Labor MP Andrew Leigh wrote in 2013 that 'Australian society prides itself on being one where people can move from one social class to another'. Liberal MP Malcolm Turnbull wrote in 2012 that 'most if not all Australians would agree inequality is a legitimate matter for politicians to be concerned about'.

Declining connections between people and jobs in our cities are making Australia a place where people are less likely to get ahead through hard work and effort, regardless of where they were born.

We've seen that the economy has changed over the last fifty years to become more knowledge-intensive, less dependent on manufacturing, and with opportunity and prosperity increasingly concentrated in city centres. Yet patterns of where population growth is happening are more in line with a 1960s manufacturing economy than a twenty-first century knowledge economy. Consequently, Australia's big cities are not performing one of their most important roles—connecting people with jobs—as well as they should.

The Committee for Sydney wrote in 2013 that current arrangements 'deliver neither the housing people want or can afford in the locations in which they want them nor the best settlement patterns to support Sydney's modern economy. It has also left too many communities too far from the "economic action" with all the associated human and environmental consequences. [This] is the main source of spatial and intergenerational inequity in Sydney'.

We've also seen that it hasn't always been this way. The growing divide between people and jobs in Australia's big cities is bad for the economy, and bad for the fair go.

Chapter 4

Cities and social connection

IF YOU ASK PEOPLE to close their eyes for a second and visualise what is most important to them, the answer is most likely to be the people they are closest to—children, partners, friends, family. As well as meeting our economic needs, cities affect our ability to meet our fundamental human need to have meaningful, positive interactions with other people.

Social connection is not an optional extra in our lives. There is no opposite for the word 'lonely' in the English language, just as there is no opposite for the word 'thirsty'. When we are *not* lonely a fundamental need is being met. It's no surprise that solitary confinement is considered among the worst of punishments. Similar neurological processes create the sensations of loneliness and of physical pain.

Cities are places where large numbers of people come together to benefit from interacting with each other. These interactions can be economic and they can be social. Residents can experience social isolation if the location of their homes or a lack of travel options narrow the opportunities for social interaction available to them.

Social connections happen at a number of levels: intimate personal and family relationships; a broader network of friends, relatives and colleagues; and our feeling of belonging in communities. These connections are all important, from close, regular contact with loved ones to incidental interactions in the street.

Just as cities and the economy have changed a lot over the past fifty years, there have been big changes in how we live our lives and how we connect with others. Many of us frequently use social media. But we're less likely to get social connection today from belonging to organised groups such as sporting clubs, churches, school parents' and citizens' groups, volunteer organisations, political parties, trade unions or business associations than people were fifty years ago.

Household structures are also changing. Figure 4.1 shows that single-parent families have become increasingly common over recent decades. Single-person households are also increasingly prevalent, and now make up one in four Australian households. The population is ageing. We are partnering and having children later, and increasing numbers of us aren't doing it at all. As more and more women have joined the workforce, they have gained more choice about their living arrangements, and some are choosing to live alone.

More people are expected to live alone in the future. The Australian Bureau of Statistics predicted that the number of single-person households would increase from around two million in 2009 to 3.1 million

Figure 4.1: Changes in household composition across Australia, 1976–2011

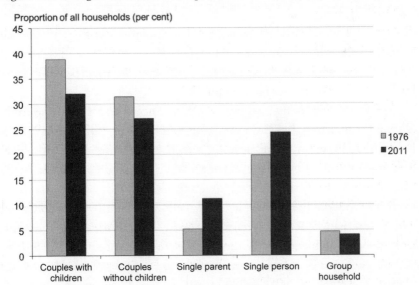

in 2031. The number of one-parent families is also expected to increase by between 40 and 77 per cent over the same period.

Many single-parent and single-person households value their living arrangements, and the freedom to live in a way that may have been impossible fifty years ago. But single-parent and single-person households are also at greatest risk of social isolation. Single parents are almost twice as likely to experience loneliness as people living as part of a couple.

People who live by themselves are much more likely to experience loneliness than are people in larger households. Loneliness is especially high among men living alone, most notably those aged twenty-five to forty-four. Women on lower incomes are also disproportionately likely to be lonely. One study found people living alone are more than three times as likely as people in larger households to experience loneliness more than once a day, and about twice as likely to experience loneliness at least once a week.

The situation can be particularly difficult for older people living alone. A UK study found that nearly half of all older people consider the television to be their main form of company, and in 2006 more than half a million older people spent Christmas Day alone.

* * *

The need for social connection is as old as humanity itself. Neuroscience research suggests that over tens of thousands of years our need to deal with other people has fundamentally influenced the structure of the human brain. We are social animals.

Different people obviously have different needs. Privacy and solitude are important, and very different from loneliness or isolation. There is no such thing as an 'ideal' level of social connection. But some level of connection is critical to everyone's wellbeing and satisfaction with life. A recent study found that loneliness detracted more powerfully from how people rated their level of wellbeing than being in physical pain or on a low income. There is growing evidence that people with strong social connections live longer because of those social connections. Loneliness is up there with high blood pressure, lack of exercise, obesity and smoking as an indicator of shortened life expectancy.

Social connections also make us part of society. Through them we share information, resources and skills. Interacting with other people informs our expectations of them and teaches us about social norms. Without social interaction and connection, we could not establish the mutual expectations and trust that are the foundation for our market economy and liberal democratic system of government.

There is an ingrained idea that people will always seek to satisfy material needs before worrying about psychological needs such as the need for human contact. Yet fieldwork undertaken by the UK's Young Foundation revealed young people going without food in order to keep their mobile phones topped up, leading the foundation's former chief executive Geoff Mulgan to conclude that 'the human need for connectedness' outweighs 'almost everything else'.

So social connection is incredibly important, in fact fundamental, to being human. But what does it have to do with cities? The relationship between cities and social connection is not as well understood as the relationship between cities and material prosperity. Nonetheless, cities can increase the number of social connections available to us, and offer people a wider choice of possible partners. In contrast, the popular reality television show *The farmer wants a wife* is about a farmer who wants to meet and settle down with a partner but has little opportunity to do so in the local area.

Within cities, the housing market shapes whether people can live near friends and family and other networks. Connecting with friends and family also depends on being able to get around. Long commutes mean less time with family and friends, as Hiren and Meera Suratwala (whom we met in Chapter 3) can attest.

Of course cities—their populations, housing markets and transport systems—are far from the only influence on social connection. A person's health, level of income, gender and whether or not they have children are all vital influences on whether they experience loneliness. But cities matter, too. Being able to live near family and friends, and being able to travel to meet them, remain critical. Face-to-face contact, so important to nurturing business relationships and complex problem-solving, also remains the essential way to develop and sustain our personal relationships. The qualities at the core of social connection—trust, sympathy, respect, understanding, loyalty and cooperation—come more easily through direct contact.

While social media use has increased exponentially over the last few years, new research has found that it does not have the same beneficial impact on 'increasing positive mood and … social belonging needs compared to face-to-face interactions'. Having friends online whom we haven't met in real life doesn't appear to benefit our overall wellbeing. Online relationships complement, rather than replace, direct contact.

Housing and social connection

After a long career running restaurants and pubs, and often living at the back of them, Caroline Maloney (names have been changed) needed a new home. She needed a place where her 97-year-old mother, Sofia, could live out her last years and where her friend Michelle, another restaurateur, could stay on her visits to Melbourne. But Caroline did not want to live in a share house or 'anything hippie-dippy'. Nor did she want to join a body corporate, being 'a control freak … with an obsession with privacy'. She had to find a place that would give her company when she wanted it, but also allow her to be autonomous and alone.

She looked for some time in Melbourne's northern suburbs and in the CBD. But none of the houses were right and the apartments in the CBD did not appeal. Many of the latter were isolated and cramped; some had open areas that were built to accommodate communal life but looked as if they were never used. 'They were bad machines for living in,' she says, reworking the architect Le Corbusier's phrase for what a modern dwelling should be. Then she found a shopfront for sale in a main street in the inner suburb of Fitzroy. The upstairs area was dark and decrepit but also large and deep, and it gave Caroline an idea. She bought the property and, working with an architect, transformed it.

A sliding door separates Sofia's large living room from the front room Caroline spends most of her time in. The door's frosted glass increases privacy, while a curtain can also be pulled across if Caroline is entertaining and wants to keep the noise down. But if she is holding a large party, she throws the door open and creates one big, bright space. At those events, Sofia might come out to say hello then retreat to her bedroom. 'I think she enjoys the sound of people talking and having fun; it makes her feel comfortable,' Caroline says. In Sofia's bedroom a long, high window enables her to lie in bed and watch the sky.

Two galley kitchens side by side enable the residents to cook separately, or to join the kitchens into one if a party is planned. The kitchens use every centimetre of space, with compact fridges, dishwasher drawers and cupboards that go nearly to the ceiling. Behind the kitchens is a laundry, the only shared room in the dwelling.

Michelle's small, two-roomed apartment is off to the side. 'When Michelle is here the place buzzes and really takes life—it's terrific,' says Caroline. 'Michelle thinks I'm too private, though. Sometimes she'll give me a ring and ask if I will deign to have a cup of tea with her.'

The architectural trick was to make minimal structural change to the dwelling, in part to preserve its value for resale. Skylights lighten rooms; a sliding door and thick curtain can muffle sound as well as a wall can, and are more attractive. Caroline sees a time when homes like hers exist not just in the inner city but in newer and more conventional dwellings in the middle and outer suburbs. It just takes a little extra cash and some imagination.

Two trends could drive the change, she says. The first is an economic downturn that leaves people owning homes they cannot afford to live in alone. The second is the large and growing number of single people. She imagines cohousing developments in which people have privacy, including separate entrances, but might share a washing machine, a car, a garden and a pet.

'Once the idea is out there, once people start talking about it and realise we are not talking about a hippie share house, I think it might take off,' she says. 'It's about people being emotionally secure, to have company when they need it, and to be on their own when they don't.'

* * *

The average household size has been declining over most of the past century, and our population is ageing. More people are living alone. The number of Australians aged eighty-five or over is predicted to quadruple from 0.4 million in 2010 to 1.8 million in 2050. In light of these demographic trends, it is worth considering whether new housing options can better support social connection.

There are many traditions of households living together in a combination of shared and private spaces. One familiar example is the large, multi-generational extended family.

As the population ages, increasing numbers of older Australians will live alone in houses built to accommodate entire families. New sublease arrangements could be created to allow older Australians to share their homes with tenants. The potential benefits could include extra income, extra support, an increase in the availability of affordable housing and more social connection.

One contemporary example of innovation in residential arrangements is cohousing, which emerged in Denmark in the 1970s. Cohousing has now spread beyond Denmark, particularly in northern Europe and America. Most cohousing is closer to conventional household arrangements than it is to communal living. In some cases, it is simply a row of houses where the fences between backyards have been removed to create a shared garden, shed and laundry.

Shared facilities, paths and green spaces can bring people together. Successful cohousing often uses semi-private spaces, such as verandahs and patios, as a buffer between private homes and common areas. This helps to balance community life with personal privacy. Joint input into decisions about the community, shared meals and social events can provide both incidental and planned social interaction. Together these elements can generate a strong sense of connection and greater wellbeing.

Cohousing gives residents opportunities for meaningful social interaction, but it doesn't need to dominate their lives. In a cohousing complex in California, people spend on average just under 6 per cent of their time in communal spaces, and a little less than that interacting with other members of their community.

Retirement villages and independent living units in residential aged-care facilities can be seen as contemporary examples of cohousing. Residents continue to enjoy the privacy of their own home, while sharing facilities, communities and services. In Europe and America, cohousing is becoming a prominent option for older people who want to stay independent but who also need greater support from others. In Denmark, most of the newest cohousing developments target older people.

But very little of this kind of innovation is happening in Australia. Dwellings for single-person households, notably in blocks of flats or apartments, rarely include shared or communal areas. Cohousing is extremely rare, partly because of constraints that lead the Australian housing industry to be risk averse and conservative, an issue examined in the next chapter.

Keeping a pet also helps some people feel less lonely and isolated. A pet provides company, and gets its owner out and about. Pet owners report fewer annual doctor visits and are less likely to be on regular medication. Pet owners are also found to have greater self-esteem, higher levels of physical activity and fitness and to be less lonely than non-owners. People find that walking their dog is a great way to meet people, especially other dog owners.

Rental leases and strata title conditions for blocks of flats or apartments often heavily restrict ownership of household pets. This means many people who want to own a pet forgo doing so, despite the benefits it would bring. Rather than managing the very low risks that most domestic animals present, body corporates and real estate agents often impose a blanket ban. Other countries are more lenient: in Germany, for instance, renters can ordinarily keep small animals. Western Australia has a special pet bond, allowing landlords to charge an extra bond for tenants with a pet. Although a landlord can still refuse pet ownership at a rental property, the bond is seen as a way of reducing the financial risks from any damage. No other state has this arrangement.

Getting around

Several times a week, for twenty-six years, Lili Szalisznyo made the long trip from her cottage in the Brisbane suburb of Corinda to a radio studio at Kangaroo Point, across the Brisbane River. The studio was home to ethnic radio station 4EB FM, where Lili presented a Hungarian-language program twice a week.

The 79-year-old took the job after the Hungarian consul in Brisbane, who was involved with the program, suggested it needed 'a woman's voice'. Lili learned how to operate the control panel, took to the airwaves and never looked back.

'It was a good station,' Lili recalls, 'and I know my country, all its traditions and customs, inside out.

'At the station, people came from fifty-seven nations. Everybody understood me because they've all been foreigners. If I took some Hungarian food to the table they never asked, "Oh my God, how could you eat that?"'

But being unable to drive, Lilli struggled to get there. She would broadcast for an hour and a half on Thursday morning and on Wednesday night for forty-five minutes to 9 p.m. There were also regular team meetings on Monday evenings.

Lili had an hour's walk from her home to Corinda train station. She would travel twenty minutes to the city, then walk another fifteen minutes to the ferry station at Brisbane River. She caught the ferry, disembarking at Kangaroo Point under Story Bridge. To reach the studio on the main road she had to walk another ten minutes, the traffic roaring in her ears. Lilli had to get up at 5 a.m. on Thursday mornings, rain or shine. Wednesday nights were even harder. Sometimes her husband picked her up, other times she braved the journey home.

'There is a park under the bridge. When I'd walk to the ferry station it was full of drunk people. They hassle you for cigarettes and things like that. It was dark. There was absolutely no security really,' she says.

On those nights, Lili rarely made it home before 10.30 p.m. As she got older, the night trips grew more difficult and unpleasant. So in 2000, she relinquished her Wednesday night spot. Despite the many challenges, she persisted with the early morning slot. After her husband died in 2004, the radio show became Lili's escape 'from a horrible world'. But the transport hassles finally defeated her. On Anzac Day 2013 she quit the program entirely. 'I love to walk, but I'm getting older,' she explains.

Since she left the show, her world has shrunk. She relies on her neighbours for companionship and a lift to the shops—the nearest retail strip is an hour's walk from home, and the buses are infrequent and unreliable. She grieves for the old sense of community and purpose: 'I miss it, the show, terribly … it was my life. The listeners still ring me up to tell me how much they miss me.'

* * *

People need to get around a city in order to get to work and to shop, to travel to see friends and family and to participate in sporting, cultural and community activities. All these activities can strengthen material and psychological wellbeing. But being able to get around also improves people's sense of control over their life and their sense of connection with the community.

The shape of our cities can make it easier or harder for people to see each other. In many parts of Australian cities, not having a car is a huge barrier to mobility. Often the people at greatest risk of social isolation are the ones with least access to transport. One study found that more than half the carless households in outer Melbourne were single-person households, with single-parent families also over-represented.

Another study found that one in three single parents in Sydney lived in an area with poor access to public transport (defined as more than 800 metres from a stop with a service running at least once every half-hour during the day). Even those who could access public transport did not always find it suitable for travelling with small children, prams, bags and groceries. One single parent from Claymore in western Sydney said: 'I do a big shop once a fortnight at Campbelltown and get a cab home, then I get smaller amounts every couple of days down at Eagle Vale. If you've more than two bags, forget it, you can't get them on the bus. The buses don't have enough room'.

For single parents with no car and poor access to public transport, taking their children to after-school sporting or leisure activities is 'out of the question', as one woman put it. Getting to doctors or hospitals

Figure 4.2: How far you can travel on public transport in forty-five minutes from two different starting points, Adelaide

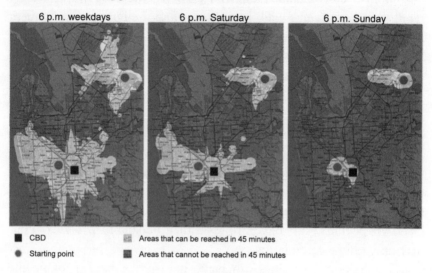

using public transport is also extremely difficult, and virtually impossible on nights and weekends.

Being able to get onto public transport does not guarantee mobility over a wide area either. People living in outer suburbs regularly find themselves with a far more limited choice of destinations within a given travel time than people living closer to city centres.

An additional problem is access to public transport on weekends, when many social trips happen. The maps in Figure 4.2 show that even in areas with rich public transport options, such as central Adelaide, the distance people can travel in forty-five minutes falls sharply on weekends.

Commuting and social connection

We saw in Chapter 3 that many households face difficult trade-offs between long commutes to work and time with family. Hiren and Meera Suratwala are just one of many outer-suburban households that endure long commute times in order to make ends meet or secure their financial future.

Long commutes corrode social connection and wellbeing. More than half of commuters say they would spend more time with their family and friends if their commuting time were significantly reduced. Many would also spend more time exercising or sleeping.

People who commute for long periods also report lower levels of wellbeing and satisfaction with their life than people whose commutes are shorter. Research in both the United States and Germany found that longer commutes lead to declines in how people rate their own well-being. Low wellbeing in turn also makes us less likely to connect with other people—it's a vicious cycle.

Long commutes are also bad for health. A 2012 US study found that as commutes get longer, people's physical activity and cardio-vascular fitness drops, while blood pressure and weight increase. The study also associated commuting by car for more than 16 kilometres each way with an increased risk of high blood sugar and high choles-terol. Swedish researchers concluded that having a job far from home is linked to increased exhaustion, stress, lack of sleep and days off work, irrespective of whether people commute by car, train or bus.

Longer commuting times also mean less time socialising, and less involvement in sporting groups or community organisations. In the United States, researcher Robert Putnam found 'a simple rule of thumb: every 10 minutes of commuting results in 10 per cent fewer social connections'.

Social connection is typically an afterthought, if considered at all, when major decisions about transport infrastructure and land use are made. Yet some groups, particularly people who rely on public trans-port, face increased risk of social isolation because it is hard to get around. More can be done to balance social connection with other objectives of transport systems, such as growing the economy and reducing traffic congestion.

* * *

The housing we live in and our capacity to get around cities are impor-tant influences on the quality and degree of social connection we enjoy. Housing and transport also shape the job opportunities we can access, the time we spend commuting to work, the strength of the economy and the trade-offs we have to make between working, spending time with family, friends or on leisure activities.

The next two chapters take a detailed look at the housing market and transport systems in Australian cities to identify why they're creating an increasing divide between people and jobs, forcing people into trade-offs between financial security and family time, and making social connection much harder.

Chapter 5

Housing

MORE THAN ANY OTHER issue covered in this book, housing stirs up strong emotions. Housing gets a lot of media coverage, but there is little insight amid the noise, which might be serving only to increase our levels of uncertainty about the right thing to do—both in our own lives, and for the nation as a whole.

In any given year, around 100 000 people in Australia become home owners for the first time. They would benefit from any policy that leads to lower house prices. Politicians talk often of the need to improve affordability for younger home buyers, yet the 5.8 million households who already own at least one home are wary of any change that might push prices down or slow price growth. Increasing house prices are a problem; so are decreasing house prices. John Howard famously remarked that he had never had anyone complain to him about the price of their house going up.

Nonetheless, the longest housing boom in Australian history has collected plenty of victims. Homes are harder to buy than they were twenty or thirty years ago. House prices have grown much faster than incomes. Younger households and lower-income households are increasingly unlikely to own their own home.

We tend to assume that all Australians want a detached house (preferably on a mythical quarter-acre block), but in fact, Australians have a diverse array of preferences about where we live and the kind of home we want to live in. These diverse preferences shouldn't be a surprise—they reflect the diverse attitudes, backgrounds, demographics and circumstances of the Australian community. Yet in some of our cities, the assumption that everyone wants a detached house on a quarter-acre block has helped to drive development patterns that further increase the distance between people and jobs.

The way the housing market works is a big culprit in the declining access to jobs and increasingly divided cities we've discussed in previous chapters. Home prices have been growing much more quickly in inner than outer suburbs, making areas with the best access to jobs increasingly inaccessible for many households. Even within a given budget, people's choices are further constrained by the limited range of housing options the market is offering them.

Meanwhile, increasing numbers of people are renting, and renting for longer periods of time. Renters get an especially raw deal, having to move much more frequently than they would like, and missing out on government support such as tax concessions that benefit home owners and investors in housing. Renters on low incomes are especially badly served by the housing market, with many having to make extremely difficult compromises just to put a roof over their heads.

What we want from housing

In Chapter 3 we met the Suratwalas, who live in Epping North in Melbourne. We saw how challenging their family life is, with two long and complicated commutes to jobs far from where they live. The Suratwalas had looked in other suburbs for housing they could afford to buy, to no avail.

'We would 100 per cent move, even to a house that was smaller, if we could be closer to public transport,' says Hiren. 'At least public transport actually exists further in, as opposed to the false promise of public transport out here,' he says, referring to a train line that was planned but not built.

The Suratwalas are not alone. A large and rising number of Australians are struggling to find homes that allow them to work and raise a family without heavy strain on their time, bank balances and quality of life. More of them are being forced to the city fringes, thwarted by a housing market offering limited choices and growing prices that are placing home ownership in areas with good access to jobs increasingly out of reach. To understand what needs to change, we need to look at how the housing market works—and doesn't—for Australians in search of a decent home.

'Everyone wants to live in a big house on a quarter-acre block'— these words are said so often in Australia that they have passed into legend: unquestionable, self-evidently true. They have shaped housing policy, as generations of developers, planners and politicians have assumed that our cities can go on expanding without limit, since new buyers will always prefer a detached house, requiring new land beyond the existing city limits.

There are many assumptions, but very little actual data available on the housing preferences of Australians. The only certainty seems to be that when people are asked to choose anything they want, they typically say they'd like a large detached house near the centre of the city. But people also know that in the real world, we don't get everything that we want. We make all sorts of considered trade-offs every day. Of course, unrestricted choices are easy—most of us would jump at the chance of being given an enormous house set within extensive gardens within easy walking distance of both serene parks and the buzz of downtown. While we're at it, we should throw in a large garage for the sports cars.

In reality, most people start looking for a home with a sense of where they want to live, the space they need and what they can afford. But unless we are really lucky, the place we end up with will often be smaller, in poorer condition, further from transport or in a less appealing suburb than the one we hoped for. Sometimes it will be all four. These are the kinds of compromises the world imposes on us.

In 2011, the Grattan Institute conducted research to establish what Australians would choose when they had to trade off their priorities against their actual housing budgets. We hoped to find out if the current market was giving them the housing they wanted. We asked focus groups in Sydney and Melbourne to explain what the phrase 'owning your own home' meant to them. People often responded by describing a detached house on a block of land. The dream is deep in the psyche of many Australians, as one respondent made plain: 'We're born and bred in Australia—we're ingrained and conditioned to have that attitude towards detached homes ... I've worked hard and earned the right to own my own place—it shows I've done well'.

Home owners may feel a sense of achievement and psychological reassurance because they are part of the Australian majority in a country where ownership is considered normal, and anything else seen as requiring explanation. As one focus group participant put it: 'you want to be reassured you've made the right decision'.

'Self-worth is equated to the type of house you have' was how a middle-aged Sydneysider put it. Housing is often also the most valuable purchase we ever make, and so justifying our choices is important to us: 'it's part of what you're meant to do—it's the dream'.

Developers and builders know they're selling dreams. Billboards advertising new housing on cities' outer fringes promise a bucolic wonderland that sits improbably alongside people cycling to work and buzzy cafes. One shows a beautiful young couple in a paddock, one sitting on a Vespa scooter, the other holding a caffe latte in a glass. The homes are described as 'within easy reach', with 'everything at your doorstep'. House models come in portfolios with names like 'The Aspirations Series'.

In Australia, home ownership is seen as the norm. Yet in the years after World War II, only about half of households owned their homes. Postwar government policies led to home ownership rapidly increasing. By the early 1960s, three-quarters of households owned or were buying their home. That figure stayed relatively stable for a long time, then more recently started gradually declining. Today 68 per cent of households are home owners.

To get a handle on what matters most to people when they choose housing, we conducted research with a representative sample of home-buying adults in Melbourne and Sydney. First, we asked them to choose their priorities among fifty-six different characteristics of dwellings and neighbourhoods. The number of bedrooms was most frequently chosen as their top concern. What was more surprising, though, was that most of the top ten characteristics that people valued in a home concerned its location rather than its size. Living in a safe neighbourhood, being close to family and friends, shopping and public transport were all very important.

We also examined how different kinds of households responded. Older people, in particular, considered the neighbourhood more important than the dwelling itself. For them, proximity to friends and family, shops and health services were all prime considerations. Single-person households also ranked the location over the home. Unsurprisingly, couples with children saw the size of a dwelling as central. Parents aged eighteen to forty-four rated the number of bedrooms as most important, while 45- to 64-year-old couples without children saw it as eighth most important.

In other words, the preferences of couples with younger children look most like what we assume everyone wants—a big, detached house with a garden. Public debate about housing—not to mention advertising from real estate agents and property developers—focuses disproportionately on this household type. Yet couples with children make up less than a third of Australian households. Couples aged eighteen to forty-four with children make up less than a fifth. Since the mid-1970s, couples with children have declined as a proportion of all Australian households, while the proportions of lone-parent and lone-person households have increased. These changes should be reshaping the housing market, but it is struggling to keep up.

When Grattan asked the people in its survey to mimic real-world decisions that consider the type of house and location they can afford on their real budget, they turned out not to have a fixed desire for a detached house above all other considerations. Instead, they had a range of preferences, as Table 5.1 shows. Faced with actual property prices and actual budget constraints, fewer than half the Melbourne people said they would prefer to live in a detached house. About a quarter of people surveyed said they would choose semi-detached housing such as townhouses, units or terraces, and another quarter would choose a flat or apartment, if they could live in the kind of neighbourhood they wanted. In Sydney, the preference for detached houses in a real-world scenario was even less. About 40 per cent preferred it. A quarter preferred semi-detached townhouses, units or terraces, and about a third preferred apartments or flats.

Table 5.1: Homebuyers' preferred dwelling type and location with real-life budget constraints, Sydney and Melbourne, 2011

	Detached	Semi detached	Flat up to 3 storeys	Apartment 4 storeys +	TOTAL
Sydney					
Inner	9%	4%	2%	5%	**20%**
Inner-Middle	9%	7%	4%	5%	**26%**
Outer-Middle	12%	7%	4%	6%	**30%**
Outer	10%	6%	5%	4%	**25%**
TOTAL	**41%**	**25%**	**15%**	**20%**	**100%**
Melbourne					
Inner	8%	6%	3%	5%	**22%**
Inner-Middle	14%	8%	4%	4%	**30%**
Outer-Middle	14%	8%	3%	3%	**26%**
Outer	12%	6%	2%	2%	**22%**
TOTAL	**48%**	**26%**	**12%**	**14%**	**100%**

Overall, the trends were surprisingly similar across groups and cities. They showed that contrary to myth, not all Australians want to live in detached houses. The housing people actually want is a much more varied mix than our cities currently provide. A significant proportion of people want to live in a semi-detached home or an apartment in locations that are close to family or friends, to shops and to transport options.

The survey was repeated in Perth in 2013, with similar results. Presented with real-world scenarios, 56 per cent of residents of Perth opted for detached houses, 35 per cent for semi-detached homes and 9 per cent for flats or apartments.

This diversity shouldn't be a surprise. Yet in Australia today, there is a great mismatch between people's preferences expressed within their real-world budgets, and the actual stock of housing. There are large shortfalls of semi-detached housing and apartments in the established areas of both Sydney and Melbourne. Semi-detached homes represent only around one in ten homes in both cities. One in five Sydney households expressed a preference for an apartment in a building four storeys or higher, but these represent only one in ten homes in Sydney. This leaves more than 150 000 Sydney households whose preferred trade-offs cannot be accommodated by the housing stock in that city.

Melbourne has more recently seen the construction of a large number of high-rise apartment developments in and around the CBD, mainly with one and two bedrooms. These do not suit many households, who would like to be able to choose semi-detached homes or low-rise apartments in established inner and middle suburbs. But very few of these are being built.

Housing stock in cities

One reason for this mismatch between the housing available in cities and our current preferences is that once housing is built, it endures for a very long time. Most of today's housing was built decades ago when costs were lower, cities smaller, families larger and preferences were different. Most parts of Melbourne with the best access to jobs were developed before 1965. The western Melbourne suburb of Altona, for example, was on the city fringe when it was built in the 1960s, at a time when suburban manufacturing was the backbone of Australia's economy. Today it is a middle-ring suburb made up almost entirely of detached houses for families with children. Yet Altona contains many older childless couples and single people, among others. The dwellings are a poor fit for this diverse population.

Australia's accumulated stock of housing is dominated by detached houses. This mix has changed little over recent decades: in 1976, detached houses comprised 78 per cent of Australia's housing stock; in 2011 the share was 74 per cent.

We aren't building what we want

We have to take the housing built in previous years as given. Wiping a city clean and starting again is hardly an option. But even the housing being built today does not match the preferences of home buyers today.

Our research found that only 12 per cent of Melburnians, given a full range of choices within their budget constraint, preferred a family-size detached house on the city fringe. Yet detached houses represented more than two-thirds of homes built in Melbourne in the decade to 2010, with most of these houses built on the fringe.

Meanwhile, in Australia's largest cities almost none of the demand found in our surveys for semi-detached housing and low-rise apartments in established suburbs is being met.

To understand why this is happening, we need to consider the market from a developer's perspective, how they go through the steps required to build and sell new housing. These include obtaining land, finance and permission to build the housing, and then getting it built. As it turns out, developing the terraces, townhouses, units, flats and apartments that many people in our survey preferred is slower, more difficult, more expensive and involves more uncertainty than building detached housing on the outer fringes of cities.

Getting permission to build

State and local governments determine where and how new homes can be built. They use rules and processes for determining how land gets used—including zoning rules and the planning system—to try to meet particular goals for cities. Some of these are uncontentious: nobody wants a chemical plant in a residential street. But these rules and processes also create major problems for people looking to build housing. While specific arrangements differ between Australia's big cities, a common experience is too much complexity, too much cost and too many delays.

Partly the problem is a bias within the system against building new homes in the places most people want to live. Many established suburbs are zoned for minimal redevelopment. Where zoning rules allow for development, permission from the local council is usually still required to build homes. In applying for permission to build homes, developers are required to show how the homes that they intend to build comply with relevant local and state government planning rules.

Getting permission to build new housing in established suburbs is typically expensive, time-consuming, complicated and uncertain. A typical application to build any kind of home other than a detached house takes more than four months to be decided on in Queensland and Victoria, and almost as long in New South Wales. Many take considerably longer. Holding land that sits idle while this occurs is expensive. The interest costs on money borrowed to finance new housing keep adding up, whether the project is going ahead or stalled in bureaucracy.

In a 2011 report, the Productivity Commission found 'the regulations and agencies involved in planning, zoning and development assessments constitute one of the most complex regulatory regimes operating in Australia'. Examples of this complexity are not hard to find. Adelaide City Council—home to just 20 000 people—has eleven different residential zones, each with different rules about what housing gets built in that area. The land use planning rules set by Queensland local councils include confusing jargon such as zones, precincts, precinct classes, area classifications, domains, constraint codes, use codes and planning areas.

Different rules and plans for how land gets used apply to different areas and are made by different levels of government and other bodies. Western Australia alone has eight different levels of planning instrument. Moreover, changing a higher-level plan will usually have consequences for lower-level plans. It has taken as long as twenty-three years for local plans in that state to be updated to reflect changes to city- or state-wide plans. A flatter hierarchy of plans is only part of the solution though. There is no hierarchy among New South Wales' forty-seven different state government environmental planning policies. But this does not make them easy to follow.

Decisions about how land is used can also be referred to specialist government agencies. These include bodies charged to conserve a state's heritage or protect the environment. In New South Wales, 101 different local and state rules provide for referrals to these agencies. In South Australia, there are nineteen different agencies to refer to. In Queensland, fifty-five different situations can trigger a proposal to be referred to a specialist agency.

In many states, local residents are also able to formally object to developers' applications for council permission to build new homes. The consequences of these objections, and who can object, vary from state to state. In Victoria, anyone can object to (and then subsequently appeal) such an application. People objecting in New South Wales and South Australia must have a relevant interest, such as living sufficiently close by.

Like convoluted planning and zoning arrangements, rules about objections make it hardest to build homes in inner and middle suburbs that our research identified as having the biggest shortfalls of housing. They also disproportionately hamper construction of the housing types with the biggest shortfalls compared to what people say they want— semi-detached homes, such as townhouses and units, as well as flats and apartments. A recent study found that between 2002 and 2008, almost no proposals to develop detached housing in the Melbourne suburbs with the lowest house prices attracted objections. About one in five proposals to build townhouses, units or apartments in those areas attracted objections. Where house prices were highest (mostly in established inner and middle suburbs), more than half the proposals to build townhouses, units or apartments were objected to.

After a development application has been approved, in some states that decision can be appealed in a tribunal or court, leading to further cost and delay. Appeals are especially frequent in Victoria, and again much more common in established inner and middle suburbs with the best access to jobs.

Developers report that delays getting permission to build housing, and the uncertainty and costs involved, are a significant disincentive to building anything other than detached houses on cities' outer fringes. These often do not require approval or can go through an accelerated approval process. There are no neighbours in these 'greenfield' sites, so no-one to make legal objections to housing being built next door. For example, Debra Goostrey, CEO of the Urban Development Institute of Western Australia, stated in 2010 that 'it is significantly more expensive to do infill [building homes in established areas] in WA than greenfield development'.

Complex rules and processes for getting permission to build housing create other problems too. The NSW Independent Commission Against Corruption identified that that state's convoluted, uncertain and time-consuming planning system greatly increases incentives for corruption among developers, local council staff and elected officials. For example, decision-makers identified thirty different plans, policies or other documents that could have informed the determination process for the Quattro development in Wollongong, which was a subject of the commission's 2008 inquiry into the Wollongong City Council.

Scarce land

Land is the biggest contributor to the overall price of housing. For example, in 2014 the typical price for a detached house in North Perth was $860 000, about double that for Rockingham, near Perth's southern fringe. Most of this price difference comes about because land in North Perth is more valuable than land in Rockingham, not because of what is built on it.

Land is also the biggest contributor to the increases in house prices that have occurred in recent decades. In the decade from 2003, house prices in large cities have increased much more quickly than the cost of building new housing. One reason for this is that land in established suburbs with good access to jobs is scarce. Sydney, Melbourne, Brisbane, Perth and Adelaide together have about 1400 square kilometres of land within 10 kilometres of their city centres, and more than twice that amount between 10 and 20 kilometres from their respective city centres. There is as much as thirty times that amount of land more than 20 kilometres from large city centres, depending on how city boundaries are defined.

Of course, a fixed amount of land doesn't inevitably require that a fixed amount of housing be built there. One way to get around the scarcity of land in inner and middle suburbs is by building homes that allow more people to live in areas close to jobs—such as semi-detached terraces, units and townhouses and flats and apartments. As these kinds of homes are built, the amount of people given the choice to live in an area can grow, even if the amount of land is fixed.

We've seen that building housing in established areas is difficult, expensive and slow, due to the various rules and processes involved in getting permission to build new homes. In effect, these rules exacerbate the scarcity of land in our cities, driving up the prices of housing in established inner and middle suburbs. Recent research by the Reserve Bank of Australia shows that restrictive zoning pushes up the price of housing right across the city. Less restrictive zoning results in more affordable and better-located housing, with more choice for residents. This experience is also borne out in the United States: housing costs are much higher in places with tight restrictions on building new housing, such as San Francisco or Boston, than in places with fewer restrictions on building new homes.

* * *

It is also harder to build new homes in established areas because developers find it more difficult to find sites large enough to build on. As in most other industries, developers and builders operate more efficiently and at a lower cost when they build larger amounts of housing at once. This is easier on the fringe of a city. Developers typically need to buy farmland from a small number of owners, on which they can build a lot of homes.

In contrast, building a larger number of homes at one site in an established area will often involve buying housing from many individual home owners. Only some may be interested in selling their home at the time the developer wants to build. Developers either need to wait until home owners are ready to sell, which can lead to considerable delay, or convince home owners to sell by offering above-market prices, driving up costs.

Sometimes large former industrial sites can offer developers and builders the necessary scale to build new housing efficiently in established areas. But developing these sites is not always straightforward either. For example, they may need expensive and time-consuming decontamination.

Building in established areas

In addition to a finite amount of land and onerous requirements for getting permission to build housing, construction costs, financing practices and a risk-averse building industry also make it harder to build the housing Australians want in the places they want it.

Material and labour costs make buildings higher than four storeys more expensive to build than other housing types. For example, in Brisbane it costs around $1450 per square metre to build a basic flat or unit of up to three storeys. To build a basic apartment in a Brisbane building of up to ten storeys costs around $2000 per square metre.

Timber and bricks—the main materials used for buildings under three storeys—are far less expensive than the steel and concrete required for higher buildings. High-rise apartment blocks, which require lifts, cranes and underground excavation, cost more again.

Labour costs also depend on building type. Detached buildings and small blocks of flats don't require as many skilled workers, such as crane operators, as buildings of four or more storeys. Building projects of four or more storeys are also much more likely to involve a unionised workforce. Industrial practices may have some impact on the costs of some projects in some states, though robust evidence is difficult to find. However, construction of semi-detached homes and low-rise flats is not unionised, so industrial practices are not stopping these kinds of homes getting built, whatever the situation for medium- and high-rise apartments.

Finance to develop and build flats and apartments is harder to obtain and more expensive than for detached housing. Detached houses can be built and sold, one dwelling at a time. This can't happen with apartments, so banks require developers to pre-sell as much as 90 to 100 per cent of the properties before they build. Many developers are reluctant to accept so much risk.

It's no surprise that the Australian housing industry is cautious and conservative. Banks prefer to finance developers with a track record; real estate agents resist any proposal that departs from the norm and, in their view, will be hard to sell. It's an industry marked by both 'inertia and momentum', noted one housing expert we interviewed. 'There is plenty of business to be had from doing the same thing we've done for a while.'

A sign of this conservatism is the paucity of new ideas in medium-density construction. The dominant Australian housing innovation has been the streamlining of construction processes and costs for detached houses. New ideas that could make construction of other types of home better and cheaper are employed much less frequently. For example, modular or unitised apartment construction involves prefabricating some or all of the apartment off-site at a factory, with much less construction on the building site. This can enable a more efficient production process, speed up construction time and reduce waste. Less on-site construction also reduces the potential for delays due to bad weather, and disruption to neighbours and traffic. Yet getting finance for developments built this way is reportedly difficult, and uptake in Australia is much slower than in many other countries.

The result is housing projects that adopt newer ideas are funded outside mainstream financing avenues for a lower return, by developers who, as one developer described, are 'doing it for the love rather than for the money'. Unsurprisingly, there isn't a lot of that going on.

Recent housing trends

In recent years, nowhere near enough new housing has been built anywhere in Sydney. Between 2001 and 2010, 222 000 homes were built in Sydney, almost 40 per cent less than the 307 000 built in Melbourne. The pace of construction has picked up a bit more since 2010, but not dramatically.

Until recently, greenfield development—dogged by issues of fragmented land ownership and high infrastructure contributions that developers must pay—has been seen as unprofitable in Sydney. Some larger developers left New South Wales altogether. Most construction in Sydney has been in established areas, but not enough homes are being built anywhere. The overall result has been limited choices for Sydney residents.

In contrast, more homes are being built in Melbourne. Most of them are detached houses on the city's outer fringe. Four of the nation's top ten fastest-growing local government areas are on Melbourne's fringe—Wyndham, Whittlesea, Melton and Casey. The City of Melbourne, in the very centre, is also among the nation's fastest growing local government areas. There, most recent construction has been high-rise apartments. Most new development is split between premium apartments, for buyers who can afford the higher development costs and land prices associated with being close to the city centre, and small apartments sometimes aimed at international students.

While high-rise apartments in the CBD work well for some households such as students and young professionals, most families don't want to bring up their children in a small city apartment. Like the Suratwalas, though, many would like to be able to choose a somewhat smaller home—for example, a townhouse, unit or terrace—if it means they can be closer to jobs and transport.

But building new homes in established areas is difficult; the risks and costs are considerably higher. Other than high-rise apartments very close to city centres, relatively few non-detached homes are getting built in Melbourne either. Developers say that the costs, delays and barriers associated with obtaining land, finance, getting permission to build and construction mean the numbers often don't add up.

Many commentators regard the scale of Melbourne's recent housing construction, mainly on the city fringe, as a success. Undoubtedly it has contributed to housing in Melbourne being somewhat more affordable than in Sydney. But this pattern of growth at the very outer fringe has not been without cost. According to Marcus Spiller and Terry Rawnsley, Melbourne 'is afflicted with relentless pressure for low-density housing expansion into districts which are increasingly distant from the main concentrations of employment ... Regrettably, trying to solve the affordability problem by cutting up more land on the urban fringe may be like trying to fix a flagging economy by printing more money'.

Brisbane and Perth are facing similar challenges as their populations increase.

Locked out of established suburbs

Over time, home buyers on average incomes have had little option but to enter the housing market at points increasingly distant from the city centre. For example, in 1995 a Melbourne household on a typical income could afford a \$170 000 home. At the time, this was enough to buy a house in most suburbs 10 kilometres from the Melbourne CBD and beyond—and closer if one was willing to buy in places such as the then unfashionable Footscray. By 2000, a typical house was generally only affordable to a household on a typical income in suburbs such as Mordialloc or Hoppers Crossing, 24 kilometres or more from the CBD. By 2009, the equivalent household could afford to spend \$382 000; but with that amount of money they could generally only afford a house in suburbs as much as 40 kilometres from the CBD, such as Berwick or Melton.

This trend is occurring in all Australia's big cities. It is happening because there is such a dearth of new housing in established inner and middle suburbs with good access to jobs. This scarcity drives up house prices. Meanwhile, the economy has become more knowledge-intensive with opportunity increasingly concentrated in city centres. As Australia's population has continued to grow, there is no shortage of people wanting to live in these areas. The higher prices people are willing to pay in these areas—those that can afford them—show that people value areas with good access to jobs and transport, even if the homes in these areas are smaller than those further out.

Consequently, in recent decades house prices in inner-city areas with the best access to jobs have climbed sharply. From the early 1980s onwards, average annual growth in house prices has been about 2 per cent higher in suburbs within 5 kilometres of the CBDs than on the fringes of Australia's five biggest cities. The gap between inner and outer suburban house prices is widening fastest in Sydney and Melbourne, which are geographically larger and have greater concentrations of knowledge-intensive activity near their city centres.

Another factor making it harder for first home buyers to buy near the city centre is that there is less variation in home prices within suburbs than ever before. There are fewer chances to buy a cheaper home in established inner and middle suburbs. In 1976, about one in six

Melbourne suburbs could be described as 'mixed price'—meaning that the numbers of cheap and expensive property sales in these suburbs were relatively even. By 2009, only one in fifty Melbourne suburbs were mixed price.

These trends are locking in long-term inequality. Many people can only afford to live far from city centres. But moving to outer areas where house price growth is slowest reduces people's prospects of moving later on to areas with better access to jobs.

Left unchecked, this polarisation will almost certainly continue. As city populations grow, housing close to jobs and public transport will continue to appreciate in value more quickly than housing in outer areas. Wealthier households will generally seek to live in these more central locations, and will increasingly be the only ones able to afford the requisite higher housing costs. Less well-off households will increasingly be locked out of these areas, and out of the larger numbers of accessible jobs with higher incomes and greater security that inner and middle suburbs offer. It is an alarming scenario, made possible by the way Australia's housing market works.

Declining home ownership

After their landlord raised the rent for the third time in two-and-a-half years, Alexandra and Andrej Babic decided the time had come for them to vacate their two-bedroom apartment in North Strathfield, in Sydney's inner west. Though technically it was the landlord who gave notice first, their minds were largely made up.

The Babics had moved into the property in 2010 as newlyweds. At the start of their tenancy, the fortnightly rent was a manageable $760; by the time they moved out, in January 2013, that figure had soared to $1100. At that time, Andrej was clearing $2200 a fortnight as an IT network engineer and Alexandra about $1100, working casual shifts in retail and at the local NRMA call centre.

The Babics shifted to a renovated three-bedroom apartment with a balcony and garage in North Parramatta, further out, in Sydney's west. At the time, the location made sense, at least for Andrej, who worked a short drive away in Castle Hill. It was trickier for Alexandra, whose retail job was in the inner-western suburb of Burwood.

The rent on the apartment, in which they still live, is $1100 a fortnight, the same as in North Strathfield. During their previous tenancy the couple had invited Andrej's brother, Miles, to move in with them. Having arrived in Sydney from his childhood home in the NSW town of Armidale, he needed a place to stay, and the couple needed to ease the rent burden. When they shifted to North Parramatta, Miles shifted with them.

'He's a good flatmate,' Alexandra says of her brother-in-law. 'He gives us privacy and things like that. But it does mean that since we got married we haven't lived alone together for more than six months.'

Still, the help from Miles came as even more of a relief when, a year after their move to North Parramatta, Andrej was made redundant. He soon found another job, but in North Sydney—'and here we are, way out west,' Alexandra remarks—and for less pay. These days he clears $1900 a fortnight and Alexandra brings in $800. She's taken a new job in a call centre close to home, and can now walk to work, but the finances have taken a hit. Without Miles' contribution, more than 40 per cent of the couple's income would go on rent. Alexandra says they're simply treading water as it is.

'After rent, after bills—and we were both paying off a HECS debt— after all that there's not much left over,' she says.

Alexandra isn't hopeful about the couple fulfilling their aspirations for home ownership any time soon:

> We do track the property market quite intensely. Initially we wanted to buy a nice house in a vaguely decent area that had a good school, that kind of thing. Raise a family. Ideally in the northern beaches of Sydney where Andrej's aunty and uncle and cousins live.
>
> And we've decided we're not going to let this stop us from having children.
>
> But to buy a $400 000 property, which would get you a slightly newer two-bedroom apartment in the western suburbs or maybe a three-bedroom house somewhere outside of the greater Sydney

area, we would need at least $120 000 in savings, and we don't have anywhere near that. We've only got about $30 000. And the closer we get in our savings, the more property prices increase.

She and Andrej are determined to enter the market, however. They consulted a mortgage broker and a financial planner and both suggested the couple aim for an investment property.

'We're focused on that now. We'll buy whatever, wherever, as long as it's a good investment. We'll buy and then rent out the property,' Alexandra says.

In the meantime, the Babics have made an art form of austerity. Alexandra says she's only been away twice in the past decade, including her honeymoon. 'So we don't go away and we don't eat out. Occasionally we go to the movies. And that's pretty consistent with all our friends: when we want to catch up we have drinks at someone's place.'

Alexandra veers between optimism and resignation when she contemplates the future. 'Sometimes you feel, "Okay, we'll find a way to do this." Other times you don't feel all that good about the future. You feel that you work, work, work and don't get anywhere.'

* * *

Statistics suggest young people are finding it increasingly difficult to buy their first home. Figure 5.1 shows that in 1981, more than 60 per cent of households where the oldest member was aged 25–34 owned or were purchasing a home. By 2011, the equivalent figure had dropped to 48 per cent.

It isn't certain whether this decline is simply due to younger households deferring buying a home, just as people today are marrying and having children at later stages than they were thirty years ago. But home ownership rates have also been declining among middle-aged households. This suggests most younger households aren't 'catching up' later in life. Younger households with access to parental help with their first home purchase are obviously in a much better position than those without.

Home ownership is also out of reach for more lower-income households. In the mid-1970s, home ownership rates across income groups

Figure 5.1: Home ownership rates from 1981 to 2011—younger households and overall

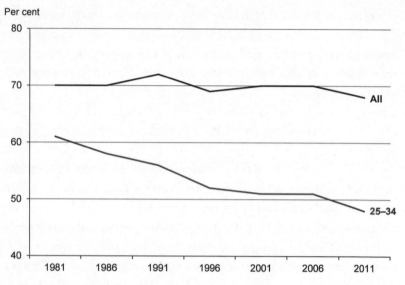

were fairly similar. People in lower-paid jobs were just as likely to own their home as people in highly paid jobs, even if it may not have been as nice a home or in as desirable a location. But today there is a growing divide.

Home ownership is an important way households build their wealth and save for retirement. Government tax settings reflect how central home ownership is to growing household wealth in Australia. Owner-occupied housing is not subject to land tax, and receives concessional treatment in determining whether someone is eligible for a government pension. Proceeds from the sale of owner-occupied housing are not subject to capital gains tax. Because they are in higher tax brackets, households on the highest incomes with the most expensive homes benefit most from these arrangements.

Tax concessions such as these reduce the amount of tax the government collects. This means one of three things: renters who don't benefit from that concession pay more tax; governments have less money to spend on other priorities; or governments need to collect more revenue in other ways, such as through the goods and services tax (GST).

Anne Power and Laura Lane of the London School of Economics observe that policies paid for by all taxpayers that support home owners to grow their wealth create 'a big financial gulf between owners and renters, bestowing on owners considerable wealth and security, allowing them to borrow and also to help their children become owners in their turn. For renters, the converse is true'. In this way, government policies are exacerbating the impact of divided access to home ownership.

Increasing house prices

A major contributor to increasing divides in home ownership levels has been house prices that have grown more quickly than incomes. The Reserve Bank of Australia estimates average house prices grew from two and a half times the average household disposable income in 1985 to be four and a half times the average household disposable income in 2012.

Some contributors to this house price growth are not changes we would want to reverse. More women have entered the workforce, spending some of their earnings bidding up house prices. Interest rates declined from the heights of the 1980s and early 1990s, and people buying housing have used the increased borrowing capacity this has given them to bid up prices. On average, households that did manage to buy a home devoted a fairly steady proportion of their income to servicing their mortgage over this period.

A more problematic cause of house prices growing relative to incomes is that demand for new housing is outstripping the new housing being built. Australia's population is growing by roughly 400 000 people a year, all of whom need somewhere to live. Moreover, the average number of people living in one home has almost halved over the last century. Both of these trends contribute to a need for new homes to be built.

But not enough homes are being built to meet the demand for housing in Australia. One government estimate put the shortfall of homes in Australia at around 228 000 homes, with the shortfall having increased at a fairly steady rate since about 2005. In 2014, Commonwealth Treasurer Joe Hockey noted that rising house prices were a reaction to lack of supply, since 'Australia fundamentally doesn't produce enough houses to meet demand'.

Sometimes rising demand for Australian real estate is attributed to foreign buyers. Foreign investors can buy housing in Australia, though only new dwellings or vacant land for redevelopment. These rules aim to ensure foreign investment stimulates new construction of homes, rather than bidding up the prices of existing homes. Temporary residents can buy one home to live in while in Australia, subject to the approval of the Foreign Investment Review Board (FIRB). The FIRB has acknowledged that prosecutions for breaching these rules are 'very rare'.

sReserve Bank analysis suggests the value of foreign investment as a proportion of the local market has slightly increased in value, mainly in Melbourne and Sydney. But it also found that new housing built for foreign investors and approved purchases of established homes by temporary residents each represent around just 1 per cent of total turn-over in the Australian housing market. To the extent that regulations aren't being enforced, this needs to improve. But claims that foreign investment is having any more than a marginal impact on Australians' capacity to buy their first home are inaccurate, and are a distraction from the real and growing barriers to home ownership in Australia.

One consequence of rising prices is that it is harder for people to buy their first home than it was thirty years ago. Raising a deposit is more difficult than it was. For most of the 1980s, a home buyer needed to have saved around the equivalent of a full year's average income in order to secure a loan they could comfortably repay but that was still large enough to purchase a median-priced dwelling. By 2010, the median house price had gone up so much that the corresponding deposit size had increased to roughly four times the average annual income, though banks are now often willing to accept smaller deposits, for instance if a borrower takes out mortgage insurance.

First home buyers let down

Government policies to support first home buyers into the housing market have largely failed to achieve their objectives.

Over the last fifty years, governments have put in place a range of measures aimed at improving affordability for first home buyers, including various grants, boosts, bonuses, tax breaks and savings accounts co-contributions. Economist Saul Eslake estimates that these measures have cost more than $22 billion since the 1960s. Despite this assistance, home-ownership rates have declined since 1961. Eslake says: 'It's hard to think of any government policy that has been pursued for so long, in the face of such incontrovertible evidence that it doesn't work, than the policy of giving cash to first home buyers in the belief that doing so will promote home ownership'.

First home buyer assistance has largely enabled households who were already going to buy a home to do so a little earlier, rather than enable more households to own a home. These grants and concessions are usually too small to help people pull a deposit together, and they don't help buyers meet regular mortgage repayments. Grants and subsidies for first home owners are also tiny compared to the tax breaks and subsidies that existing home owners and property investors receive.

Tax concessions for property investors are another kind of government policy affecting the housing market, and first home buyers in particular. Tax concessions such as discounted capital gains tax and negative gearing are often cited as mechanisms for getting more housing built. For example, the Real Estate Institute of Australia was reported in 2013 as advocating negative gearing because it 'helps in the provision of rental accommodation'.

Negative gearing allows investors in housing and other assets to deduct the interest costs of borrowing from their taxable income, including income from other sources such as wages. This allows negatively geared investors to reduce their overall tax liability. The Commonwealth government forgoes between $2 and $4 billion in tax revenue each year through negative gearing.

Tax concessions from negative gearing are more generous in Australia than in most other advanced countries. A comparison by the Reserve Bank found tax concessions arising from negative gearing were more generous in Australia than the other countries it analysed: the United States, United Kingdom, Canada and the Netherlands. Notably, homes in the United States, United Kingdom and Canada are all more affordable than in Australia, according to a different study carried out in 2014; the Netherlands was not part of the study. Meanwhile, other advanced countries such as Germany, France, Switzerland, Sweden, Denmark and Finland do not offer negative gearing to housing investors at all.

In addition, capital gains tax rules were changed in 1999 so that investors in assets such as housing pay half their normal tax rate on the profits from selling that asset. Discounted taxation of capital gains, compared to income from other sources such as wages, costs the Commonwealth government about $4 billion a year in forgone tax revenue, though not all of this arises from discounts on housing investment.

These tax concessions are not resulting in much new housing being built. Almost 95 per cent of loans for housing investment are for people to buy established houses, rather than build new ones.

Tax concessions for housing investors disproportionately benefit people on higher incomes. In 2011, more than half of all capital gains were accrued by people earning more than $180 000 a year. Most investors reduced their taxable income by about $10 000 a year through negative gearing, but this figure increased to about $13 000 a year for people earning over $80 000 a year, and increased further to $25 000 a year for people earning over $180 000.

In some ways this is unsurprising—higher-income earners in higher tax brackets get more financial benefits from reducing their taxable income than lower-income earners in lower tax brackets. But it is problematic if the tax concessions are hardly getting any new housing built. Again, these tax concessions don't exist in isolation. The end result is that either people who don't benefit from the concessions pay more tax, and governments have less money to spend on other priorities, or governments need to collect more revenue in other ways.

While they stimulate very little new construction, tax concessions for investors are driving up the prices of existing housing. The tax benefits on offer encourage investors to spend more than the underlying value of the housing they buy. These subsidies seem to be helping investors muscle first home buyers out of the market. Loans to investors accounted in 2014 for close to half of all new housing loan approvals, and in New South Wales investor loan approvals increased by about 90 per cent from 2012 to 2014.

These tax concessions may also represent risks to the broader economy. In 2014 the Commonwealth Government's Financial System Inquiry, chaired by former Commonwealth Bank CEO David Murray, concluded that the tax treatment of investor housing 'tends to encourage leveraged and speculative investment ... Housing is a potential source of systemic risk for the financial system and the economy.'

So far we've looked at how the housing market works for home buyers, investors and the businesses involved in building housing. Next we consider its impact on the more than two million Australian households who rent their home.

Renting can be very insecure

For six years, Simon Khamara and his wife Chérie have negotiated the hazards of Sydney's rental market. After an extended period working overseas, the couple returned to the city in 2008 so that Simon, aged forty, could take up a position at the Sydney Theatre Company. Soon after, Chérie, a 37-year-old social worker, landed a job in the health sector. Being English, she always envisaged settling down in London. Sydney 'was only supposed to be for a couple of years', Simon explains. 'But I guess this is what happens when you get a really good job, like I did. We never really entertained the idea of buying a place in Australia even though we could have, and in hindsight probably should have.'

For the first eighteen months they rented a one-bedroom flat in harbourside Kirribilli. Then they shifted to a $620-a-week, two-bedroom terrace in Balmain East, in Sydney's inner west. As the expiry date on the Balmain lease approached, the estate agent told them it would be fine to stay on. But two weeks before the formal end of the lease, they heard that the overseas-based landlord had other plans. They were given notice to vacate when Chérie was six months pregnant.

They scrambled to find somewhere else. 'We wanted to stay in the same neighbourhood,' says Simon. 'We were two pretty well paid professionals; there was nothing dodgy about our applications. And Chérie was heavily pregnant. But there was no sympathy.

'I remember there was a silent bidding war for one property in [nearby] Annandale. We rang the agents and they said, "Well, we've had someone offer more for this property." When we asked how much more, they said, "We can't tell you."'

At the time, NSW law entitled tenants to only two weeks' notice before they had to vacate. The couple begged for more time and got an extra fortnight, but the landlord became 'quite nasty'.

'We were pleading that Chérie was pregnant and the market was weak. But he threatened to sue us,' Simon recalls.

The landlord was eager to sell. Simon and Chérie woke one morning to find two tradespeople removing a blind on their balcony. No-one had bothered to obtain their consent. A tenants' advocacy service advised the couple to fight the termination notice in the Consumer, Trader and Tenancy Tribunal, pointing out that at least the legal manoeuvring would buy some time. But the thought of protracted proceedings was too much; the pair were 'already stressed enough' and began packing their stuff into boxes.

Their estate agent had one listing for a flat, and the couple applied, assuming they would get first preference. They weren't considered. Then they noticed a listing on the agency's website for a two-bedroom furnished short-term rental in inner west Glebe. The rent was a punishing $770 a week, but they grabbed it anyway, put their belongings into storage and kept looking for another place. By now Chérie was seven months pregnant.

Some five weeks later they inspected a house in Summer Hill, 8 kilometres west of Sydney's CBD, for $720 a week. It was further from the CBD and the cost was much higher than they wanted to pay, but their options were few and the clock was ticking. They moved to Summer Hill, Chérie gave birth, life settled into a stable rhythm—until the year-long lease neared its end, and 'the same thing happened'. They were told to vacate, albeit with more notice than previously thanks to changes in the law.

'By now we were wise and jaded,' recalls Simon. 'So we took a place even further out, in Ashfield.' At $520 a week, it was considerably cheaper. But a year later the family was again sent packing. They had been forced to shift three times in three years. Now the family rents a townhouse in inner west Leichhardt for $725 a week. 'We had to pay to be closer in,' Simon explains. 'We accept that.' But he also believes that renters in Australia face a raw deal; a problem that's as much cultural as it is economic.

'I've lived in a number of cities, in London, in Paris, but I've never experienced anything like Sydney. The quality is so low and the demand so high.

'In Europe renting is very common. In Australia you're seen as something of a pariah, someone who can't get their life together,' he says.

For now, Simon and his family are crossing their fingers. 'We are about to come to the end of our one-year lease in Leichhardt. We're not contacting the agents. We don't want to tempt fate.'

* * *

Simon and Chérie are among the many Australian households that choose to rent. Some rent because they value the better access to jobs, schools and amenities that established inner and middle suburbs offer, but cannot afford to buy a house in these areas. Renting avoids many of the costs that buying a home involves. Others rent because they value the flexibility it offers and do not want to commit to buying a home.

Still other households rent because they cannot afford to buy. While public and community housing assists a small number of the most disadvantaged, for many, renting is the only long-term option.

Households renting their home represent one in four Australian households, a proportion that is steadily increasing. It's widely thought that most renting is temporary: what people do while studying or saving for a deposit. But more than half of renters have rented for more than five years, and a third for more than ten. It is outdated to think of renting as a transitional state on the way to the Australian dream of home ownership. Yet these stereotypes might well be contributing to a culture that makes renting in Australia unstable and insecure.

When people start renting, they generally sign a 6- or 12-month lease, then rent month-by-month once the initial lease expires. There are no legal restrictions on longer leases, but low vacancy rates, and the pressure on many tenants to reach agreement and get a roof over their head, give landlords substantial bargaining power. As a result, the length of residential leases in Australia is usually the legal minimum, giving landlords maximum flexibility to raise the rent or sell the property at the end of the lease period. Landlords can also generally terminate leases with thirty to sixty days notice in order to move in themselves or sell the property.

The result is that renters move much more frequently than home owners do, and much more frequently than they want to. Of renters who had moved home in the previous five years, a third characterised the move as forced or constrained. The gap between owners' and renters' frequency of moving home in Australia is the widest in the developed world.

Renters want stability and security of tenure for the same reasons owners do. A stable location enables children to stay in the same schools, and households to stay connected with their family, friends and community. Moving frequently is inconvenient and expensive. It makes it harder to plan for the future, as does the ongoing threat of having leases terminated or not renewed.

In many other advanced countries it is possible to rent without the instability and insecurity that Australian renters regularly face. Figure 5.2 shows that renters in places such as Germany, France and the United Kingdom enjoy longer lease terms, more narrowly defined reasons for eviction and longer notice periods than renters in Australia. Australian commercial leases—including those to small businesses and sole traders—also typically involve longer terms and frequently include options to renew. Commercial property is also frequently sold to investors with a tenancy underway, whereas residential sales can be preceded by eviction of tenants.

Renters also do not enjoy the same scope as owners to personalise their accommodation, so that it feels like home. Usually they can only make minor alterations at the discretion of the landlord. There are few rewards for tenants who improve their housing or devote time and money to keeping it in good condition.

Many renters want to keep pets, just as many home owners do. Pets provide companionship and can play an important role in mitigating

Figure 5.2: Typical rental conditions in some other developed countries

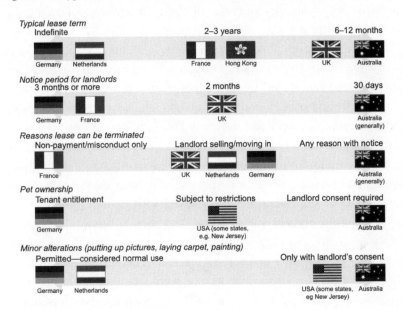

loneliness and the serious problems it can cause. Yet many landlords and property managers have blanket rules against pet ownership, even when it presents little or no risk.

Renters also often report that real estate agents conducting inspections do not respect the fact that they are in the renters' home. In one survey, many renters said they wanted 'to be treated with more respect'.

Figure 5.2 shows that other advanced countries do not so severely restrict tenants' capacity to make a home of their rental property. For instance, in Germany renters can ordinarily make small holes in the wall to hang pictures.

Lower-income renters squeezed

Lauren Beaumont (name has been changed), a 33-year-old single mother of six, grew up in Mount Druitt in Sydney's west. Eight years ago she found herself in housing limbo, forced to live with friends as she inched up the state's public housing waiting list. After a stay in Orange, New

South Wales, she returned to Sydney, figuring her prospects would be better there. She could get short-term help from her immediate family, and in turn assist them.

'My mum was going through some dizzy spells and I wanted to help her, get some things from the shop, that kind of thing. I'm the only one of her kids who has a car,' Lauren explains. Lauren assumed employment would be no problem and she was right: she now works as a room attendant at the Novotel hotel in Rooty Hill in Sydney's west.

What Lauren hadn't banked on is Sydney's expensive and ferociously competitive rental market. Since their return six months ago, she and her children, aged between seven and sixteen, have been sleeping on floors and living out of suitcases. First they stayed with Lauren's sister in the western Sydney suburb of Glendenning, and then at her mother's place at nearby St Marys. For the past three months they've been staying at the same suburb with another of Lauren's sisters and her eight-year-old son.

Lauren works shifts five to six days a week, earning $570 after tax. She receives just over $500 a week—$1029 a fortnight—in family tax benefit. She does not receive child support. To accommodate her family she needs to find a place with at least four bedrooms, 'two kids each room'. She is looking for a house in the west, no more than twenty minutes drive from the Novotel. 'I'm not spending money on petrol,' she explains. Nor does she want her kids to move schools again.

The cheapest place she's applied for was $340 a week, 'and I've gone as far as $550'. Even with her entitlement to $73-a-week Rent Assistance, rent would chew up roughly 30 per cent of her income—at worst, 48 per cent. Balancing the budget is hard enough already. She's received some food vouchers and parcels from Anglicare Sydney; her mother, a volunteer for the agency's emergency relief team, facilitated the contact. For a gold coin donation Lauren has also obtained fruit and vegetables through the Fresh Fruit Thursdays program at Anglicare's Mount Druitt centre.

For now, the estate agents and landlords won't give her a chance. Lauren reels off the suburbs where she's applied for rentals: Seven Hills, Erskine Park, Penrith, Kingswood, St Clair, Werrington. Before she started working at the Novotel, she even ventured as far as Richmond, northwest of Sydney, and Blackheath in the Blue Mountains. Lauren says:

I've applied for fifty houses. It was number fifty this week.

I rang this place up in Werrington where they help you out with getting private rental and they said, "Oh, we can't put you on the list until something comes up." And then they never got back to me.

Sometimes I'm the only applicant, the only person turning up for an inspection, but then they'll tell me they gave the place to someone else. No explanation, that's it.

I think it's because of my children. We've been to a house where the property manager said, "The owner doesn't like kids." Because in the past the tenants have destroyed the house. But then, what's the point of putting a four-bedroom house on the market?

She suspects her modest income also plays its part. 'There's nothing wrong with my credit history,' she stresses. 'But I guess some of the other applicants make more money.'

In the meantime, she has no choice but to endure the cramped and unsettled existence at her sister's 3-bedroom public-housing home. Her eldest son sleeps on a mattress in the lounge, the teenage twins have a couch each, Lauren and two daughters share two single mattresses pushed together. Her 14-year-old son occupies the third bedroom, hemmed in with their clothing racks. Their furniture and other belongings sit in storage, waiting for a new abode.

Lauren is grateful for her sister's generosity, but the strain on everyone is enormous. 'It's horrible,' Lauren says, 'living like that. Not having your own place where you can live by your own rules.' Still, there's no going back to Orange and 'public housing has a 10-year wait list', so Lauren perseveres in the hunt.

'Number fifty', Lauren's most recent application, is for a place in St Marys for $360 a week. 'The rooms are small but it's a cute little house,' she says, a slight lift in her voice. 'So I'm waiting to hear back on that one.'

* * *

The experience of Lauren Beaumont and her children shows some of the more acute human consequences of the problems with Australia's housing market. The overall shortage of housing in Australia has also led to a shortage of rental housing. Rental vacancy rates are at historically low levels—typically around or below 2 per cent in recent years—indicating a significant shortage of rental properties.

In light of such a shortage, it's no surprise that lower-income earners are spending more of their incomes on rent. Since the early 1980s, rents have increased more quickly than incomes, with the gap widening fastest for lower-income earners.

Lower-income renters' affordability problems are exacerbated by stiff competition for the lowest-cost rental housing. Some households on moderate incomes may prefer to live in lower-cost housing and spend the money they save on other things. But lower-income renters typically don't have the option of living in higher-cost housing, or they have to make big sacrifices in order to do so.

Consequently, many households on lower incomes find it a struggle to pay the rent. The proportion of Australian lower-income households spending more than 30 per cent of their incomes on rent (a common affordability measure for households with limited capacity to spend more money on housing) has been increasing since the early 1980s. These rental affordability difficulties are most acute in big cities.

Some have to make big sacrifices and compromises just to keep a roof over their heads. Common responses to affordability difficulties among lower-income renters included borrowing money from family or friends, selling or pawning possessions and seeking support from a welfare agency. More than a third of lower-income renters also identified that housing affordability problems had contributed to their children going without adequate health or dental care.

Moreover, lower-income renters have to make greater compromises about the location, size, type and quality of their home than most other households. Most lower-cost rental housing in cities is located in outer and fringe suburbs. The result is that lower-income earners are increasingly cut off from opportunities to access the more secure and high-paying jobs that tend to cluster near the centre of cities.

In Sydney and Melbourne especially, low-cost rental housing was historically located in inner suburbs, but has retreated outwards as economic opportunity has concentrated inwards. For example, Surry Hills in Sydney and Richmond in Melbourne were once considered slums, but rental housing in these inner suburbs is now very expensive. In 1994, the typical rent across all kinds of home in inner Sydney (suburbs such as Ashfield, Marrickville and Lane Cove) was $210 a week compared to $170 a week in outer Sydney (suburbs such as Liverpool and Fairfield). By 2014, the gap between rents in these areas had widened. The typical rent in the inner city was $585 a week, compared to $420 a week in Sydney's outer suburbs.

The shrinking supply of public housing adds to the problem. Fewer than 4 per cent of households now live in public housing in Australia, a proportion that has been steadily declining over recent decades. People seeking public housing face long waits. In Melbourne, for example, the average wait time for public housing is around four years.

Governments once played a major role in building new housing. Between 1947 and 1976, Commonwealth and state governments contributed more than 20 per cent of the growth in new housing. Since the mid-1970s, governments have reduced their role in building new housing. Policy has instead shifted to measures that provide money to buyers and renters, such as grants for first home buyers, tax concessions for investors and Rent Assistance for renters on income support. Over this time, the target group for public housing has narrowed. Public housing once provided a home for many low-income workers and returned soldiers, but today mainly serves very disadvantaged households with special needs.

One consequence of this shift is that lower-income earners today have little option but to look for housing in the private rental market, where households in a similar position several decades ago may also have had the option of seeking public housing to meet their need for shelter. The resultant increased demand for private rental housing contributes to intense competition for the lowest-priced rental homes, and to increases in rents.

Housing is dividing Australians

Rather than bridging divides between Australians, the housing market is widening them. Home owners in inner suburbs enjoy good access to jobs, and many have grown their wealth through strong house price growth over recent decades. In contrast, most of the opportunities for people to buy their first home today are in places far from city centres. This leaves them cut off from jobs and transport in a way their parents never experienced. The housing market is not providing the options people want, notably semi-detached terraces, townhouses and units, and low-rise flats and apartments in established inner and middle suburbs.

Younger people are increasingly locked out of home ownership, as are lower-income earners. The home ownership divide between young and old is widening, as is that between rich and poor.

The large and growing number of households renting their home don't enjoy anywhere near the stability, security and control over their lives that Australian home owners and many renters overseas do. For many, home ownership is increasingly unattainable. Like first home buyers, many renters are pushed into areas with poor access to jobs due to price constraints and a shortage of new housing. Renters on low incomes are doing it especially tough.

Government policy is making these divides worse, or in some cases even creating them. Convoluted rules and processes for getting permission to build housing make it difficult and expensive to build the kinds of home that many people want to live in. These rules contribute to a shortage of new housing in Australia, especially in established suburbs with good access to jobs.

Tax concessions for investors inflate the price of established housing, but get few new homes built. They also contribute to declining rates of home ownership. Tax concessions for home owners do help many households build their wealth and provide for their retirement, but they also exacerbate the wealth divides between renters and home owners, and between home owners in inner and outer suburbs. These tax concessions are funded by the whole community, yet the greatest benefits accrue to wealthy households who need them the least.

Legal settings for residential tenancies, and deeply entrenched cultural norms about renting, contribute to renters' second-class status. Both are looking increasingly outdated as more and more Australians rent their home.

One critical divide, the one between people and jobs, could be ameliorated by good roads and public transport that enable people to get around quickly and easily. Yet in the next chapter we will see that a gulf in access to public transport deepens—rather than narrows—the divide between inner and outer parts of Australia's big cities. Meanwhile, traffic congestion continues to grow, causing frustration among commuters, cutting into free time, restricting access to jobs and holding back the economy.

Chapter 6

Transport

THE CLOSER THE DISTANCE between where you live and work and shop, the happier you'll be, goes 'Triangle of happiness', a song by the Australian harmonic vocal group Tripod. The luckiest people in the song live above the milk bar they run. To everyone else who lives in cities, the struggles of getting around—the commute to work, getting kids to school, seeing friends and family, going to the cinema, doing the shopping, visiting the doctor—are all too familiar.

Cities draw their power from bringing many people together to do things they could not do alone. But congestion and poor public transport systems can prevent a city from fulfilling its most basic functions: connecting people with each other and with jobs. This is precisely what is happening in Australian cities today.

This chapter considers how well our transport systems are doing, and for whom. It examines why congestion happens, and why commute times are increasing, especially to many outer suburbs where residents have fewer transport choices and nearby employment options. It explores the roles of cars and of public transport.

Our largest cities were settled when horses were still the main way to travel. But horses were largely reserved for the rich. Horses need stables, land and lots of food. So most people walked. Australian cities started small and compact, and most people went on foot to work.

Later, suburbs developed along tram and train routes as these extended outwards. At the end of World War II, Melbourne was still the recognisable child of the 1880s, writes Graeme Davison in *Car wars*, his book on how the car changed Melbourne. 'Seen from the air, it looked like a giant hand, the palm representing the central business district and the core of closely settled industrial suburbs, and the fingers, the web of railway and tramway suburbs.'

After the war, owning a car became accessible to many, at the same time that manufacturing was moving to the suburbs. The car's comfort and convenience transformed urban transport and reshaped Australian cities. We were able to live on bigger blocks of cheaper land, further from the city centre, and drive to work on new roads. Homes were no longer within easy walking distance of a train station or a tram stop. A new suburban landscape emerged.

At this time, getting to work by car suited our economy. The car provided manufacturers with a large workforce and opened up opportunity for many. But now that the economy has changed, the car is no longer the answer it once was.

Debates about transport tend to be polarised in Australia. Commentators love to get on soapboxes and advocate in favour of cars or public transport. For example, the City of Yarra in Melbourne campaigned against the proposed East West Link road tunnel in that city with the slogan, 'Trains not toll roads'. But it's not that simple. If large cities are to function well, they need networks of good roads and good public transport.

Longer commutes

We have seen that the fastest population growth is occurring in new suburbs far from city centres, largely because of the way the housing market works. But the shift to a more knowledge-intensive economy means that jobs and opportunity aren't following at anywhere near the same rate. So for many people living in these suburbs, connections to jobs and opportunity are poor and getting poorer.

Commuting times are increasing in all Australia's large cities, especially in outer suburbs. From 2002 to 2011, the average weekly commuting time for full-time workers in Australia's large cities increased by almost 20 per cent, to five hours and forty-five minutes a week.

People living in large cities' outer suburbs commute on average for around 20 per cent longer than people in inner suburbs. While this gap is not as big as you might expect, inner-city residents usually take more time to travel shorter distances because there is more congestion and they are more likely to walk, cycle or use public transport.

The gap between commuting times in inner and outer areas is also less than it might be because some people living in outer areas—people such as Alice Osborne, whom we met in Chapter 2—give up skilled work further from home because the commute takes too long.

Longer commutes are particularly tough on women caring for children, and people in part-time or casual work. Spending more than two hours a day commuting to a full-time job may not be ideal, but spending just as much time commuting to a 3-hour shift scheduled around school or child-care hours is even worse. And many people in outer areas commute for much longer than the average, as the Osbornes and Suratwalas (whom we met in Chapter 3) can attest. In 2002, one in six people spent more than ten hours a week commuting. By 2011 this proportion had increased to one in four.

* * *

When Alice Osborne worked as a medical researcher in the city she woke at 5 a.m. She drove to Laverton train station, arriving before 6.30 a.m. to nab a parking spot. Leave home any later, and Point Cook is in gridlock. Only three main roads—Point Cook, Palmers and what the locals refer to as Boardwalk Boulevard—lead to the freeway. Start the journey during peak hour and it can take a very long time just to get out of the suburb, let alone make progress in the city-bound lanes of the M1, crammed with commuters from other growth suburbs in Melbourne's west.

Catching the bus to Laverton was never an option for Alice. It would make an already long journey longer and the bus connections with the train line are unreliable. Commuters who miss their bus home in the evening often wait forty minutes for another.

So Alice caught an early train from Laverton. Then from Flagstaff station in the CBD, she caught a tram to her work at the Murdoch Childrens Research Institute, located on the top floor of the Royal Children's Hospital. At 7 a.m., she arrived at work and swiped her card on the back door to let herself in.

On the days Alice worked, her husband Jason dropped their son William at the new childcare centre at nearby Sanctuary Lakes at around 8 a.m. He then had to battle the now-clogged streets of Point Cook, inching his way to Laverton station, which was overflowing with cars. Sometimes he'd find a park in the 'mud pit', the dirt patch on the road near the station. Often he'd have to backtrack to Aircraft station.

On those days, Jason rarely made it to work before 10 a.m. Often he had missed an important meeting or conference call. Tense and frustrated, he spent the rest of the day playing catch-up. He began to worry about his performance, convinced his productivity was suffering.

Longer travel distances

Transport can only go so far to bridge the gap between jobs and opportunities and where people live. Australia's outer suburbs have far fewer jobs than working-age people, so many people have to commute long distances to work. Some outer suburban residents are able to commute to their local area, but the lack of local jobs means many have to travel further afield. This may be to established suburbs closer in, as Meera Suratwala does in travelling from Epping North to Blackburn. Other outer suburban residents have to commute all the way to the city centre, as Hiren Suratwala and Jason Osborne do.

In Wyndham, Melton and Cardinia—Melbourne's three fastest-growing outer suburban local government areas—the typical commute to work is about 25 kilometres. Average commutes in outer western and south-western Sydney are about as far. By contrast, the average commute among all Melburnians is about half that distance, and a bit longer at 15 kilometres across all of Sydney.

City centres are where economic opportunity and employment growth are concentrated. But getting to them from outer suburbs takes a long time, especially from places where public transport connections are poor. In Wyndham in Melbourne's outer west, the local council organised a competition to highlight poor transport connections to the area's fast-growing suburbs such as Tarneit, Wyndham Vale and Point Cook. Local councillor Peter Maynard was part of a team that took an hour and thirty-seven minutes to drive the 27 kilometres from Point Cook to Federation Square in Melbourne's CBD. Progress was painstaking. The team averaged a speed of about 17 kilometres an hour. Peter observed that 'for the first 10 to 15 kilometres, [the driver] Marie didn't get out of second gear'.

Other modes of transport were not much quicker. Driving a car to a nearby station then catching a train took about an hour and ten minutes. Taking a bus to the station then catching a train took between an hour and ten minutes and almost an hour and a half, depending on what suburb people started from. These times probably understate the typical commute from these suburbs to the centre of Melbourne: like Alice Osborne, many commuters have a walk or another trip after catching the train into the centre. Unsurprisingly, a relatively small proportion of outer suburban residents of Australia's big cities commute to city centres at present, despite the greater opportunities on offer in these places.

Congested roads

Traffic is a by-product of a healthy economy and a connected community. Cars, trucks and buses on the road are people going to work, businesses making deliveries and family members visiting each other.

But too many of these journeys at the same time leads to congestion, which chews up a lot of time that people could spend in other ways. Across all Australian cities at all times of day, driving on the road takes on average almost a third longer than it would if there were no traffic. Of course, congestion levels vary greatly across the day. Sydney drivers are delayed an average of thirty-eight minutes for every hour they drive on weekdays in peak times. And this is a citywide average: in some places the congestion is worse again.

Traffic congestion is getting worse. Between 2006 and 2011, the average speed on the M5 from south-western Sydney to the airport slowed from 44 to 35 kilometres an hour during the morning peak. Average travel speeds fell also in peak periods over the decade from 2003 in Melbourne. Motorways in particular are seeing increased use, though average speeds are getting slower on all major roads, especially in inner suburbs. Congestion is also increasing at off-peak times: for example Melbourne's lunchtime traffic is heavier on Saturdays than during the week.

Congestion is not entirely predictable either. Some days are worse than others. For example, on a good day Meera Suratwala's commute from Epping North to Blackburn in Melbourne takes fifty minutes, but on a bad day it stretches to an hour and twenty minutes or more. This uncertainty increases the frustration that congestion causes and the amount of time people have to allow for travel.

An extreme example of how this uncertainty plays out can be found in Alice Osborne's suburb of Point Cook. Pregnant women choose to induce labour before their due date, lest they risk giving birth while stuck in peak hour on the freeway. Alice has a friend who was booked to give birth to her second child at one of the private hospitals in the inner city. The woman's first labour had been fast so she decided that leaving the timing to nature was too big a risk.

The costs of congestion—to Australia as a whole, and to individuals, families and businesses—are high and increasing. We saw in Chapters 3 and 4 that long commutes take their toll on family life and social connection. In 2005, the Bureau of Infrastructure, Transport and Regional Economics estimated the costs of congestion to individuals and the economy at $9.4 billion. One tradesperson quoted in the Commonwealth government's 2013 *State of Australian cities* report observed how traffic forces him to either forgo income or charge higher prices: 'If you quote for a two-hour job but it takes you two hours to get there, it's really a four-hour job'.

Causes of traffic congestion

A large amount of congestion arises from the way jobs are concentrated close to each other, especially in inner-city areas. Bottlenecks caused by the design of a city's transport system also contribute, as does the way the transport system is managed.

There is only so much road space to accommodate cars that want to go to employment centres at peak times. It is not surprising that as our cities' populations grow, both the morning and the evening peaks are starting earlier and lasting longer. In Melbourne, for example, traffic volumes are growing fastest on motorways and other main roads between 6 a.m. and 6.30 a.m.

An increasing number of seemingly discretionary trips are also contributing to peak-hour congestion. Recreational and shopping trips made up only 3 per cent of morning peak car travel in Melbourne in 1978, but thirty years later represented 17 per cent of these trips. About one in every six cars on the road during the morning peak is someone heading to or from shopping or leisure activities. More people are using cars rather than public transport for recreational and shopping trips, and many more of these trips are happening at peak times. This shift appears to be occurring Australia-wide; for instance, in Sydney 19 per cent of peak-period trips are for recreation and shopping.

Congestion caused by a finite amount of road space near employment centres is likely to get worse in future. The total distance driven, and total number of car trips being taken, in Australian cities are increasing more slowly than they did in previous decades. But car use is still growing overall, and does not appear to be slowing in outer suburbs. Moreover, Australia's population will continue to grow, and knowledge-intensive activity will continue dominating the economy. The amount of travel by trucks transporting freight is also expected to increase substantially over coming decades.

Congestion can also be caused by bottlenecks in the system—when, for example, commuters have to drive through a busy area (such as an inner-city employment centre) in order to reach a destination on the other side of the city (such as a port). Or a natural feature can create a bottleneck. In Sydney the harbour makes it harder for people and businesses in different parts of the city to connect with each other by road.

Bottlenecks can also stem from how a city's transport system is managed. For example, on-street parking on main roads causes unnecessary congestion. Often almost half the available road is taken up by cars that are standing still, and congestion inevitably ensues. For example, the average speed for trams sharing roads with cars in Melbourne's sub-urban shopping strips is just 15 kilometres an hour.

Level crossings where train lines meet roads also create congestion. Indeed, traffic congestion increases as public transport improves, because more trains passing level crossings means more delays for cars. The Koornang Road level crossing on Melbourne's busy Dandenong line, for example, is closed for a total of almost an hour across the 2-hour peak period. One nearby resident indicated that 'if you ever get through the Clayton Road level crossing during peak hour with two trains or less going through, you've done really well'.

Traffic bottlenecks at level crossings are bigger problems in some cities than in others. Melbourne still has about 170 level crossings on the electrified suburban train network, while public works projects during the Great Depression replaced most of Sydney's level crossings with bridges and tunnels. The Sydney suburban train network now includes only a handful of level crossings.

Good or bad road management can make a surprisingly big difference to congestion. A recent Victorian auditor-general's report found that road authorities were failing to make the most of technology such as intelligent traffic light phasing so that cars can move more quickly through intersections. Because such technology can substantially reduce congestion at very low cost, traffic lights are supposed to be reviewed every five years to make sure they are handling traffic flow as effectively as possible. But the report found Victorian authorities only do so about every twenty years.

We can't build our way out of congestion

Roads connect lots of people with lots of jobs. Car travel enabled Australia's cities and the manufacturing-based economy to develop. At the end of World War II, one in five trips was made by car. By the 1980s, four in five trips were made by car.

Cars continue to be the main form of transport for most Australians, especially in outer suburbs. Cars are always available and enable people to travel directly from their home to where they want to go.

They are more flexible than other forms of transport: you can drive to work and shop on the way home, or collect children from school. You can travel further more quickly, at least when not too many other people are sharing the road.

Cars are especially important for trips to middle and outer suburbs, where jobs are more dispersed. Nine in ten commuters to jobs located 10 or more kilometres from the centre of Australia's big cities travel by car.

Motorways in particular connect large numbers of people and jobs, and businesses, customers and suppliers, in reasonable travel times. They are a vital part of a modern city's infrastructure.

A new motorway doesn't just speed up trips that people were already making before the motorway was built. They enable new travel patterns by allowing industries requiring lots of land or connections to ports and airports—transport, warehousing or wholesaling companies, for instance—to move away from congested inner locations.

Since 2005, the 40-kilometre-long M7 has linked western Sydney suburbs such as Wetherill Park, Fairfield and Ingleburn with each other and with other parts of Sydney. A 2008 evaluation of the motorway by consultants Ernst and Young found that it better connected such places to other parts of Sydney, supporting commercial and industrial growth, and improving employment opportunities for people living in areas served by that road.

While motorways can help distribute jobs around cities and enable drivers to bypass congested areas, their cost is considerable. For example, inner Melbourne was very congested in the late 1980s. Motorways were poorly connected, often ending in inner suburbs and pouring traffic onto congested roads, especially around the CBD. The CBD was a thorough-fare for people driving from one side of the city to the other, while also serving as a major employment centre.

In response, the government built CityLink. Between 1996 and 2000, the Tullamarine Freeway in the north-west and the Monash Freeway in the south-east were upgraded, and the two freeways linked so that cars and trucks could bypass the CBD. CityLink connected north-west and south-east Melbourne; it also connected both areas with knowledge-intensive jobs and industries in the CBD and inner city.

This did not come cheaply: CityLink cost an estimated $1.5 billion to build in 1993 prices. Adjusted for inflation, this would be about $2.6 billion in 2014.

New roads also fill up fast. This inevitability is known as the 'fundamental law of road congestion'. Much as we'd like to, we simply cannot build our way out of congestion by continually adding road space. New roads enable more people to travel around, but the savings in journey times they offer are fleeting. There are always more people wanting to drive in peak periods than there is space on the road. For instance, the authority responsible for Melbourne's proposed East West Link tunnel acknowledged that local traffic would return to current levels within twelve years of the new tunnel being built, notwithstanding its estimated cost of $6 to $8 billion. It was estimated the proposed tunnel would reduce the total time drivers across the whole city spend in their car by only a tenth of 1 per cent.

Every square metre used for roads is also expensive, and land in inner-city areas is finite. Land used for roads and for parking is not available for more productive uses such as shops and offices, which create jobs and economic growth.

Driving makes enormous sense for individuals, but if too many of us do it at the same time, it stops making sense: too many drivers ultimately turn city streets into a car park. We think of congestion as something we have to cope with, not as something we create. Yet that is what we are doing. As cities expert Ed Glaeser puts it: 'Soviet Russia used to charge artificially low prices for consumer goods, and the result was empty shelves and long lines. That is basically what happens when people are allowed to drive on city streets for free'. We seem to think we have a right to travel on roads for free. We used to think the same about parking.

Public transport

Public transport can carry many more commuters into job-rich areas than cars can. There is only so much road space to accommodate cars that want to go at peak times to areas with lots of jobs. The Clarkson (formerly Joondalup) and Mandurah lines stretching north and south of Perth's CBD have more than three times the capacity of the Mitchell and Kwinana freeways that run alongside them. The single bus lane on the Sydney Harbour Bridge takes more people to the city during the morning peak than all the other city-bound lanes combined.

Public transport is especially useful when roads get congested, such as when lots of people are travelling to work. Public transport use declined as a proportion of all travel between World War II and about 2005, as the car became the dominant form of transport. Since about 2005, the proportion of trips to work by public transport has been increasing slightly. Trains are responsible for nearly all of this growth. Increased train use in Sydney and Melbourne appears to have been caused mainly by strong CBD and inner-city employment growth. In Perth, an expansion of the rail system has been the biggest contributor.

By enabling large numbers of people to work close to each other in a small area, public transport underpins Australia's knowledge-intensive economy. One in three commuters to jobs located within 10 kilometres of the centres of Australia's five biggest cities travels by public transport. In the Sydney CBD, a staggering 180 000 people an hour arrive during the morning peak. More than half travel by train. The Sydney CBD's underground rail loop, completed in 1956, makes this possible. Cars and even buses simply can't move as many people into small areas at once.

Dedicated busways in Brisbane, tram-only lanes in Melbourne and priority bus lanes in all large cities also help to make public transport move more quickly. They make the best use of scarce road space as buses and trams can carry more passengers in an hour than cars occupying the same amount of road.

Each person taking public transport instead of a car frees up road space they would have used if they had driven. This either reduces congestion or enables someone else to use that road space for work or personal travel. Public transport commuters also don't use up scarce CBD land with car parking. A parked car occupies about the same amount of space as a standard office work cubicle, so driving to work essentially doubles the amount of space that a city worker takes up. That space used for car-parking is not available for other more productive uses.

The Melbourne City Loop enables large numbers of knowledge-intensive service businesses and workers to cluster in the CBD. Since

1981, when trains started running through the underground rail loop, it has made the northern and eastern parts of the CBD easily accessible on foot from a train station. It is hard to be precise about how much the City Loop has opened up new jobs and business opportunities, and helped workers to become more productive. But since the 1980s, the growth in high-skilled, knowledge-intensive employment around the northern and eastern parts of the CBD has been considerable. The area is home to Telstra's national headquarters, the Melbourne office of the Reserve Bank, the Melbourne Central complex and many large government departments.

A recent report for the Victorian government by SGS Economics and Planning described the experience of international financial services business Mazzei and Burton as it considered options for opening an Asia Pacific office in the late 1990s. The company shortlisted Sydney and Melbourne as possible locations. They wanted their new home to offer strong business opportunities, affordable office space and good access to a large labour force via public transport—in other words a site very similar to their base at Canary Wharf in London. While Sydney was highly rated due to its large financial services cluster, the high price of office space concerned the company. Collins Street, Melbourne, with its proximity to Parliament station, was a far more attractive location than the Sydney CBD could offer. The company relocated a dozen employees to Melbourne and hired another dozen local staff.

Increased public transport use does mean that train services in Australia's biggest cities are operating at full or near-full capacity during peak periods, particularly on routes into city centres. In Sydney, track capacity has been reached on several rail lines during morning and evening peaks, and most peak services are crowded. A shortage of station capacity in the central city exacerbates the bottleneck in the CBD. Brisbane's inner-city rail network is also close to capacity in peak periods.

More choices

Public transport offers commuters an alternative to driving, thereby mitigating overall congestion levels. For individuals, it also provides an alternative to being stuck in traffic or unable to find a park. Some public transport passengers value the opportunity it gives them to 'switch off', for instance by reading or using a smartphone.

Public transport usually costs passengers much less money than running a car. Ticket prices are typically lower than petrol, parking and car running costs. Buying a car involves a large upfront expense; catching public transport does not.

Public transport also helps enable people who can't drive to participate in the economy and community. This is not a small group: one in ten households in Australia's five largest cities does not own a car. Public transport enables many non-drivers to get to jobs in city centres and inner suburbs, just as it supports many members of the wider population to do the same. But getting from one middle or outer suburban location to another by public transport will often involve lengthy travel times, multiple connections, or long walks at one or both ends of the journey; sometimes all three. A long public transport journey is better than not being able to make a trip at all. But public transport doesn't come close to giving non-drivers heading to most outer and middle suburban destinations the mobility and convenience that cars can offer.

Cut off

Hiren Suratwala doesn't relish the 90-minute drive from his Epping North home to his job as a chef in the Melbourne CBD. Nor does his wife Meera enjoy her long drive to work in Blackburn. But the lack of realistic public transport options gives them little choice but to drive.

Hiren would need to walk about fifteen to twenty minutes to the nearest bus stop. Buses are infrequent and unreliable. At off-peak times—when Hiren travels—the buses come twice an hour, if that. They finish running at about 9 p.m., which is no use as his work can extend well into the night. If Meera were to catch a bus to Epping station and then another to her work in Blackburn, the entire journey would take two-and-a-half hours one way.

A proposal for a spur line to branch off the Epping line towards Epping North at Lalor was frozen under the Bracks–Brumby Labor government and continued to be under its Coalition successor. 'Go down to the walking tracks and you'll see a steel plaque,' says Hiren, growing agitated at this failed promise, with Meera nodding in furious agreement. 'It says, "This reserve forms part of a future Transport Corridor." I mean they still call it that.'

As things stand, catching a train into town from Epping, Lalor or South Morang stations would only be possible if he could find somewhere to park the car. The three stations have more than 900 parking spots in total, but all fill up by 8.30 a.m.

The few occasions when Hiren had to take the train—when his car was damaged in an accident—are memorable for all the wrong reasons. One night he managed to knock off work early and rushed to Flinders Street station to catch the 10.38 Epping-bound train. But on this night the train left three minutes early. Then, Hiren continues, the 11.08 train was cancelled. By the time the 11.38 arrived at Lalor station it was nearly 12.45 a.m. Meera had to pick him up, lifting the two sleeping children from their beds and bundling them into the car. On another occasion, he waited at one Flinders Street platform for the South Morang line, only to hear an announcement that it was immediately leaving from another platform instead.

* * *

Hiren's story is a common one. Catching the train or bus can be an alternative to driving on congested roads, but for many people in middle and outer suburbs it is not always realistic. Public transport services are too far away, they run too infrequently, they do not take people where they need to go, or they take too long to get there. Consequently, as the maps in Chapter 2 showed, people living far from city centres who use public transport have very limited access to jobs within a reasonable commute time.

Access is the first barrier many people face to using public transport. Public transport infrastructure has failed to keep pace with patterns of land release, housing development and population growth. For example, almost one in five Melburnians does not live within 400 metres of a train, tram or bus stop (a measure of access to public transport commonly used by transport authorities). Some growth suburbs are even more poorly served. In Point Cook and Epping North, where the Osbornes and Suratwalas respectively live, fewer than half the local residents live within 400 metres of a train, tram or bus stop.

A recent newspaper report described the experience of Angela Plows, aged sixty-seven. There was a bus stop one street away when Angela moved to Shalvey in western Sydney in 1973. Later there was a stop outside her house, which was very important to Angela as she has an eye condition and cannot drive. But about four years ago the weekday buses changed routes and weekend buses were slashed. The stop on her street vanished. Now when she heads to the bus stop—to go to the doctor, to the shops or to catch a train to visit her family—she takes a backpack, heavy with the weight of an emergency nebuliser for her asthma. The walk is at least twenty-five minutes, backpack on, through an unlit park or around a school. Angela is not alone in having limited access to public transport. A New South Wales government report acknowledged that from 2000 to 2010 only four in ten new homes in Sydney were built in 'transit nodes' within 800 metres of a train station or 400 metres of a major bus stop or light rail station. It forecast that this pattern would continue to 2020.

In many parts of Australia's cities, public transport runs too infrequently to offer an appealing alternative to car travel. About one in ten Sydney residents living more than 20 kilometres from the city centre lives within 400 metres of a public transport service that runs, on average, at least once every fifteen minutes. In contrast, more than half the people living within 10 kilometres of Sydney's CBD live near a service running frequently. Similarly, in outer Melbourne the time gap between bus services is almost double that in inner and middle suburbs. Buses run on an average of once every forty minutes in Melbourne's growth areas— less frequently than buses in the rest of the city, even though many outer suburban growth areas also lack train and tram alternatives.

Once the bus or train arrives, the length of the journey puts people off. More than a third of car-based commuters in Sydney avoided public transport because it was too indirect. A quarter preferred their car because public transport was too slow.

Congestion slows down many bus services, making travel times longer and less predictable than if there were no congestion. Bus services on the relatively short journey between Spit Junction and Wynyard in Sydney can vary from the timetable by up to twenty minutes. The 28-kilometre trip from Mona Vale to the city can take up to ninety minutes. Similarly, Melbourne's trams are getting slower in peak periods; the city's tram system is one of the slowest in the world.

Buses further from city centres are much more likely than inner-city bus routes to meander indirectly along circuitous routes to their destination. The bus routes in Wyndham in the west of Melbourne are more than twice as long as the most direct route from their origin to their destination. Such bus routes are unsuitable for peak-hour commuters. Research in Sydney found that buses mainly permitted very local travel.

It is perhaps not surprising, then, that buses can be seen as a service of last resort, to be avoided if another choice like driving a car is an option. More than two-thirds of Melbourne's bus users don't have a driver's licence. When the Western Australian government replaced trains with buses on the route to Fremantle, patronage dropped 30 per cent. The slower speed and poorer reliability of the buses appear to have been key factors. The proportion of people taking the bus to work across Australia's big cities has remained steady at about one in twenty commuters since the mid-1990s.

The introduction of dedicated busways, separate from other traffic and largely avoiding traffic lights, has helped Brisbane to increase bus patronage in recent years. Busways, like train or light rail lines, give bus passengers a congestion-free trip. But even so, increased bus use in Brisbane has been modest, growing 1 percentage point as a proportion of all trips between 2006 and 2011.

* * *

For most of the twentieth century, building and expanding train lines, then roads, improved people's mobility and access to jobs. The combination of a growing population and the shift to a more knowledge-intensive economy, with opportunity and prosperity more concentrated in city centres, means that the old approaches are not enough.

But there are strong incentives for governments to avoid being honest about the trade-offs involved in our cities' housing markets and transport systems, and to avoid the hard decisions needed to keep them working for all residents. The next chapter outlines these in detail.

Chapter 7

Why our cities stay broken

LIMITED HOUSING OPTIONS AND inadequate transport networks are big problems not only for cities but for the nation. They hold back our cities' capacity to give people higher living standards, more economic security and more choices. They limit many people's opportunities for the kinds of social connection they value.

So why aren't we dealing with these major challenges facing our cities and citizens? Mainly because they have underlying causes that are extremely hard to address. Three in particular stand out.

First, decision-making about cities is fragmented. Big Australian cities don't have a single institution that decides for the city as a whole. Instead, they are caught between Australia's three tiers of government.

The second challenge is how we deal with change. While many city residents accept in principle that the status quo is not working, that our cities are going to grow and we have to find a way to make their growth manageable, we often oppose change in our own neighbourhoods. Sometimes we feel change is being imposed on us, without our having any say in it, and the only response is to resist. The result can be what one former council official referred to as a 'public sullenness'. Sometimes our opposition stems from self-interest. Understandably, nobody wants to lose out from any change.

The third is that the challenges we face simply aren't being addressed by our leaders. Fixing our cities isn't easy for politicians, but too often they deny that problems even exist. Or politicians and public servants respond to the difficult politics involved by offering easy answers that don't work in the real world, by failing to implement plans to improve cities, and by pursuing quick fixes at the expense of lasting solutions.

This chapter examines these challenges in turn. The next chapter considers ways to address them.

Fragmented decision-making

Cities, when working properly, connect people and jobs across their whole area. Because local changes affecting housing and transport have citywide effects, decision-making on these issues should take the whole city into account. Most big North American, European and Asian cities have governments, led by mayors or city governors, which are responsible for many aspects of their whole city. New Zealand's Auckland Regional Council is responsible for a city of around 1.4 million people. No body—government or otherwise—does this in Australia.

Housing policy exemplifies how fragmented decision-making is bad for cities. Despite housing's central role in people's lives and the economy, no one part of government is responsible for understanding housing as a system. Dispersed accountability frequently means no accountability. Each level of government is comfortable passing the buck to the others.

The Commonwealth government is far removed from the day-to-day realities of cities. It is responsible for tax settings that affect home ownership, such as capital gains tax and negative gearing rules. Yet the Commonwealth pays little regard to the impact of these settings on housing costs, on what housing gets built where and their implications for how people get to work. Before becoming prime minister, Tony Abbott said in 2013 that housing 'is essentially a state government matter'. This is despite cities being critically important to the national economy, and generating most of the Commonwealth government's tax revenue.

The Commonwealth also decides the nation's immigration intake, then leaves state and local governments to deal with the ensuing demand for housing, roads and public transport. Commonwealth and state government ministers for housing, where they exist, are generally responsible for public and community housing as an arm of welfare policy. Such housing is important, but it only makes up about 4 per cent of Australian homes.

State governments set broad parameters around what land can have housing built on it, and the processes that have to be followed in doing so. They are responsible for building main roads and train lines, and operating public transport services. To raise revenue, state governments charge land tax and stamp duty, both of which influence how the housing market operates.

Yet state governments have tight budgets. They see themselves as mendicants to the Commonwealth, which collects most of the tax paid in Australia. State governments also have rural and regional constituents. It can hurt a state government to be seen as too focused on the needs of their state's biggest city. Queensland governments, for example, ignore rural areas at their peril. The Kennett Liberal–National Government lost the 1999 Victorian election in part because people in regional Victoria saw it as too 'Melbourne-centric'.

Local governments are responsible for granting permission to build new homes. They also set rules and processes governing how and where this occurs, on top of those set by state governments.

Local governments are too small to shape a city's destiny. They represent small parts of cities, and tend to pursue parochial agendas that benefit their area, sometimes at the expense of the city as a whole. In most large cities they are responsible for only a small fraction of the wider city population and area. The lord mayor of Adelaide, for example, heads a municipal area with a population of around 20 000 people. Greater Adelaide's population is more than sixty times this amount, at around 1.3 million people.

The City of Brisbane is a partial exception. Established in 1925 with the merger of twenty councils, it is responsible for 1.1 million residents and the area within about 20 kilometres of the city centre. The

Queensland government is responsible for major roads and train lines. But the City of Brisbane is large enough, with a big enough democratic mandate, to be a credible advocate to the state government about transport infrastructure. In the mid-2000s when Campbell Newman was mayor, the City of Brisbane played a major role in advocating for road tunnels and busways that the state government then built.

The City of Brisbane still falls short of making decisions that take the whole local area into account though. When it was first established, the city council was responsible for the entire city. But greater Brisbane has grown to encompass 2.2 million residents, and the City of Brisbane is responsible for only half this population. People from the Sunshine and Gold Coasts also commute to Brisbane, and vice versa. People and jobs are connected across the whole of south-east Queensland and its 3.5 million residents, and decisions about how land gets used, and when and where transport gets built need to take the whole region into account. Yet the City of Brisbane is just one of ten councils responsible for different parts of south-east Queensland.

* * *

Sometimes state and local government approaches to housing policy don't work well together. The recent introduction of new zoning rules for building housing in Melbourne provides an example. In March 2013, the Victorian Liberal–National coalition government announced new rules giving power to local councils to plan how and where new housing is built in their area. So far, so good. New housing is needed as Melbourne continues to grow, and the way it gets built should respect local communities' wishes.

The rules set out three zones into which each local council must divide their area. 'Residential growth' zones enable the highest levels of new housing growth near train lines, shopping strips and the like. 'General residential' zones should be used in most residential areas to preserve character while enabling moderate housing growth. Finally, 'neighbourhood residential' zones tightly restrict housing growth.

The rules were sensible in theory. But the state government did not bind local councils to share the responsibility to accommodate more people, which would have ensured all parts of the city did their bit to house Melbourne's growing population. The response was predictable. Councils representing inner and middle suburbs—places with the best access to jobs—quickly declared that they wanted hardly any population growth. Glen Eira council, in Melbourne's south-east, zoned about 80 per cent of residential land to restrict growth in housing. In Boroondara in Melbourne's inner-east, 76 per cent of the council area was zoned so that any building proposal higher than two levels would be blocked. In inner southern Bayside, 83 per cent of the council area cannot have any housing higher than two storeys. Almost no residential land in Boroondara—less than one per cent of the municipality's total area—was proposed for the residential high-growth zone.

The Government's own demographic projections for Melbourne, based on the new zones, show more than half Melbourne's population growth occurring in outer and fringe suburbs. If this does occur, the costs to the economy and to the quality of life of many people, stemming from poor access to jobs and limited housing choice, will get worse, not better.

The then Labor opposition promised during the 2014 election campaign to review the new zones. At the time of writing this review was yet to commence.

Local parochialism can also compromise big cities' transport networks. In 2008, the Victorian Government extended clearways—parking bans on main roads during peak times—in congested inner suburbs. One hundred and fifty clearways within 10 kilometres of the CBD were extended and standardised to operate from 6.30 to 10 in the mornings and from 3 or 4 to 7 in the evenings. The new times were strictly enforced, with the number of vehicles towed away often exceeding 500 a month. The measures improved commuter travel times by almost 10 per cent while costing the government $13 million, a tiny figure compared to the cost of building or expanding roads in those areas.

However, the inner-city councils of Yarra and Stonnington fought a rearguard action, seeking to have the Supreme Court declare the clearway extensions invalid. They lost, but their campaign appeared to encourage the then Liberal–National Coalition opposition to oppose the clearway extensions to boost their political prospects in these areas. After the

Coalition won power in 2010 it abandoned the clearway extensions. It favoured the concerns of a small number of local councils and local traders about on-street parking over the needs of car and public transport commuters, and the wider metropolitan economy.

This example also illustrates that opposition parties—of both political persuasions—are willing to oppose local change for short-term electoral gain, even if the change is in the interests of the wider city. This kind of political opportunism is another impediment to improving Australia's cities.

Resisting change

We may not always want change, but it is inevitable. Cities change because the world changes, the economy changes and people's lives and needs change. Indeed, the character of a city—and of all its individual neighbourhoods—is the result of how it has changed over time.

The story of two Sydney suburbs shows how much the needs of an area can change. Auburn and Ryde are on different sides of the Parramatta River but shared many similarities in the past. Both suburbs are located about 15 kilometres from the CBD, were established in the late nineteenth century and saw intense development in the post-war period. By 1981, Ryde had a bigger and slightly older population. But the two suburbs were fairly similar. It would have been very difficult to predict how radically their paths would diverge in the next thirty years.

Since 1981, Auburn's population has grown much faster than Ryde's, particularly as a result of immigration (two in three Auburn residents were born outside Australia). The number of under-15-year-olds has grown by 40 per cent, while the population aged over sixty-five has grown more slowly. Ryde, by contrast, has had a dramatic increase in the number of older residents, but the number of under-15s has barely grown at all. Of course, the housing and other needs of an extra 3000 children in Auburn are very different from those of 4500 extra elderly residents in Ryde. These diverging needs would have been hard to predict when the suburbs were first developed.

We've seen that most people today want to be able to live in areas that give them good access to jobs and transport. In order to do so, many would be willing to live in smaller housing, such as semi-detached townhouses, terraces, units and flats, if such housing were available. Many parents want their children to be able to live nearby when they move out or buy their first home. Some older people would like to move out of their large family homes as they grow older, but stay in their suburb. But there is only a finite amount of land in inner and middle parts of cities. Nearly all of it is already used for housing and for shops, parks, businesses and roads. So if more people are to live in these areas, neighbourhoods inevitably need to change.

Areas that evolve to create greater diversity of housing also allow people to stay connected to family, friends and their local area as their own lives change. For example, some older people don't want to stay in a large house with a big garden to maintain once their children move out. But they usually want to stay in the same neighbourhood.

The experience of Ken and Maureen Barrell shows the problems that arise when a neighbourhood doesn't change, even as the lives and the needs of its residents do. The Barrells are just two of many people who want to see change in their old neighbourhood so they can stay part of it.

Nearly forty years ago, Ken and Maureen built their own home in Engadine, in Sydney's south. The two-storey brick house, testament to the young couple's hopes to settle down for the long haul, has given them many happy years.

Three daughters were born and filled the house. During long summers, the children played on the trampoline and in the swimming pool. The double garage at the end of the sloping driveway had two cars. Ken drove to factories for his work as an inspector with the NSW Electricity Commission. Maureen drove to the train station and then caught the train to the state attorney-general's department, where she worked in the court transcription service.

The girls finished school, then one by one left home. Ken retired; next year Maureen plans to do the same. Now in their sixties, the couple have decided it's time to move to a new house, though not to a new suburb if they can help it.

'Nearly two years ago we started talking about downsizing,' Maureen says. 'We don't need four bedrooms any more, the pool never gets used, there's a lot of maintenance. And one of my daughters is a paramedic and she's already saying, "Mum, get out of that house before you fall down those stairs and have to be carried out!"'

Ken and Maureen want a new house with three bedrooms: one for them, one to accommodate the grandchildren or Maureen's sister who visits regularly from the country, and one for 'me to retreat into so he can watch the football,' Maureen explains. The block must be flat; no rise in the driveway, no flights of stairs, and no pool. And their new home should be in the suburb they know and love.

'When you've educated young children in the area and they've played sport and that sort of thing, you don't even realise how many people you know,' says Maureen. 'We have really great neighbours and many friends in the area.' Ken agrees: 'We don't want to move too far away'.

Having decided to downsize, the Barrells began leafing through local real estate brochures, checking email alerts and attending inspections for anything 'vaguely suitable'. Disenchantment set in fast.

'I don't mind if I need to put a new kitchen in,' Maureen says of the houses on offer. 'But I don't want to do a complete refurbishment of a house. But you find that Engadine is about fifty to sixty years old as a suburb, so there's a lot of old, old houses that have either been extended and done up or they're still really old. Or you'd find places that tick the boxes for some things but then there'd be a pool. Or it would be a single-level dwelling, but it might be down a steep driveway. For my thinking, they're the things you want to avoid in old age.'

The Barrells also mull over the big stamp duty bill they would have to pay. 'You're looking at about 25 to 30 000,' Ken says. 'These are all things you have to take into account.'

At one stage the couple found a villa that ticked all the boxes. It was in the next suburb; one home in a complex of four and no body corporate or strata fees. They contacted the agent to put in a bid. But another interested party soon outbid them. The problem, says Maureen, is that other people of a similar age in their neighbourhood have had the same idea at the same time.

'We all built at the same time,' she says. 'Our neighbours are still the original ones from forty years ago. Now the young people are coming into the suburb again, and they'll put their kids through school. And everyone else seems to be downsizing at the same time; it's very competitive. We've come to the decision that we've had enough.'

Ken says: 'We looked for twelve months and got a bit depressed.'

The Barrells are taking an extended break from househunting. They'll start searching again once Maureen retires and has more time and energy for the task. They plan to find a suitable place first, access their superannuation to put down a deposit, then place their family home on the market and hope for the best. Sadly, says Maureen, 'we even have to rethink staying in the area'.

Imposing change

Change must respect the interests of people who live in an area. Too often it doesn't. It is hardly surprising that some local residents resist change when they have no real say over its form, no sense of why it is necessary and no idea of what they get in return for having more households in their street.

In a large 2010 survey of residents across all Australia's main cities and a number of smaller ones, most people did not consider that governments were concerned about residents' preferences when they planned and decided how land gets used. Most residents thought that local government consultation on these issues happened only sometimes or not at all.

There is a big mismatch between what communities want and what governments are doing. For example, in the same survey, communities around Australia identified their top priorities in relation to land use as personal safety, public transport and traffic congestion. But government agencies surveyed at the same time reported their own priorities as 'accommodating higher population growth', 'transitioning to higher population densities through greater infill' and 'managing greenfield development'.

Experts and opinion leaders often fail to acknowledge that change can be difficult, or fail to identify ways to make change easier for people. Nor do they always accept that the views of existing residents of inner and middle suburbs should be respected, often dismissing them as

'NIMBYs' (Not In My BackYard). But existing residents have legitimate concerns, and their fears can be well-founded.

This mismatch of community, government and expert priorities and
approaches makes many residents of established areas doubtful that
change will be in their interests, or accommodate their wishes. People
resent having plans and decisions thrust upon them. If plans are not
supported by the community, they tend not to endure and make a difference. So existing patterns of housing development and population
settlement largely continue, notwithstanding the increased congestion
and limited housing choice and poor access to jobs these bring about.

In Victoria, two city plans for Melbourne have been developed this
century. In 2002, a Labor government introduced *Melbourne 2030* as a
30-year plan to manage land use and population growth. It was updated
in 2008 with the title *Melbourne at five million*.

In the lead-up to the 2010 election, the Liberal–National opposition
denounced *Melbourne 2030*. They stated 'it has failed to achieve its targets, it has divided communities and it has seen a wrecking ball approach
to planning become the dominant culture within government'. The crit-
icism appeared to resonate with sections of the community, no doubt
in part because *Melbourne 2030* had been produced with little genuine
community engagement. Yet in government, the Coalition also did not
engage seriously with the community before, in 2014, it released *Plan
Melbourne*, its vision to guide the city's growth to 2050.

By contrast, when a citywide plan was developed in the 1990s for
Vancouver, a city of more than two million residents on Canada's west
coast, a significant proportion of the population was consulted. People
were asked to consider the trade-offs involved with any decisions and
to recognise that everyone had to compromise for the city to work. A
source closely involved with the Vancouver reforms whom we interviewed on condition of anonymity remarked that 'if the Vancouver
public had been given a plan as finished as the draft of *Melbourne 2030*
they would have revolted'. We draw out the lessons Vancouver's experience holds for Australian cities in the next chapter.

Similarly, when authorities in Portland, Oregon, in the United States
developed an overarching Regional Framework Plan in the 1990s, their
engagement process was very thorough. One source in Portland, also

interviewed on condition of anonymity, emphasised the value of 'taking planning back a step and asking people what they want'. They contrasted the approach to engagement in Portland with that in cities in Australia, where 'there seems to be a culture that consultation is about telling people what the planners have decided'.

People in big Australian cities are rarely meaningfully involved in making the trade-offs that are required to keep a lid on congestion and expand housing choices and access to jobs for more people. 'Consultation' by governments is too often superficial window-dressing, rather than genuine engagement. For example, in 2013 Kym McHugh, president of the Local Government Association of South Australia, expressed concern at the limited consultation underpinning the *30 year plan for greater Adelaide* released by the SA government in 2010. He wrote that the plan 'was developed in isolation from the community and a draft document was launched on a public that had missed the start of the conversation and was expected to take a leap of faith to board the urban renewal train. For many the train has never left the station'.

When genuine engagement doesn't happen, officials and politicians are in danger of paying too much attention to noisy lobbyists and protesters. Small numbers of residents can be very active, but unless a much larger proportion of residents are engaged, we have no idea how representative the loudest advocates are.

Low levels of trust in politicians and other decision-makers exacerbate the problem by making residents doubtful that change will respect their interests. State and local politicians and property developers can indeed be untrustworthy, as the NSW Independent Commission Against Corruption has shown all too clearly.

But state government failure to engage residents isn't the only problem. Local governments can resist change if it threatens their interests. And, if we are to be honest, so can ordinary citizens.

Nobody wants to be the loser

Often people are wary of change because it can involve giving up a benefit—especially one paid for by other members of the community. Such benefits include tax concessions for property investors or subsidised public transport fares. In addition, people are often understandably wary of giving up a benefit they receive now for less certain benefits in the future, even if the future benefits would leave them and the community better off.

It can be hard to identify who pays for—and who benefits from—some of the government policies that shape Australia's cities. But it is worth trying to do so, because it helps to explain why our cities are the way they are.

Home owners benefit financially from slow growth in the supply of new housing. The failure to build enough homes—especially townhouses, units, terraces and low-rise flats in inner and middle established suburbs—means many people can only afford to live on city fringes, and so have poor access to jobs. An inadequate supply of housing also makes it hard for first home buyers to enter the market, and pushes rents upwards, putting many low-income renters in a very tough situation.

But a shortage of new housing in established inner and middle suburbs benefits owners of existing homes in those areas by helping to drive up their price. It's no surprise that objections and appeals to new housing are far more frequent in suburbs where house prices are high. Growing the supply of new housing in established areas and improving housing choice would benefit all city residents and the economy by giving more workers access to more jobs, and by giving everyone more choice about how and where they live. But there is also a trade-off between the financial interests of home owners and investors in established suburbs and the interests of potential residents of those suburbs, and of the wider city. Changing the patterns of housing development and population settlement we have pursued since manufacturing was at its peak isn't easy, despite the benefits a shift would bring.

Similarly, the substantial tax concessions that benefit housing investors—namely discounted capital gains tax and negative gearing—make it harder for first home buyers to buy a home. The community as a whole pays for these tax concessions: either people who aren't eligible for the concessions pay more tax, or governments need to collect more tax revenue in other ways, or they have less money to spend on pensions, schools and hospitals.

But people benefiting financially from the concessions are unlikely to want them to stop. More than a million Australians have negatively geared investment properties, reducing their overall tax bill. Governments are therefore reluctant to make any change to tax rules that could be seen to disadvantage such a large group of people, even though tax concessions for property investment are getting very little new housing built, and come at great cost to the rest of the community.

* * *

Identifying who benefits from—and who pays for—different kinds of transport can also help us understand why things are the way they are.

Three overlapping groups of people benefit from any improvement to roads or public transport that increases access to jobs. People using the infrastructure benefit most because they have more and better ways to get around. For example, a recent report prepared for the Victorian government described the experience of Marcus, who finished high school at St Albans Secondary College in 1999. The following year, Marcus kept working at his part-time job at a local restaurant as he was unable to find a job with more hours nearby. But in 2001 the Western Ring Road—a major motorway connecting western Melbourne—opened. This enabled Marcus to widen his search for employment, and he found a better job near Melbourne Airport, providing inflight meals to airlines.

Similarly, businesses in areas well-served by transport also benefit from nearby road and rail infrastructure because it lets them connect with larger numbers of customers and potential employees. This is why businesses such as those we discussed in Chapter 2—BCG, Deloitte and SKM—locate in CBDs, despite the higher rents they have to pay.

The second group benefiting from improved transport infrastructure are people who own homes (whether as home owners or investors) in those areas. This is because better nearby transport increases the value of their home. Deputy governor of the Reserve Bank Philip Lowe explained in 2013 how this comes about:

When housing prices are high, it is largely because land prices are high. And land prices are high when there is a shortage of

well-located land. We cannot do much about the physical supply
of land, but investment in transportation infrastructure—by
making it easier to move around the city—can increase the supply
of well-located land. And when supply increases, prices adjust.
This means that underinvestment in transportation networks
tends to put upward pressure on housing costs.

Third, taxpayers as a whole benefit from improved transport, even
when they do not use new motorways or train lines themselves. Better
transport links between people and jobs grow a city's economy and
create employment opportunities for everyone in it.

Yet the way we pay for transport infrastructure and services doesn't
match the way its benefits are distributed between users, nearby property owners and the general public. There are two main reasons why.

First, property owners grow their wealth when property values go
up in places where transport is improved. But they don't always pay
much tax on these increased property values to contribute to the cost
of the improved transport that led to them. Home owners are exempt
from land tax, and also from capital gains tax on their primary resi-
dence. Some residential landlords pay state government land tax, but
there are many exemptions and loopholes that allow people to minimise their land tax bill. State government stamp duty is only paid
when a home changes hands. Increased property values will usually be
reflected in higher local council rates, but these generally go towards
local government garbage collection, libraries, parks and local community services rather than main roads, motorways or train lines.

Second, users of public transport only contribute to a relatively small
proportion of its costs. Full fare public transport tickets only cover part of
the cost of running these services, and none of the costs of new lines and
other infrastructure. The revenue collected from public transport fares in
Sydney in 2011, for example, was more than $3 billion less than the cost
of operating the system. Sydney's public transport system recovers about
a quarter of its operating costs through fare revenue, compared to 31
per cent in Melbourne and 38 per cent in Perth. Australian public transport systems do worse than most systems overseas, such as those in US
cities, at covering costs with fare revenue. For example, public transport

systems in Washington DC and San Francisco recover about 80 per cent and 73 per cent, respectively, of their operating costs.

The community as a whole pays much of the cost of transport infrastructure and services through general taxation. Of course, commuters and home owners are also taxpayers. But people pay income tax, the GST and other taxes—and through these contribute to paying the costs of transport infrastructure—irrespective of whether they own a home. The upshot is that non-home owners subsidise the property values of home owners through their taxes by paying for transport improvements near those properties. And people who don't drive or catch public transport subsidise the people who do.

These complicated financial flows are undoubtedly abstracted from the gritty reality of cars, roads, trains and buses. But they have real effects. Many people have poor access to public transport because governments can be reluctant to expand services and thereby spend more money subsidising public transport. Renters help pay for the tax concessions that contribute to a growing divide between home owners and renters. And the divide between residents of public transport–rich inner suburbs and poorly serviced outer suburbs is made worse because outer suburban residents' taxes subsidise the public transport services that give inner suburban home owners greater mobility and higher property values.

Leaders who don't face up to the challenge

Politicians make many big decisions about our cities. But often they don't even try to make the changes our cities need. Sometimes this is because they fail to grasp the reality of life in today's cities, which is often different from life when they were growing up—when cities were geographically smaller and had smaller populations, roads were less congested and the suburban manufacturing economy was stronger. Sometimes they pursue easy answers that don't solve problems. Sometimes they are more focused on short-term pay-offs in the media or at the next election than on pursuing more substantial measures that offer genuine and enduring benefits.

Today's economy is very different from how it was decades ago, as is the experience of people who live in cities. But the mindset of many politicians and opinion leaders can lag behind our own everyday

experience. Hangovers of our nation's rural past can exert a disproportionate influence on decisions today. For example, while the federal
Liberal–National Coalition government committed to fast-tracking
an 1800-kilometre Inland Rail project through regional Queensland,
New South Wales and Victoria, in 2013 it ruled out funding new public
transport in cities, where most Australians live and work. The Inland
Rail initiative is unlikely to be much comfort to the millions of commuters in big cities with poor access to public transport and little choice
but to spend long hours stuck in traffic.

Similarly, the relative importance of manufacturing in our economy
has declined since its heyday fifty years ago. When state governments
promote housing on cities' outer fringes with little access to jobs or adequate transport infrastructure, it is as if they are replaying the approach
of a bygone era, when opportunity was more dispersed through the city
and the outermost suburbs weren't as far from the centre.

Distance from the day-to-day problems of large cities can also cloud
decision-making. While most politicians themselves live in large cities,
the expert advice that Commonwealth government ministers receive
comes from public servants and ministerial advisers living in Canberra,
a place remote from the lives most Australians live. While undoubtedly
well-meaning, the perspectives of Canberra-based experts and advisers
can be skewed by living somewhere with a disproportionately small private sector economy and almost no traffic congestion.

Official statistics and data also give national leaders a poor understanding of the spatial implications of their decisions. Official economic
statistics in the United States and many countries in Europe track the
economic performance of individual cities. Yet the Australian National
Accounts compiled by the Canberra-based Australian Bureau of
Statistics do not do this. Nor in 2014 do we collate nationwide statistics
about housing supply or access to jobs.

The media's priorities also explain why some of the problems in
cities are not on the radar of decision-makers. Large broadcast and
print media organisations are invariably located in or near the centre of
big cities. Media organisations struggle to give issues emerging on the
fringes of big cities as much attention as those emerging in inner-city

areas (or in regional areas in the case of broadcast stations' regional affiliates and the ABC). Tight budgets mean that media employees often have to contribute multiple stories in a day, making it harder to travel longer distances to the outer suburbs. Thus, the growing divide between inner and outer suburbs of Australia's big cities doesn't get as much media attention as it would if media organisations' locations were more geographically dispersed. The level of media attention the problems of cities receive in turn affects how much politicians and other decision-makers focus on them.

Even worse than failing to understand the problems facing city-dwellers is complacency or denial. Yet this is far too common. Local and state governments frequently tout Australian cities' high rankings according to 'quality of life' indices, failing to mention that the index is oriented towards wealthy, globally mobile professionals rather than whole city populations. Former Victorian premier John Brumby said in 2010 that he believed the state was 'travelling well', citing as evidence Melbourne's place in the world's top ten most liveable cities. Four weeks later his government had been voted out of office, with many voters unhappy about its performance in managing Melbourne's population growth. Unreliable and overcrowded public transport was a major concern in many middle and outer suburbs.

Sometimes politicians abdicate responsibility for solving the problems of cities. When Premier of New South Wales Bob Carr declared in 2001 that Sydney was 'full', he was effectively admitting that he and his government were unable to manage its growing population. Yet Sydney's population has grown throughout Australia's history, and failing to deal with it doesn't make the problems go away. Chair of the Productivity Commission, Peter Harris, has said: 'Even if you don't build the roads (or) ... expand the rail signalling, expand the station car parks, rezone the regeneration areas, the population growth still proceeds. It's like putting the cap on the toothpaste tube but continuing to squeeze'.

In the decade after Carr's comment, growth in Sydney's supply of new housing slowed, with fewer homes being built than in the 1990s. Sydney had easily the most expensive housing market in the country, and little progress was made in giving people access to public transport. During the decade from 2000, Sydney's economic growth generally lagged the nation's, having led it in the 1990s.

Easy answers that don't work

Politicians and other opinion leaders avoid tackling the issues facing Australia's cities by offering solutions that sound appealing but don't actually work. These include claims such as releasing more land will solve all our cities' housing problems, proposals for new cities, and schemes to relocate jobs to employment-poor areas.

First, a common cry is that the housing supply shortages (and thereby higher house prices) should be solved by releasing more land for housing at the edge of our cities. In 2014, former Commonwealth treasurer Peter Costello stated that 'what's driving house prices ... more than anything else is land releases in our big cities'.

In the 2000s, Melbourne released much more land on its fringe than Sydney. And house prices are lower in Melbourne than Sydney, though still very high by world standards. But in Chapter 3, we met the Suratwalas and the Osbornes, both of whom bought houses on newly developed land. Their experience shows that local residents can end up cut off from the kinds of opportunities people living in inner areas take for granted. More housing on city fringes won't give many households the choices they would like to make, notably living near jobs and transport.

Trying to solve the problem of housing supply by further spreading our cities outwards will only increase the distance between people and jobs, heightening the transport challenge and the problems this divide causes for people and for the economy. Building most housing on cities' outer fringes is easier than building new homes in established areas, since it doesn't involve dealing with the objections of neighbours, but over time the whole city will pay the price of poorer connections between people and jobs.

Second, the difficulties of managing large cities can prompt calls to establish new ones. Western Australian Premier Colin Barnett and former Australian Workers Union leader Paul Howes both suggested a new city up north as a way to manage population growth. It is a well-meaning idea, but a bad one. In 2009, the World Bank studied new cities, many of which were built as a result of a political decision to alleviate population pressure on existing ones. They found that few met their goals, saying:

> New cities do better when they are located near larger successful cities. But they often suffer from the same government-related failures that led the government to establish them, especially the failure to manage large cities well. That is, governments that do badly in managing large old cities also do badly in managing small new cities.

Advocates of new cities also struggle to identify just who would live in them, or what residents would do for a living. It would ordinarily be unrealistic to expect employers to move their business from an area with a large customer base and an established network of suppliers to the complete unknown of a new city.

The promise that large numbers of jobs can easily be moved to where people live, especially in employment-poor outer suburbs, is a third idea that sounds appealing. Unfortunately, in practice it rarely works. As housing expands outwards in cities, jobs do not follow at the same rate.

Some do gravitate to outer areas. Supermarkets, schools and hairdressers will always be needed wherever people live. Some outer areas have manufacturing, logistics or transport businesses for whom cheap land and access to freeways are more important than proximity to the inner city. But businesses selling to the whole city, the nation or the world tend to cluster in city centres and around ports and airports. Overall employment growth has been much higher near city centres. The minimal net private sector employment growth in western Sydney in recent years has not happened by accident.

It would solve a lot of problems if outer suburban employment growth could be stimulated in other ways. But unfortunately it's not that easy. Businesses will locate where they consider it's best for them. It's very difficult to order them around and tell jobs where to go.

Job creation schemes in areas with limited employment opportunities are not uncommon. Yet there is limited evidence that such policies create significant numbers of long-term jobs or are cost-effective. The few rigorous evaluations of past Australian efforts suggest that politicians are happier spending money on these kinds of initiatives than on finding out if they actually work. Where they have been evaluated, job creation has generally fallen short of targets.

Governments are also frequently called on to relocate government offices to outer suburbs to boost local jobs. For example, demographer Bernard Salt advocated taking knowledge-intensive jobs out of the city centre to suburbs around the city, and stated 'the former [Victorian] state government was on the right track with its decentralisation of the Transport Accident Commission (TAC) from Melbourne's Exhibition Street to Geelong'.

But relocating government offices away from suppliers, contractors, partner organisations and current and potential employees is at best a risky move. For example, a feasibility study for the relocation of the Victorian TAC found it would lead to 'little or no net economic benefit to the state', and would only be feasible if about sixty jobs were cut. As it turned out, more than 400 staff—out of a workforce of about 650—opted to take a redundancy or be redeployed within the public service rather than move to Geelong with the TAC. Such an enormous loss of corporate knowledge and institutional memory can undermine how productive and effective an organisation is for years to come.

It can also be incredibly expensive for other taxpayers. Incentives for the TAC staff who did relocate to Geelong included a $15 000 'loyalty bonus', $30 000 housing assistance, payment of stamp duty and legal fees, a 10 per cent salary bonus, and reimbursement of some school and childcare costs.

Many government agencies doing specialised or knowledge-intensive work locate in city centres for the same reasons that drove BCG to stay in central Sydney and SKM to relocate from Armadale to the Melbourne CBD.

Governments do have a critical role in enabling economic activity to occur in outer suburbs. In some places, governments' failure to provide adequate infrastructure or services may stifle job creation. They have a responsibility to redress these gaps. Barriers to creating new jobs— unreasonable restrictions on businesses using land, for instance—should be minimised. Outer suburbs should not be short-changed in their access to infrastructure, services or social spending. But government services and infrastructure alone will not fix low and declining access to jobs in many outer parts of Australia's cities.

Failing to deliver

Far too often governments announce grand plans for cities that don't turn into reality. State government plans for housing frequently fail to come to fruition because they lack implementation mechanisms. For example, from 2006 to 2011, only around 15 000 homes were built each year in Sydney, barely more than half the target set in the NSW government's 2005 metropolitan strategy.

Promises to build transport infrastructure often turn out to be just as empty. The many transport plans that have been developed for Sydney in recent decades include *Metrowest* in 1990, *Action for transport* in 1998, the *Metropolitan Rail Expansion Program* in 2005, the 2009 *Sydney transport blueprint*, the *Metropolitan transport plan* just one year later and the 2012 *NSW transport master plan* after the election of the Liberal–National Coalition government. All bar the last—which is too recent to be assessed—include promises that have not turned into reality. A new underground train line between Redfern and Wynyard has never been built, after first being promised in 1990 and then again in 2010. Nor has a promised extension of the Eastern Suburbs line to Bondi Beach (promised in 1998 for completion by 2002), nor a rail link between Epping and Parramatta, among many others.

Victorian governments have produced some impressive documents describing their aspirations for land use and new transport in Melbourne. But too often they have been statements of vision or aspirations, not linked to clear implementation plans and funding. The 1969 *Melbourne transportation study* identified a need to electrify the rail line between St Albans and Sunbury. This project was completed in 2012, forty-three years later. A rail line to Doncaster in Melbourne's east was first proposed in the 1929 *Plan of general development*. It has yet to be built. Public Transport Victoria's 2012 *Network development plan* suggests it will be completed by 2027, just under a century later. Yet no funding has been allocated to the project; current and prospective residents of the area should not hold their breath. The 2012 plan also promises that a line to Rowville will be completed by 2027, fifty-eight years after it was first proposed in the 1969 *Melbourne transportation study*. Again, funding for the project has not been allocated.

Major projects aren't the only kinds of improvement being promised but not delivered. Hiren and Meera Suratwala's neighbourhood, Epping North, was developed as a residential area by the state government planning body VicUrban, later renamed Places Victoria. It installed a number of bus shelters in the area, but never introduced a bus route. The state government Department of Transport blamed Places Victoria, saying that 'new shelters in Epping North were installed without consultation with the Department of Transport and don't necessarily reflect future public transport routes'. Places Victoria says its public transport plan for the new estate was 'signed off by the Department of Transport'. Meanwhile, families like the Suratwalas are still waiting for the bus.

Short-termism

Politicians make bad decisions for the same reason they make promises that don't get delivered. Promising a new train line brings popularity at the next election. Delivering on the promise is someone else's problem, well into the future. The short-term electoral benefits of announcing a new project mean that these announcements often occur before enough work has been done to identify how much the project would cost, or even whether it's a good idea. Chair of the Productivity Commission, Peter Harris, observes:

> If our infrastructure planning systems were valued, they would be regularly churning out detailed published assessments of cost and benefit in advance of announcements, and these would be given to the community to justify the immense size of some of the commitments being made. This would be in-depth analysis in advance of press release.
>
> Whereas the norm in major projects is that the announcement precedes the detailed planning. Then if there is time a cost-benefit

assessment may be done but often won't be published due to confidentiality concerns. Following that, there is a rapid move to tender in order that the promise is not overtaken by the appearance of delay.

Before the 2013 federal election, the Liberal–National Coalition committed that all Commonwealth infrastructure spending exceeding $100 million would be analysed by Infrastructure Australia, and to regularly publish cost-benefit analyses for all projects being considered. (Infrastructure Australia is an arm's-length body established in 2008 to provide advice to governments on Australia's infrastructure needs and on the merits of proposed projects.) A good idea, if done well.

Yet the same Coalition policy document also included major funding commitments not underpinned by this kind of analysis—$1.5 billion towards Sydney's WestConnex project and $1.5 billion for Melbourne's East West Link, for example. In December 2013, Infrastructure Australia assessed WestConnex as merely being at an 'early stage': the first of four stages of readiness. The East West Link was slightly more advanced, having 'real potential', but still a long way off being 'ready to proceed' and meriting billions of dollars of taxpayers' money.

Separately, the then opposition leader, Tony Abbott, said the Commonwealth government should only fund road, not rail, projects in cities. It would be better to fund projects that offered the best value for money and the greatest benefits to individuals and the economy, regardless of the mode of transport involved or the size of the project.

Big projects are expensive, and usually end up costing even more than forecast. Often the promised benefits don't stack up, or the projects turn out to be more expensive than first thought. Early cost estimates are often based on speculative analysis and guesswork. Too often governments change their mind about what they want after a contract has been signed, driving costs up.

Examples of cost overruns associated with big projects include unrealistically optimistic traffic forecasts for the Clem7 Tunnel in Brisbane, Cross City Tunnel in Sydney and EastLink in Melbourne, and similarly wishful passenger forecasts for the Sydney and Brisbane airport trains. Revenue from road tolls and train tickets was much lower than expected, taxpayers and investors wore the cost and the money lost on these projects wasn't available for other much-needed transport improvements.

Decisions about how to improve transport systems are very important. Getting them wrong wastes large amounts of money that could have been spent on other improvements to roads and public transport. This in turn contributes to traffic congestion, poor access to public transport and people struggling to get around their city.

* * *

This chapter has reviewed the main reasons that the decisions needed to turn our cities around aren't being made and implemented. Muddied accountability for cities makes a big difference. Our wariness of change—because too often change is imposed on us or because of short-term self-interest—is another problem. So is an inadequate understanding of how important it is to manage cities well. Politicians' willingness to promise what they can't deliver also contributes, as does their bias towards short-term decisions.

The next chapter outlines some ways to overcome these problems. It recommends steps that governments can take to help cities improve our material prosperity and our quality of life.

Chapter 8

How we can fix our cities

PROBLEMS WITH OUR CITIES aren't being solved—if anything, they are getting worse. This chapter outlines some ways to turn them around.

All Australian cities are different, and each will find different solutions. So rather than providing a detailed blueprint or implementation plan in this chapter, we describe the kinds of change that would have the biggest benefits.

First, we look at decision-making—who should make the decisions and how. Second, we look at ways to improve our housing market. Third, we look at how our transport systems could be made better. Finally, we look at how the way we pay for improvements in our cities could be made fairer and more transparent.

Decision-making

Improving how decisions about cities are made will help to ensure that the right decisions are made, that the community has ownership of them and that they last. Australian and international experience shows that the decision-making process must be better in two critical ways, even if the specific changes will vary among Australia's cities.

First, decision-making must take the whole city's needs into account. This doesn't necessarily require new organisations. Less formal mechanisms—such as improved cooperation among governments, businesses and civic institutions, and good relationships among the various players, including across political divides—are critically important in making this happen.

Second, if changes are to endure, residents need to have much more power to shape decisions that affect them—both at a citywide and at a local level. The community engagement that precedes decisions affecting cities and the living in them needs to extend far deeper than the perfunctory exercises that Australian governments usually conduct.

In 2010, the Grattan Institute looked closely at decision-making in Dublin, Copenhagen, Vancouver, Toronto, Seattle, Portland, Chicago and Austin—eight cities with similar demographics, population growth and political systems to large Australian cities. Each of these cities had made and sustained hard decisions to better manage population growth or to turn around economic decline. Our interviews with decision-makers in these cities revealed that debates about the future of cities are fraught everywhere. A former senior official in Seattle said that 'planning is the most political thing a society does'.

The interviews showed that it is vital to find a way of making decisions that make sense for the city as a whole. What happens in one part of a city affects residents in another. Therefore everyone needs to get a say in decisions that affect housing and transport across the city.

Cooperation between different levels of government is essential. Cooperation does not necessarily require a single organisation. In Vancouver, for example, decision-making operates through local governments voluntarily participating in a federation, Metro Vancouver, which has no power to raise revenue. Decisions are negotiated. Local governments retain the freedom to apply regional goals in ways that work best for them.

Other cities have had to make relationships work under even more complicated circumstances. Copenhagen in Denmark and Malmö in Sweden make up one labour market connected by the Øresund Bridge; these relationships had to work across national boundaries. Interviewees in both cities recognised that the successes of each helped the other grow.

This culture of cooperation and good relationships is just as vital in Australia as overseas. During an interview with a recent Queensland

government minister, he strongly confirmed the importance of relationships, including across political parties, for getting things done.

Collaboration between governments, business and civic institutions also helps cities succeed. It avoids a government-against-citizens
dynamic. In Toronto, the Toronto City Summit Alliance brings together
business, government, community groups and unions to deliberate and
consider the future of Toronto. Focused on both sparking conversation and enabling practical solutions, the Summit Alliance 'galvanised
a whole lot of interest in the civic realm in the largest sense', according
to a senior member of the Alliance.

Cooperation across party lines contributes to a further charac-
teristic of successful cities—consistency of political direction across
political cycles. In Portland, they call it 'stickability' of direction. A
Portland senior public servant commented that policy 'has managed to
survive political generations. A mayor leaves office, a new one comes
in—and the agenda doesn't change dramatically'. This consistency was
ascribed partly to the extent of public engagement, but also appears to
be a result of bipartisan cooperation, starting with Democratic mayor
Neil Goldschmidt and Republican governor Tom McCall forming an
'unusual alliance'. Their motives were different, but both articulated a
set of values for Portland in 'clear and charismatic' terms.

A former mayor of Copenhagen said: 'It is crucial to see that to
change the course of cities is a long-term project. You have to have a
vision, you also have to have the will'. He described the effort as like
trying to lose weight: 'Over time, there are hundreds, even thousands
of decisions that have to be made, all heading in the same direction'.

Changes to decision-making structures can sometimes help, especially when they solve a particular problem and reflect a shared view
among the community. But changing structures will not produce success
by itself, and can be a dangerous distraction from the reform process.

There is no single kind of structural change that would work for
all Australian cities. Some people advocate for citywide mayors, com-
missions or governments, in the hope that one of these can speak for
big cities, and make decisions that take their interests as a whole into
account. But setting up metropolitan governments would be tough, and
experience overseas shows that they are not a panacea. The benefits

they offer are uncertain, and no Australian state or local government would want to hand over their powers to such a body. Few Australians would welcome a fourth layer of government that would still need to work with all the others—for example, with the Commonwealth on national infrastructure such as airports and interstate roads.

Giving everyone a say

All of the overseas cities in the study had a different story to tell. But a recurring theme was early, sophisticated, sustained and deep engagement with the community. This was especially the case in cities that needed to make hard decisions and did so successfully. Engagement seems to make tough decisions possible, and to make them stick.

Yet most Australian residents feel they have little control over changes to their neighbourhood. If decisions to make our cities better are to be made, and made to last, people need to have more of a say in them. Too often in Australia, governments 'consult' residents to provide a veneer of respectability to a pre-determined outcome, rather than to genuinely respond to residents' priorities.

Many of the overseas cities we examined faced challenges similar to our own. But in Toronto, Copenhagen and Chicago, and especially in Vancouver, Seattle and Portland, residents were engaged in making difficult but necessary trade-offs far more often than in any similar exercise we have seen in Australia.

What does this engagement look like? Two cities are examined closely in the boxes below, but all the overseas cities in our study had a few things in common. A metropolitan-level discussion about the future of the city came first, so that choices about individual neighbourhoods could take place when residents understood the consequences of these choices for the wider city. Engagement had to happen early, before decisions were made or decision-makers' minds largely made up.

Residents needed to be presented with real choices and their long-term consequences. In Vancouver, officials discussed how they were careful not to present a clearly preferred option. 'People were not presented with two leper colonies and a Club Med,' said one senior official.

Residents needed information about the consequences of each of the choices they faced about the future, and what these choices meant for how they wanted to live.

The nature of engagement was also important. One official involved with Vancouver's engagement observed that it was largely characterised by debate among residents—'very much citizens speaking to citizens' in scores of public discussions rather than 'pontificating by staff or politicians'.

And a significant proportion of the population was involved. In Portland, development of an overarching Regional Framework Plan involved 182 public meetings. A survey of every household in the Portland metropolitan region drew 17 000 responses.

Vancouver's City Plan

Vancouver's development of its CityPlan in the 1990s directly involved more than 20 000 people, with an extra 80 000 feeling they had contributed in some way by the end of the process.

Residents were initially asked about the direction of the city overall. The trade-offs involved in choosing different growth strategies were made clear, but there were no 'preferred options'.

Once the overall direction of the city was more settled, engagement continued on what would happen at the neighbourhood level. The city invested the time and effort to do this properly—the plan progressively developed from 1992 to 1995, including several stages of intensive community engagement.

Engagement did not promote a favoured approach, or necessarily seek consensus. People were presented with real choices and their pros and cons.

While the planning process was still underway, the council acted quickly to make immediate changes in response to overwhelming support for increased greenways and community policing, for example. Immediate implementation gave the council credibility and grew community buy-in. People felt as if they had been heard, and that the enterprise was a joint one.

Being clear about the benefits of change to a neighbourhood was also critical to the success of engagement. Each neighbourhood was told that the more households it had, the bigger the contribution it made to governments' tax revenue and therefore the more money it would receive to improve the area. Working with developers and builders, residents frequently opted to get more of the amenities they valued by allowing some buildings to be even higher than required for the area's housing targets, which had been agreed in the citywide engagement phase. A senior public servant closely involved in developing the CityPlan said residents took the view that 'if we had a little more density here, we could have an even larger library'. They were willing to add 'another floor on this building in return for that'.

People need to be able to 'see a benefit to the new growth coming in', said the same public servant. 'We've been able to show that the level of population growth is not the problem, it's how you manage the growth ... you need to have high quality amenity and high quality public spaces.'

The resulting CityPlan sought to maintain popular features of the city, but changed the types of housing in it, and allowed development of industrial sites in return for services such as community policing and better transport. The process has been recognised around the world for its involvement of citizens in building a shared vision for the future. Vancouver was the only city we studied to have reduced commute times while increasing its population.

Today, new technology can make engagement easier. Traditional community consultation can fail to engage many people, especially those with children or demanding jobs or both. People with the time and inclination to participate in town hall meetings do not necessarily represent the community as a whole. Government discussion papers can be dull, jargon-laden or so vague and insipid that there is no clear indication of what the choices and trade-offs are. But three-dimensional visualisation tools and online consultation have the potential to reach beyond the loudest voices to a far broader cross-section of the community than would otherwise be possible.

Currently, neighbours have to read technical written descriptions of proposed new housing near their home. But it's hard to tell exactly how something will look and feel, and how it fits with the character of an area, from a written description. The uncertainty involved can lead people to fear the worst.

Three-dimensional visualisation tools are much more effective at conveying what proposed new housing will actually be like. One Australian state government official said that 'this tool is moving us from year-long to hour-long negotiations'. A project manager at a construction company explained how much easier these tools made it for local people to get a sense of how a proposal might turn out. 'Previously it was all plans and words—and they didn't understand. Now they can see it clearly, as plain as day.'

Involving the community in Seattle

The Seattle City Council established a Neighbourhood Planning Office in 1995, and gave it the task of connecting with the community. Its engagement process directly involved more than 20 000 people in thirty-eight neighbourhoods. Following the metropolitan-level process, a common framework of targets was developed, then each neighbourhood decided how it would accommodate extra households. In effect, as one senior official put it, residents said: 'We'll take more into the neighbourhood, but we want a big say in how'.

Each neighbourhood was funded to hire the resources it needed to develop its own values and vision for their neighbourhood within the citywide targets, and to then work on the land-use issues, design and anything else needed to make the vision work. It was a difficult task, and needed investment to be done well. In this period, about three quarters of Seattle's planning budget was spent on public engagement.

The process often started with identifying what each neighbourhood wished to preserve: open space for children to play, or shops a safe walk away, for example. During the planning stage, these priorities were constantly referred to, so that these aspects of the neighbourhood would either stay the same or improve. A running storyline of what had changed as a result of feedback, what hadn't, and why, was critical to people feeling that their participation had been honoured.

Of the 4200 recommendations generated by residents for the neighbourhood plan, 80 per cent have since been implemented. In a survey conducted by the Office of City Auditor, a majority of both those who participated and those who didn't felt it had been good for Seattle.

Intensive, genuine community engagement is neither easy nor cheap. But it seems to make tough decisions possible, and to make them stick. Who might take responsibility for this kind of community engagement and keep it going over time as cities face up to the challenges of growth? Again, no one type of institution is always successful. Australian cities are different from overseas cities and from each other, and they will find different solutions. But the lessons from overseas point to a clear set of characteristics that any organisation will have to embody.

First, whatever organisation carries out community engagement and brokers decisions needs to do so at arm's-length from government. That is because its role needs to endure across political cycles, since change in cities takes time. An independent body reduces the incentive for opportunism by opposition parties, and has a better chance of setting a culture of collaboration that leads to good relationships between politicians of different parties, across different parts of society and different parts of the city. The organisation need not be completely outside government, but should at least be at arm's-length from the political process, not subject to direction from a government minister.

Second, the organisation needs to take into account the whole city, and the interests of all its residents. To do this, it would have to bring together different sectors, including state and local governments, civic institutions and businesses.

If community engagement is to work it requires decision-makers to have a genuine commitment to doing it properly, even if it takes them towards results that they wouldn't have favoured. It requires expertise and, as one former Sydney councillor put it, 'nerves of steel'.

Different cities might have different triggers to setting up such an effort; for example it might be a change of state government or the establishment of a new organisation, such as the Greater Sydney Commission announced in 2014.

Housing

The way our housing market works is cutting increasing numbers of people off from options they would like to have—notably to live closer to jobs and transport, and to live in the kind of home they want.

More and better options

Enabling people to live closer to jobs and transport, and to choose the kind of home they want, inevitably requires more homes in inner and middle suburbs, especially semi-detached terraces, units and town-houses, and low-rise flats.

Critics of building new homes in established suburbs sometimes conjure up images of downtown Shanghai, or of high-rise apartment towers dwarfing suburban homes. But development does not have to be bad, and residents do need protection from poorly designed new housing. Examples of substantial amounts of housing close to jobs and transport can be found in Potts Point in Sydney, South Yarra in Melbourne, New Farm in Brisbane and Subiaco in Perth, among other places. These are some of Australia's most populated areas, but also desirable and often prestigious places to live.

The benefits of giving people more housing options are substantial. Households wouldn't get everything they want, but a wider range of choices would make a great difference to many people's lives. The whole community benefits, too. Enabling people to live closer to jobs would help grow the economy by giving people a wider choice of jobs and employers a better choice of employees. And if new housing doesn't get built in places with good access to jobs, it gets built in areas with poor access to jobs, exacerbating the growing social and economic divide.

The biggest barrier to building new homes near employment centres is the system of state and local government rules and processes that dictate where and how new housing gets built, and how permission to do so is obtained. These include planning, zoning, referrals, assessments, objections, appeals and other processes that shape decisions about how land is used and where and what kind of housing can be built. The inbuilt complexity and delay in these processes can make getting permission to build new housing expensive, uncertain and frequently impossible. Dramatically simplifying and streamlining them is urgently required.

All states can simplify these arrangements within their own systems. Fewer levels of planning rules should apply across cities. Proposals to build homes should be confronted with fewer referrals to fewer agencies. Decision-making should be more streamlined, transparent and faster.

Less complexity shouldn't mean lower standards. In fact, higher standards for development are essential if the community is to accept a simpler, faster and less costly system.

At present local residents' interests are protected by arbitrary barriers that slow down all proposals to build housing, and make them more costly or completely unviable. A better way to achieve clearer and higher standards is through clear codes or standards that determine approval for more kinds of home development. Housing codes can protect existing residents from badly designed developments while reducing the costs of long planning approval processes.

Compliance with the code could be assessed by a builder, surveyor or consultant, and permission to build would not have to be sought through an authority such as a local council. This does not mean a free-for-all: buildings that are later found not to comply with the code can be demolished or modified at the developer's expense, with substantial penalties for the professional who endorsed it. Planning approval could alternatively be granted by an authority such as a local council, but through an accelerated process.

Codes cover aspects of the scale and appearance of buildings and how they integrate into a street. These include height and overshadowing in outdoor areas, privacy and the appearance of new developments from the street. They cover internal features, such as how much sunlight can enter living areas, and the amount of private open space. Homes that comply with the relevant housing code will be well designed and respect neighbourhood character.

Some state governments are using these kinds of code already, but largely for detached houses or in limited locations. They are not yet enabling the mix of housing in the mix of locations that people want, especially terraces, units, townhouses and low-rise flats in inner and middle suburbs. Applying housing codes to all residential areas would make a substantial difference: in many established areas, small developments of just a few homes provide most new housing. In the City of Monash in south-eastern Melbourne, for example, more than 98 per cent of housing developments built from 2000 to 2006 were between two and seven dwellings. These smaller developments provided around nine out of ten new homes in that area.

Sometimes governments call their rules and processes 'codes', but in practice allow for a lot of discretion and uncertainty. If codes are to offer certainty, compliance must be mandatory. Developers and builders should not get discretion on whether to apply them. In states where objections and appeal rights against new housing are common, these should only be possible when proposed developments are inconsistent with the relevant housing code. Local communities' interests should be respected from the start by the government involving them in developing the housing code that applies to their area. In most cases communities shouldn't need to go to a tribunal or court to enforce local rules.

Similarly, in states where this still occurs, state government planning ministers need to be less active in deciding whether individual developments can go ahead. Ministers who intervene in the approval process for individual developments erode the trust local residents have in the system, giving them little reassurance that their interests will be respected. Planning ministers should decide the content of the rules, guided by deep community engagement. Indeed they have a democratic mandate to do so. Planning ministers should not be the umpire as well. Court cases are not decided by the same politicians who wrote the laws that govern the outcome of the case. The same principle should apply to getting permission to build new housing.

Another beneficial side effect of a simpler, less convoluted and restricted system was identified by the NSW Independent Commission Against Corruption: clarity and simplicity reduce the risk of corruption.

Respecting communities

To succeed, any change needs to work for existing residents of established suburbs, as well as for prospective residents and the city as a whole. Genuine engagement is essential to achieving change that ensures everyone has their interests respected, even though not everybody will get everything they want.

The first step is citywide engagement to allocate responsibility for managing population change and building new homes across the city. This should reflect the broader needs of the city and the interests of all its residents. Plans should identify where housing to accommodate a changing and growing population will be built, and what new transport connections are required to improve residents' access to jobs. If they are built on good engagement that creates a real sense of community ownership they will also help different levels of government and different organisations work in the same direction, rather than opportunistically opposing things for short-term political gain.

To turn the plan into reality, each local council must have realistic housing targets. Every area needs to accommodate its share of population growth. Housing targets distribute growth fairly, while keeping local councils from only thinking of short-term benefits to local residents at the expense of people living elsewhere in the city.

Local communities can then agree on how to meet their housing target in a way that works for their area. As in Vancouver and Seattle, local residents should decide on design guidelines that are sensitive to the existing character of their neighbourhood. Buildings that house the same number of households can look and feel very different.

The community should also be involved in deciding what mixes of housing should go where, so that different types of household can live in the area, including older downsizers, young couples, families and single-person households. Finally, issues that existing residents rightly care about—such as maintenance of privacy, minimisation of overlooking and overshadowing, and placement of garages—should be built into local codes.

State governments have a critical role to play. They have the authority to push local councils to stick to their housing targets. They can require local plans to include enough land zoned to allow new housing. They can offer praise and extra funding to those that are succeeding, while naming and shaming laggards, and if necessary applying financial penalties. Another option is to reduce the council rates of residents in areas meeting their housing targets.

In line with citywide plans, state governments also need to ensure more housing is accompanied by better transport. Depending on the location, this could involve more infrastructure, or better ways to manage congestion and parking. These transport improvements need to be paid for and implemented, not promised then forgotten.

A better chance of owning a home

Home ownership is declining, especially among younger households and people on lower incomes. Increasing the number of homes in inner and middle suburbs would make it easier for first home buyers to afford their own home. But tax concessions funded by the community are another factor keeping first home buyers out of the market.

The two tax settings that together have the most impact on investment in residential property are negative gearing and the capital gains tax discount. These artificially drive up prices because investors get tax benefits over and above the underlying value of the housing. They also create an incentive for investors to oppose the building of new housing. Keeping housing scarce makes their investment more valuable. But it deprives other people of the option to live nearer to concentrations of jobs.

Reducing the capital gains tax discount, limiting the benefits of negative gearing or a combination of both would limit the extent to which investors drive up the price of housing for tax reasons. Gradually easing these tax breaks, in conjunction with making it easier to build new housing, would enable more people to buy their first home.

Change should be introduced gradually, and acknowledge that these tax settings apply to other kinds of asset such as shares, even if their effect on the housing market is much greater than on the share market. Negative gearing could be retained, but limited to apply to income from the investor's property or properties, rather than reducing the tax investors pay on their wages. The equivalent tax rules in the United Kingdom work along these lines. Or negative gearing could be retained in full, but limited to a maximum tax deduction each year. It could be restricted to only apply to newly built homes: many state governments have wound back grants for first home buyers in this way. The capital gains tax discount could be removed altogether, reverting to pre-1999 settings. Alternatively, the amount of tax benefit that housing investors can receive through negative gearing and discounted capital gains tax could be gradually reduced.

Some in the real estate and finance industries advance false and self-interested arguments in favour of the status quo. The first of these is that negative gearing and the discounted rate of capital gains tax increase the supply of new rental housing. Peter Bushby from the Real Estate Institute of Australia was reported in 2013 as saying that negative gearing 'helps in the provision of rental accommodation'. But only about 5 per cent of money loaned for investment in housing in Australia actually goes towards building new housing. Almost 95 per cent goes to bidding up the price of existing housing. If new houses aren't being built, then one more taxpayer-subsidised investment property means one less household owning their home. Historically low rental vacancy rates also reveal a shortage of rental properties. If a discounted rate of capital gains tax and negative gearing are supposed to be getting new housing built, they're doing a terrible job.

The second claim is that restricting negative gearing in the mid-1980s caused the rental housing market to stall. Not true. Only Sydney and Perth experienced increased growth in rents over this period, yet restrictions on negative gearing applied nationwide. And Sydney and Perth had been experiencing unusually low vacancy rates before the policy change. Growth in rents actually slowed in Melbourne and Adelaide when negative gearing was restricted, while other capital cities were stable. Moreover, once the restrictions were lifted in 1987, the bulk of housing investment shifted from new homes to existing properties.

Reform of tax concessions for property investors won't—and shouldn't—happen overnight. But it's important to be clear and honest about the consequences of these policies. Current tax settings are limiting housing choice, hardly getting any new housing built and contributing to home ownership heading out of reach for increasing numbers of Australians, all at great cost to the community.

Security and respect for renters

Renters are a large and growing group. Yet many do not experience stability and security, nor enjoy anywhere near the scope that owners do to turn their housing into a home by owning pets or making small changes, such as putting a picture on the wall.

Residential tenancy legislation in Australia exacerbates renters' lack of security, as do low vacancy rates, renters' limited bargaining power and the outdated perspective that renting is only a transitional stage before home ownership.

If renters are to get more security and respect, an essential first step is to establish an inquiry to take stock of the rental sector's growth, and of its increasing importance to households and the economy. The inquiry should consider extending the minimum duration of leases, while still enabling renters to give notice and terminate their tenancies without paying out the entire lease. Other possible measures include extending minimum notice periods that apply when landlords terminate a lease, and clearly prescribing grounds for termination. There are also strong grounds for increasing tenants' freedom to make minor modifications and to own pets.

The Irish experience shows that changes can be made without unduly affecting economic returns for landlords. In 2004, Ireland moved from arrangements similar to Australia's towards improving security of tenure for renters. The standard lease lengthened from between six and twelve months to a legally prescribed four years, though landlords and tenants can terminate a lease in the first six months with twenty-eight days' notice. After that time, landlords can terminate the lease only on more narrowly prescribed grounds. Notice periods increase in line with the length of the tenure. After the reforms were introduced, the Irish private rental sector grew substantially as a proportion of all housing.

Low-income renters and people locked out of the housing market altogether are doing it toughest of all. Public and community housing levels are declining, even as city populations and the number of people needing this kind of support grow. The proportion of rental costs being met by government Rent Assistance is also declining.

For people on Rent Assistance, it is only fair that the rate be set with reference to the actual rents people pay. The 2009 Henry Review of taxation proposed the maximum rate of Rent Assistance continue to cover a relatively small proportion of recipients' spending on rent, but that the rate be indexed to movements in actual rents rather than to the consumer price index. This seems a fair starting point for considering how to improve the circumstances of an increasingly vulnerable group of people.

Arresting or reversing recent declines in the amount of public and community housing would also help Australians on low incomes struggling to find affordable shelter through the rental market. Declines in public housing have contributed to the squeeze at the bottom of the rental market. While public housing is costly, so are tax concessions to property investors through negative gearing and discounted capital gains tax. And unlike these tax concessions, government provision does get new housing built.

It is hard to see the situation for low-income renters improving in the long term if the decline in public housing doesn't turn around. Arresting this decline is likely to have benefits that affect first home buyers as well: governments' post–World War II expansion of public housing (including housing for returned soldiers) contributed to the large-scale growth in home ownership that occurred across the 1950s.

Transport

Better transport will not solve all the problems of our cities. It cannot fully overcome the increasingly long distances between housing and jobs. New roads and public transport infrastructure are expensive. Congestion can't be eliminated entirely. Indeed, no thriving city should have zero congestion, because it would suggest the economy is moribund. Nonetheless, improved transport has a critical role to play in better linking people with economic opportunity and social connection.

Enabling people to get around better involves getting more out of existing road and rail infrastructure, while also improving access to transport in areas which are poorly served.

Improving the existing network

Making much better use of the existing transport network will enable more people to travel on it, and do so more quickly. While far less glamorous than big new road tunnels and train lines, targeted investments and management improvements to transport systems can bring substantial benefits. Infrastructure Australia found that smaller projects have the biggest impact because they target specific problems that keep cities from getting the most out of their road or rail networks. A comprehensive analysis of transport projects in the United Kingdom drew a similar conclusion.

Reducing bottlenecks helps to ensure that roads are no more congested than they have to be. On-street parking on main roads unnecessarily slows down cars, buses and trams. The Victorian experience described in Chapter 7 shows that instituting and expanding clearways can make a big difference to traffic flow for a small sum of money. But it also shows the importance of respecting local interests if change is to endure. In 2013 the NSW government foreshadowed an approach to expanding clearways that contemplates replacing on-street parking on main roads with off-street parking; this may reap more enduring benefits.

Dedicated bus (and tram) lanes can help to move the largest numbers of commuters on scarce road space, especially at peak times. So can traffic signals that prioritise buses and trams over cars. Trams in the United Kingdom and France spend between 1 and 3 per cent of their journey time at traffic signal intersections, compared to 17 per cent in Melbourne's much slower system. Priority lanes and signals are also relatively inexpensive, especially compared to building new infrastructure.

Level crossings also create bottlenecks where train lines meet roads. Replacing major level crossings with bridges or tunnels substantially improves traffic flow, and in certain circumstances can also allow trains to be scheduled more frequently.

Better traffic management systems can have a surprisingly big impact on how much traffic flows through key roads. Measures that can make a difference include ensuring that traffic lights get as many cars flowing through intersections as possible, clearing away broken-down cars on motorways more quickly, adjusting speed limits according to the amount of traffic on the road and installing traffic lights to control the flow of cars on motorway on-ramps. Some of these already exist on Australian roads, but they are much more widespread in the United States and Europe. A 2006 review conducted for Australian road authorities found that better traffic management measures could lead to 20 to 25 per cent more traffic flow on Australian motorways.

Technology can help. The spread of the Internet and wireless technology—particularly smartphones—is helping to develop real-time ride pooling and peer-to-peer car rentals that could reduce congestion over time. Sensors that help people find a car park can help reduce the congestion that comes from people circling to find a parking space. Driverless cars, though still at an embryonic stage, promise even greater benefits. Better technology could improve compliance with transit and express lane rules, which typically only permit vehicles with two or more occupants during peak periods.

Targeted investments and technological and management improvements that expand the capacity of a whole network are also beneficial. For example, upgrading signalling technology so that trains can run more frequently on an existing track can be as effective as building a new train line, but at a much lower cost. So can running larger trains that carry more passengers.

In the mid-2000s, Melbourne's trains were overcrowded. Commuters were frustrated with the reliability and speed of services. Many experienced discomfort as they were crammed into trains; others were unable to get on their train at all. From 2005 to 2008, the number of Melbourne trains reporting 'load breaches' (passenger numbers at or above capacity) rose steadily. Since then a combination of new trains, adjustments to timetables and routes and improved maintenance contributed to fewer overcrowded trains on most lines.

Even so, targeted, incremental improvements are not a comprehensive fix. There are limits to the benefits that can be reaped from more efficient management without accompanying infrastructure improvements, as the persistent overcrowding on the Dandenong and Werribee train lines that serve the fast-growing outer suburbs of south-west and south-east Melbourne reveals. The increased overcrowding across the Melbourne train network that occurred in 2014 after it had abated for several years may provide further evidence that targeted investments and incremental improvements alone cannot solve the problems of a city's transport network, even if they are incredibly important.

Pricing congestion

Congestion is inevitable in areas where jobs are concentrated. If there is no price for driving on a road, more people will always want to do so at peak times than road space will permit, leading to congestion. Charging drivers a fee to drive on congested roads at peak times reduces congestion because some people will choose to avoid the charge by driving at a different time, catching public transport or not making the journey. A charge would not eliminate congestion, but it would mitigate its worst effects.

Charges to reduce congestion have been proposed for Australian cities, but swiftly rejected after public opposition. People don't like being made to pay to use existing roads. Yet we already pay to use essential services such as electricity, gas and water, often with concessions for disadvantaged people. Charging a price for these services—even those built with public funds—helps to reduce blackouts and water shortages, and limits the need to build expensive new dams and power plants. Introducing or increasing fees to use motorways at peak times is a modest application of the same approach.

In fact, many Australian industries use variable pricing to manage high levels of demand for a scarce resource (like road space). Chair of the Australian Competition and Consumer Commission Rod Sims has observed: 'All Australians understand why it costs more to rent a beach house in January than July. We just don't call it congestion pricing'.

To be effective, a congestion charge only needs to change the behaviour of a relatively small number of drivers. Small reductions in the numbers of cars travelling at peak times can lead to big improvements in traffic flow. The number of cars on the road during school holidays—when traffic is noticeably lighter—is about 8 per cent lower than during the rest of the year. The NRMA estimates that when traffic on congested roads reduces by 5 per cent, traffic speeds increase by 50 per cent.

The best-known way of putting a price on congestion is by making people driving into the centre of a city pay a fee. These kinds of congestion charges have been introduced in London, Stockholm and Milan, and have reduced traffic volumes in those cities.

A better response to Australian conditions would be to charge drivers to use motorways at peak times (or increase tolls where they are already in place), and lower or even eliminate charges at off-peak times. Time-based charges to use motorways would lead to substantially better traffic flow. Some people will prefer to pay higher tolls at peak times in exchange for being able to get home from work more quickly. Some tradespeople would be able to earn more income by getting to more jobs in a day. Reduced congestion would enable buses to run more quickly and reliably.

Other people will prefer to reduce their costs by travelling at off-peak times, or catching public transport, thereby reducing overall congestion. The increasing numbers of people using congested roads for recreation and shopping trips during peak times may be best placed to respond to variable tolls by driving at an off-peak time. A congestion charge would also create an incentive for tradespeople and other mobile workers to schedule jobs in congested areas outside peak periods.

Because congestion doesn't discriminate between public and private roads, the change would require a shift from the current system of charging tolls on some new motorways—usually the same amount all day long—to one where time-of-use charges apply on all busy motorways, no matter what their age and whether they are operated by the government or a private company. It's the variation in the price commuters pay to use a road that is likely to have the biggest impact on congestion, not whether there is a price at all. Charging a shift worker a toll to drive home on an empty AirportlinkM7 in Brisbane at three in the morning helps pay for that road to be built, but it doesn't reduce congestion.

There are several ways to test the impact of congestion pricing. Motorways that charge a flat-rate toll could be converted to a variable toll that is higher at peak times. Drivers on congested motorways could pay a toll to use an express lane, while others retained the option of travelling more slowly without paying a toll. Technology such as GPS and electronic tolling transponders can also enable more sophisticated congestion charging arrangements to be introduced. The Singapore government has put variable prices on several major roads in order to maintain an average speed of 45 to 65 kilometres per hour on motorways, and 20 to 30 kilometres per hour on other main roads.

Whatever the arrangement, it must be designed well. Variable tolls were introduced on the city-bound lanes of the Sydney Harbour Bridge in January 2009. Fees during peak periods are $4, during the day $3, and at night $2.50. This reduced peak traffic growth, but by no more than 5 per cent. It seems the prices are having some impact, but the gap between peak and off-peak prices may not be high enough to prompt many drivers to change their behaviour. One measure that would help is electronic road signage to ensure drivers are aware of the different tolls and traffic speeds in place at different times. It is not enough to put options for lower tolls and shorter commutes outside peak times on a bill someone opens much later.

A concern about congestion charging is that higher tolls during peak periods could have a disproportionate financial impact on lower-income earners. But rather than leave congestion to grow unchecked, low-income earners can be compensated with concessional rates, toll rebates and discounts on registration. Similar discounts already exist for public transport and many utilities.

In Australia, many outer suburbs where incomes are lower are poorly served by public transport, leaving residents little choice but to drive to work. Since congestion is worst in inner suburbs, and public transport is generally much better there, higher tolls for peak periods should initially be confined to inner areas.

There are also ways to smooth the transition to charges at peak periods. A trial period would get drivers accustomed to lower congestion. Many would be reluctant to return to higher congestion levels after the trial period, even if the new system meant they had to pay a fee. Evaluation of the trial would also help set the price correctly.

Roads are not the only parts of city transport networks reaching their capacity at peak times. Trains are often overcrowded, and rail networks approach their capacity during morning and afternoon peaks. Differential ticket prices between peak and off-peak periods—with appropriate concessions—would help to limit these problems.

Peak and off-peak pricing for train travel would have to be designed and implemented well. In 2008 the 'early bird' ticket was introduced to Melbourne's train network, providing free travel to commuters arriving at their destination before 7 a.m. A 2010 evaluation found that take-up of the concession was mostly restricted to those commuters who only had to shift their normal travel time by half an hour or less in order to qualify. By 2011 there was a 6 per cent decline in train patronage before 7 a.m. from the year before. Poor promotion of the scheme was blamed for its limited impact.

Expanding transport connections

Improving transport connections from middle and outer suburbs to employment centres benefits both residents of those areas and the city as a whole.

Ensuring outer areas have adequate connections to main roads and motorways is part of the answer. The outer south-west Melbourne suburb of Point Cook, where Alice and Jason Osborne (whom we met in Chapter 3) live, lacks sufficient access roads. Consequently, people can wait in traffic for forty minutes just to get out of the suburb. This kind of local congestion really shouldn't happen.

Better public transport is also essential to improving access to jobs, especially to opportunities in the inner city. Cars will remain the main form of transport in middle and outer suburbs for the foreseeable future, especially for trips to other middle and outer suburbs. But improving access to public transport would give residents of these suburbs choices that inner-city residents take for granted. It would grow the economy by giving employers a wider choice of employees, and expand the range of employment and social opportunities available to people who are unable to drive. Better public transport would also be an essential quid pro quo for putting a price on road congestion through higher tolls at peak times.

To be a credible option, public transport services need to operate within a reasonable distance of where people live. But access to a single, infrequent, meandering bus route is barely better than having access to no public transport at all. Residents need a good choice of routes that run frequently, and offer reasonably direct connections to different employment centres.

Trains and buses both have a role to play. Buses are especially useful for shorter trips, including from homes to train stations, and for travelling between suburbs. Congestion tolls, bus lanes and priority traffic signals would also help bus services to run more quickly.

Bus patronage has grown substantially in Melbourne on high frequency 'orbital' bus routes. Melbourne's train and tram lines generally run in a radial fashion to and from the CBD, or around the inner city. Orbital bus routes running along major arterial roads provide cross-town connections to train stations, tram lines, schools, universities, hospitals and shopping centres. Part of their appeal has been that they run more often and for more hours than most services, and many stops display up-to-date information on when the next bus is due.

Trains are generally more popular than buses. They travel long distances much more quickly. No other mode of transport is as good at moving large numbers of people into inner-city employment centres. Train lines are expensive to build and run, but they are essential foundations for a knowledge-intensive economy. Large cities in developed economies worldwide are continuing to improve connections between people and jobs through new train lines. These include the Silver Line that opened in Washington DC in 2014; extensions to the Bloor–Danforth line in Toronto and the new Evergreen line in Vancouver, both planned for 2016; and London's vast Crossrail project, due from 2018.

Extending existing train lines into poorly serviced growth suburbs is one way to expand access to trains without the costs and complexity of building new lines. Adequate and safe parking is an essential complement to expanded train services in outer areas, as are good connections to local buses.

Nonetheless, some transport needs can only be met by new train lines. The expansion of trains to many previously unserviced Perth suburbs shows how this can be done well, and the benefits it can bring.

Trains in Perth

In the early 1980s, Perth had little rail infrastructure. It was not a government priority: the Fremantle line had been shut down in 1979, and only two lines remained.

Public protests and a change of government in 1983 brought a shift in approach. The Fremantle line was reopened in 1983. New lines were built, with the 26-kilometre Joondalup (now Clarkson) line opened in 1992 and the 70-kilometre Mandurah line in 2007. Both have proved very popular, with passenger numbers greatly exceeding planners' predictions, and patronage increasing across the entire network. From 1992 to 2013, total rail patronage increased dramatically from seven million to sixty-six million trips a year.

Perth's railways still lag behind Sydney's and Melbourne's in how much of the city they cover, and how much they are used. (For example, 310 million trips were made on Sydney's trains in 2013.) Nonetheless, the expansion of Perth's railways has supported employment growth in Perth's CBD: 14 per cent between 2006 and 2011, in addition to significant growth in areas such as West Perth. More than three in five peak-hour trips to Perth CBD are by public transport.

The system's design responds well to passengers' needs. Fast journey times have been a priority. The distances between stations on the new lines are long by Australian standards: an average of 3 kilometres on the Clarkson line and 6 on the Mandurah line. This means the trains go faster and stop less frequently: the Mandurah line has speeds averaging 85 kilometres an hour.

Frequent services throughout the day make Perth trains comparatively easy and appealing to use. A higher proportion of Perth train trips are in off-peak periods than is the case in other Australian cities. The national Bureau of Infrastructure, Transport and Regional Economics considers that 'With frequent services, good reliability standards and high average speeds ... the Transperth network arguably delivers Australia's highest-standard CBD commuter railway'.

For non-drivers in outer areas, public transport will never offer a complete solution to the barriers to mobility they face. A public transport service to employment centres is far more likely to operate viably, with reasonable levels of patronage, than one helping an elderly person travel at off-peak times from home to the nearest hospital, to their children's homes in suburbs further out and to their friend's home in a different part of the city. The needs of Lili Szalisznyo, whom we met in Chapter 4, are typical of the problem. It would be very difficult to design a public transport system around her travel to the Brisbane community radio station, notwithstanding its importance to her life. And in most places public transport is limited at night and on weekends, when many people are free to spend time with family and friends.

Instead, improving non-drivers' access to car travel is likely to be much more cost-effective than an extremely large-scale expansion of public transport services to serve the kinds of trips that people would always make by car, if they could. Technological developments will help shape what is possible. Options include ride-sharing apps and

car-sharing arrangements, local councils providing community transport that residents can book in advance (as some already do) and
subsidising the cost of taxi services.

More dispersed housing in middle and outer suburbs is sometimes
cited as a reason against extending public transport networks. But
Perth's expansion of rail services shows how it can be done well. In that
city, a lot of effort goes into making it easy for people in nearby areas
to catch the train. Sufficient free and low-cost parking is provided at
stations. There are good bus connections to local areas, and train and
bus timetables are integrated so that passengers transferring from one
to the other don't have to wait. Interchanges shelter passengers from
the weather, minimise walking distance and provide walkways over
busy roads. On the Mandurah line, most train passengers arrive at the
station by car or bus, allowing the stations to draw passengers from a
wider area than many do in Sydney, for example.

The Committee for Perth, a local coalition of businesses, has praised
the way Perth train services have adapted 'the traditional model of mass
transit—which achieved mass through penetration into high urban densities—to a low-density model of bringing the masses to the railway
stations by bus or car'.

Another argument for not expanding public transport services
in middle and outer areas is that it is not cost-effective. Tony Abbott
lamented 'the economics of public transport in a suburban metropolis'
in his 2009 book, *Battlelines*. But the population density of the area in
which public transport services operate is only one of many influences
on the cost-effectiveness of a public transport system. For example,
Sydney's public transport system recovers about 24 per cent of its operating costs through ticket sales, while the system in much less densely
populated Perth recovers 38 per cent of its costs that way.

Better transport decisions

Finally, governments need to plan better for the infrastructure that does
get built. Options for what to build should emerge from integrated citywide planning for housing and transport, shaped by deep community

engagement. These options should be transparently assessed for their costs and benefits well before decisions are made.

Assessments of transport options—business cases, feasibility studies and cost-benefit analyses—should be publicly available. Transparency throughout the decision-making process also makes it much more likely that plans actually get followed through, and reduces the likelihood of governments changing their minds once a project has started—a major cause of cost blowouts.

Assessments of major transport projects need to consider how they will improve people's access to jobs, and how they will shape the city's economy. Since money will always be scarce, the projects that bring the most benefits for every dollar spent should be the ones that get built.

Nor is it good enough for experts to assess potential major projects only on how they would reduce journey times, even if this is easier to measure than some of the other effects of new infrastructure. Roads and train lines last for decades, even centuries. They profoundly reshape how cities work, where businesses operate, where people live and how they get around. The UK government already systematically considers these kinds of wider impact in assessing which major transport projects to build in cities. The Australian approach is much more ad hoc, with substantial room for improvement.

Paying for better cities

There is a mismatch between who pays for improvements to our cities, and who benefits from them. Property owners in areas with good access to jobs, transport and services benefit from higher property values, while the whole community pays for the infrastructure that helps to make their property valuable. People with poor access to public transport make substantial contributions to its operating costs through taxes, but are given few transport alternatives in return.

The situation can be made fairer in two ways: by adopting a land or property tax paid by all city residents and businesses that own land, and by changing the way we pay for public transport improvements.

Land tax—a fairer way to pay

Land or property taxes are the fairest way to fund improvements to transport and other infrastructure, for two reasons. First, land and property values are a strong indicator of a household's overall wealth. So such a tax falls on those households that are most able to pay. Second, in places close to jobs, land represents a large proportion of the price of housing. Much of the land's value comes from its proximity to assets and services the whole community pays for—including public transport, roads and schools. Taxing the value of land would mean those households whose wealth grows most from these assets make a greater proportional contribution to their costs. It would give those residents an increased interest in seeing that the tax they pay is used for something that improves their neighbourhood and their city.

Such a tax could be assessed on the unimproved value of land, or on the value of the entire property. In either case, to operate fairly, a land or property tax would need to apply evenly across all home owners, investors and commercial property owners. A carefully managed transition would be needed to ensure consistency and fairness.

Land taxes do exist in name at present. But home owners are completely exempt, and state government land tax rules for investors and commercial property owners include many anomalies and exemptions that enable many people and businesses with substantial land holdings to limit their tax liability. Local council rates (a form of property tax) apply more broadly, though they too have substantial exemptions, and different levels of rates are charged by different local councils.

An added benefit of applying a land or property tax evenly across all property owners would be to enable stamp duty to be reduced or eliminated. Stamp duty makes it more expensive than it should be for people to move to where they want to live, or into the kind of home they want. Governments can more fairly raise revenue by taxing the value of land, rather than drawing a disproportionate amount of their revenue from people who move home more often.

Again, a move from stamp duty to a land or property tax would need to be introduced gradually, so that people who have recently bought property would not be disadvantaged. Transition arrangements would also need to consider households with a lot of wealth tied up in their family home but on low incomes, such as pensioners. These households could be allowed to defer paying until the property is eventually sold.

Paying for extending public transport

There is no perfect way to fund a transport system. But the Australian approach can certainly be improved. A land tax would help to more evenly balance contributions between users; businesses and home owners benefiting from higher property values; and the taxpaying public.

In addition, the revenue from any congestion charge should be returned to the transport system, to ensure that public transport offers drivers a better alternative to using congested roads. Some revenue should also be returned to road users, through lower registration fees and lower off-peak tolls, for instance. The goal is to make cities work better. Governments using such a measure just to raise revenue would doom it to failure.

If public transport is to expand, it needs to operate with more financial self-sufficiency. Some subsidy for public transport users from the taxpaying public is warranted because good public transport reduces road use and air pollution and supports economic growth. Concession fares are also important because they help people on low incomes to get around. Ticket sales fund only a small proportion of the cost of running public transport services in Australia though. Over time, public transport will need to move closer towards paying its own way. Finding ways to operate more efficiently and do more with less can help, as will increased passenger numbers, but over time full fares for public transport may need to increase.

Change for the better

The challenge of turning our cities around is not just one for governments. We all need to take responsibility for where we live.

The first thing we can do is recognise the connection between the lives we lead and the cities we live in. We can help politicians to understand how important cities are to millions of Australians' lives. Politicians want to respond to public sentiment, but they first need to be aware of it. We can call or write to them, and let them know why we're voting. We can participate in—or even start—campaigns to make our local community and our city better places to live. It's a maxim of politics that decisions are made by the people who show up. We can reward good decisions and castigate bad ones. We should be suspicious of anyone offering easy answers, quick fixes or something for nothing.

We should also demand a say in the future of where we live. Cities will change—for good or for ill—no matter what, so we might as well have a say in it. We should expect genuine engagement from leaders that lets residents identify priorities and make real trade-offs about the future, not lip-service 'consultation' with lobby groups and activists who are not always representative of many residents.

Perhaps the most important thing we can do as citizens and as residents of cities is to be open to change. If cities don't change, while the world and the economy inevitably do, things *will* get worse.

Change can be confronting. Often we do not want to change. But adapting to change frequently isn't as hard as we expect it to be. Cities helped Australia navigate the great shift from an agricultural economy to an industrial one that helped to keep us one of the wealthiest nations in the world. A more recent example is the wariness surrounding the introduction of the goods and services tax in 2000. The community was hesitant and the Labor opposition ran a scare campaign against it that almost won the 1998 federal election. But after a transition period, the GST has become an accepted fact of life in Australia. In the rear-view mirror, change often turns out to have been a lot easier than we feared at the time.

Conclusion

TO WALK AROUND SYDNEY Harbour is to behold one of the most beautiful sights in the world. The view overlooking the Opera House and the Harbour Bridge dazzles Sydneysiders and visitors alike.

The roar of the Boxing Day Test crowd at Melbourne's MCG can be spine-tingling. Families play on Brisbane's South Bank beach before visiting an art gallery or eating by the river. Residents of Adelaide flock to its annual arts festival, especially the Fringe. Perth people celebrate their beaches and their sunsets. Australians love their cities, and are proud of their best qualities.

In the past, cities helped Australians benefit from a changing world. As we shifted from an agricultural economy to a manufacturing-driven industrial economy, cities welcomed millions of new residents in suburbs that expanded as factories opened nearby.

The world has changed over the last half century. Cities are now the great engines of the modern global economy. To take advantage, many countries are trying to urbanise as fast as possible. Australians should be celebrating our luck that we already have big cities, enabling us to make the most of the twenty-first century.

But our cities are not adapting to this new reality. As jobs and economic opportunity concentrate in and around city centres, growing numbers of people are locked out. The range of housing choices people have available to them has narrowed in recent decades. We're not building the homes that would give growing populations good access to jobs, and choices about where and how they live. We continue to develop our cities in ways that worked well fifty years ago, but no longer do.

Too many people are denied opportunities to secure their future and earn the best living they can. Too many households experience high living costs and long commutes that harm social connection and family life. These challenges will continue to exist at whatever rate our population grows in the future.

When they work properly, cities generate and distribute wealth and opportunity: a rising tide that lifts all boats. But they are increasingly divided: between young and old, rich and poor, home owners and renters, the outer suburbs and the inner city.

Turning around these problems is undeniably difficult. Nobody wants to lose out from change, so we resist it, or pretend it can be avoided. Decision-makers and opinion leaders often let us down. There are practical barriers. The housing market is slow to change. Transport infrastructure is expensive. Scarce land in cities—especially close to the centre—means we can't all get everything we want.

But there are solutions too. Cities that work connect people with jobs, and with each other. Housing markets that work give people real housing options, including the chance to make meaningful choices about price, location, the kind of home to live in and whether to buy or rent. Governments can make it easier to build new homes in established areas with good access to jobs and transport, improve transport in poorly served middle and outer suburbs, and involve all residents in shaping their city's future.

The challenge is not just one for governments though. Our cities will only get better if we want them to, and act accordingly. Australians are good at adapting to change, even if we are sometimes wary of it. The reward is a richer, fairer and happier Australia, as cities take us with great speed into the next phase of our economic and social life.

Authors' note

The Grattan Institute Cities Program ran for five years until 2014. Our research covered a range of issues including city economies, decision-making in cities and the housing market. The ten reports the program produced during this time are available at www.grattan.edu.au.

As the program developed, we realised that the individual topics addressed in our reports were all part of a larger story about how Australian cities work (or don't). So we wanted to pull the story together in one place, and illustrate our findings with the experience of real people living in Australia's cities today.

We have also been struck over the years by the outdated sense many of us have of the kind of country we are living in, and by how hard it can be to draw attention to the issues facing our cities. Grattan reports seek to influence government decision-makers, such as ministers and senior public servants, using an analysis-driven format. We wanted to write the story of Australia's cities for a wider audience.

The book focuses on three main issues: the economy, opportunity and fairness, and social connection. Of course this omits a wide range of important topics relating to cities, including urban design, architecture, walkability and cycling, water, climate change and the environment, among many others. They are all important, but we have chosen not to cover them in order to maintain a focus on the three big themes of the book.

Similarly, we have not been able to cover every Australian city in the same depth. Sydney and Melbourne are discussed more than other cities, reflecting their substantially larger populations.

The case studies were researched and written by journalist Julie Szego. Unless otherwise noted, real names are used.

For ease of reading, the text does not use footnotes. References are comprehensively cited and cross-referenced in the endnotes. Grattan Institute Cities Program reports provide additional detail and evidence on issues explored in the book.

City Limits uses unit record data from the Household, Income and Labour Dynamics in Australia (HILDA) Survey. The HILDA Project was initiated and is funded by the Australian Government Department of Social Services (DSS) and is managed by the Melbourne Institute of Applied Economic and Social Research (Melbourne Institute). The findings and views reported in this book are those of the authors and should not be attributed to either DSS or the Melbourne Institute.

The opinions in this book are those of the authors and do not necessarily represent the views of the Grattan Institute's founding members, affiliates, individual board members, reference group members or reviewers. Any errors or omissions are the responsibility of the authors.

Jane-Frances Kelly
Paul Donegan

Acknowledgements

We would like to thank Julie Szego, James Button, Matthew Oberklaid, Cameron Chisholm, Cameron Harrison, Pete Goss, Meredith Sussex, Marcus Spiller, Rod Glover, Glyn Davis, Jim Betts, Owen Donald, Dennis Glover, Kathryn Anderson, Michael Hannebery, the members of the Grattan Cities Program reference group, the New England and Western Tenants Advice and Advocacy Service, Tenants Union of NSW, Bill Forrest, director of advocacy, Wyndham City Council, David Hawkins, secretariat to The Interface Councils, Anglicare Sydney, Aurora Community Association, Coleen Bowen at 2233 Realty, Camille Allam of Allam Real Estate, Meaghan Amor, Louise Adler, Colette Vella and Melbourne University Press, as well as numerous industry participants, officials and experts for their input.

We appreciate the time and generosity of case study participants and other interviewees: Mat Beyer, the Boston Consulting Group, Sinclair Knight Merz, Deloitte, Jim Gardner, Caroline Maloney, Alice and Jason Osborne, Hiren and Meera Suratwala, Lili Szalisznyo, Alexandra and Andrej Babic, Simon Khamara and Chérie, Lauren Beaumont, and Ken and Maureen Barrell.

City Limits draws on all the work of the Grattan Institute Cities Program, to which many people made substantial contributions over the years. They include Beth Barlow, Caroline Blanch, Peter Breadon, Caitrin

Davis, Leah Ginnivan, John Gregson, Amelie Hunter, Jordana Hunter, Perry Jackson, Peter Mares, Helen Morrow, Daniel Mullerworth, Michael O'Toole, Owen Probert, Tom Quinn, Julian Reichl, Nathan Stevens, Madeleine Tillig, Brody Viney, Marcus Walsh and Ben Weidmann.

Jane-Frances also thanks Paul, without whom she could not have crossed the finish line. Thanks are also due to James, Hettie, Judy and the tiny medium-density kittens of Fort Langley. She owes her family everything else.

Paul also thanks Jane-Frances, Beth Abraham, Maureen and Peter Donegan, Alice Bell, and family and friends for their patience and understanding during this endeavour.

Notes

CHAPTER 1 – A NATION OF CITIES

Page 5, paragraph commencing with 'A greater proportion of Australians live in cities ...' Statistics Canada, *Population and growth rate of metropolitan and non-metropolitan Canada 2006 and 2011*; Nomis, *2011 census: usual resident population*, ref. KS101EW; United States Census, *2010 census urban lists record layouts*.

Page 6, 'The discovery of gold ...' Australian Bureau of Statistics, *Australian historical population statistics 2014*, cat. no. 3105.0.65.001, table 1.1; Australian Bureau of Statistics, 'Population characteristics: 20th century: beginning and end', *Australian social trends*, 2000, cat. no. 4102.0.

Page 6, 'The legacy of our historical dependence ...' Australian Bureau of Statistics, 'Population characteristics: 20th century: beginning and end', *Australian social trends*, 2000, cat. no. 4102.0.

Page 6, 'But we are no longer a nation of farmers ...' Australian Bureau of Agricultural and Resource Economics and Science, *Agricultural commodity statistics 2013*, 2013, pp. 14, 16; Australian Bureau of Statistics, *Labour force: detailed, quarterly—August 2014*, cat. no. 6291.0.55.003, table 4; Australian Bureau of Statistics, *Australian national accounts: June quarter 2014*, cat. no. 5206.0, p. 39.

Page 6, 'After World War II came the rise ...' Australian Bureau of Statistics, *Year book Australia 1988: development of manufacturing industries in Australia*.

Pages 6–7, 'With the rise of manufacturing ...' Grattan Institute analysis of Australian Bureau of Statistics, *Census of population and housing*, 1966.

Page 7, 'Postwar growth in car ownership ...' Marcus Spiller and Terry Rawnsley, 'Housing and urban form: a new productivity agenda', in Richard Tomlinson (ed.), *Australia's unintended cities*, 2012, p. 145.

Page 7, 'Growth in the manufacturing industry ...' Australian Bureau of Statistics, *Labour force: detailed, quarterly—August 2014*, cat. no. 6291.0.55.003, table 4.

Page 7, 'More recently, the mining boom ...' ibid.; Ric Battellino, 'Mining booms and the Australian economy', speech to the Sydney Institute, 23 February 2010, graph 2; Reserve Bank of Australia, *Statement on monetary policy*, November 2011, p. 43.

Page 8, 'While Australia's natural resource deposits ...' Jane-Frances Kelly et al., *Mapping Australia's economy: cities as engines of prosperity*, Grattan Institute, 2014, p. 1.

Page 8, 'Today, when more than three-quarters of Australians ...' Reserve Bank of Australia, 'Australia's exports of education services', *RBA bulletin*, June 2008, p. 13; Department of Foreign Affairs and Trade, *Australia's top 25 exports 2013: goods and services*, 2014.

Pages 8–9, 'Cities generate most of our national income ...' Jane-Frances Kelly et al., *Mapping Australia's economy: cities as engines of prosperity*, Grattan Institute, 2014, p. 1 and underlying data.

Page 9, 'Australia's five largest cities ...' Australian Bureau of Statistics, *Australian historical population statistics 2014*, cat. no. 3105.0.65.001, table 3.2.

Page 9, 'Although they have similar beginnings ...' Grattan Institute analysis of Australian Bureau of Statistics, *Census of population and housing*, 2011.

Page 9, 'In the thirty years to 2013...' Australian Bureau of Statistics, *Australian demographic statistics*, cat. no. 3101.0, table 1.

Page 9, 'Most of Australia's population growth ...' Australian Bureau of Statistics, *Australian historical population statistics 2014*, cat. no. 3105.0.65.001, table 3.2.

Page 10, 'Australia's large cities ...' Grattan Institute analysis of Australian Bureau of Statistics, *Census of population and housing*, 2011.

Pages 10–11, 'When lots of people own cars ...' Information sourced from websites of these businesses.

Page 12, 'Almost all migrants to Australia ...' Australian Bureau of Statistics, 'Where do migrants live?', in *Australian social trends*, cat. no. 4102.0, 2014.

Page 13, 'At the start of 2014 ...' Richard Willingham, 'SPC future secured after Napthine government tips in $22 million', *The Age*, 13 February 2014.

Page 14, 'Wanting to connect with people ...' John Cacioppo and William Patrick, *Loneliness: human nature and the need for social connection*, 2008.

Pages 14–15, 'People living in cities live longer ...' Australian Institute of Health and Welfare, *Diabetes prevalence in Australia*, 2011, p. 8; Australian Institute of Health and Welfare, *Life expectancy*, http://www.aihw.gov.au/rural-health-life-expectancy/

Page 15, 'The link between geography and health ...' Ipsos, 'Mind and mood report—big city living', in Commonwealth Department of Infrastructure and Regional Development, *State of Australian cities 2013*, 2013, p. 273; Sue Dunlevy and Lisa Cornish, 'Dying three years younger is the price of poor health services in the bush', *Weekly Times Now*, 9 June 2014.

Page 16, 'Thankfully, we have largely learned ...' Only Melbourne, *History of Melbourne: Smellbourne*, https://www.onlymelbourne.com.au/melbourne_details.php?id=13152#.UzpuA_mSySo

Page 16, 'Cities still carry health risks.' Robert Hall, 'Notifiable diseases surveillance, 1917 to 1991', *Communicable Diseases Intelligence* vol. 17, no. 11, 1993; National Notifiable Diseases Surveillance System Writing Group, 'Australia's notifiable disease status, 2011: annual report of the National Notifiable Diseases Surveillance System', *Communicable Diseases Intelligence*, vol. 37, no. 4, 2011.

Pages 16–17, 'Australia has also done well ...' Commonwealth Department of Infrastructure and Regional Development, *Vehicle emissions standards*, http://www.infrastructure.gov.au/roads/environment/emission/; Commonwealth Department of the Environment, *National standards for air pollutants in*

Australia, http://www.environment.gov.au/resource/national-standards-criteria-air-pollutants-1-australia; World Health Organization, *Urban outdoor air pollution database*, 2011.

Page 17, 'Cities are frequently associated with crime.' NSW Bureau of Crime Statistics and Research, *Crime statistics*, 2014, http://www.bocsar.nsw.gov.au/bocsar/bocsar_crime_stats/bocsar_detailedspreadsheets.html; Victoria Police, *Crime statistics*, 2014, http://www.police.vic.gov.au/content.asp?Document_ID=782; Queensland Police, *Reported crime trend data*, 2014, http://www.police.qld.gov.au/online/data/; WA Police, *Crime statistics*, 2014, http://www.police.wa.gov.au/Aboutus/Statistics/Crimestatistics/tabid/1219/Default.aspx; SA Office of Crime Statistics and Research, *Publications and statistics*, 2014, http://www.ocsar.sa.gov.au/publications_statistics.html.

Page 17, 'Yet other costs or downsides ...' Grattan Institute analysis of Australian Bureau of Statistics, *Census of population and housing*, 2011.

Page 17, 'Serious traffic congestion also only happens ...' Rosie Squires, 'Morning peak a slow, four-hour slog', *Daily Telegraph*, 20 February 2011.

Page 18, 'But Australia is a nation of ...' Grattan Institute analysis of Australian Bureau of Statistics, *Census of population and housing*, 1991–2011.

Page 18, 'The Victorian Government has put a considerable ...' Regional Development Victoria, *Regional Victoria living expo*, 2014, http://www.rdv.vic.gov.au/expo

Pages 19–20, 'Another reason that the housing market ...' Roger Wilkins, Diana Warren and Markus Hahn, *Families, incomes and jobs, volume 4: a statistical report on waves 1 to 6 of the HILDA survey*, Melbourne Institute of Applied Economic and Social Research, 2009, p. 140; Australian Bureau of Statistics, *Australian social trends: moving house*, 2010, p. 1.

Page 21 'Two well-known rankings are ...' Mercer, *Quality of living reports*, 2014, http://www.imercer.com/products/quality-of-living.aspx.

CHAPTER 2 – CITIES AND THE ECONOMY

Page 23, 'In contrast to the days when ...' Jane-Frances Kelly et al., *Mapping Australia's economy: cities as engines of prosperity*, Grattan Institute, 2014, p. 1.

Page 25, 'BCG and SKM are far from alone.' ibid., p. 11.

Page 26, 'The same phenomenon can be observed ...' ibid., p. 1. This $118 billion includes only the value of the economic activity generated by the employees who work in Melbourne and Sydney CBDs. It does not, for example, include all the value generated by companies that have headquarters in these CBDs.

Page 26, 'Central business districts have by far ...' ibid.

Page 29, 'Being close to suppliers ...' Alfred Marshall, *Principles of economics*, 1890, book IV, chapter X, p. 3; Nicholas Crafts and Nikolaus Wolf, 'Competing successfully in a globalised world: lessons from Lancashire', *Vox—centre for economic policy research*, 22 October 2013; United Kingdom Board of Trade,

The earnings and hours of labour of workpeople of the UK: textile trades, 1909; Gregory Clark, 'Why isn't the whole world developed? Lessons from the cotton mills', *Journal of Economic History*, vol. 47, p. 141.

Page 29, 'Internet company Yahoo made headlines ...' Margaret Ryan, 'Teleworking: the myth of working from home', *BBC News Magazine*, 27 February 2013.

Page 29, 'Google agrees.' Ben Grubb, 'Do as we say, not as we do: Googlers don't telecommute', *The Sydney Morning Herald*, 19 February 2013.

Page 33, 'In our jobs we're solving ...' Jane-Frances Kelly et al., *Productive cities: opportunity in a changing economy*, Grattan Institute, 2013, p. 7.

Pages 33–34, 'In order to deal with this complexity ...' Grattan Institute analysis of Australian Bureau of Statistics, *Education and work*, cat. no. 6227.0, 2003–13.

Page 34, 'Specialisation has been part of the way ...' Adam Smith, *An inquiry into the nature and causes of the wealth of nations*, 1776.

Page 35, 'An increasingly skilled economy ...' Grattan Institute analysis of Australian Bureau of Statistics, *Census of population and housing*, 2011.

Page 36, 'These trends all contribute ...' ibid.

Page 36, 'Jobs in Melbourne are similarly distributed ...' ibid.

Page 36, 'In the map of Sydney ...' Jane-Frances Kelly et al., *Productive cities*, Grattan Institute, 2013, pp. 25–6 and underlying data.

Pages 36–37, 'The situation is not quite as bad ...' ibid.

Page 37, 'Brisbane has a similar level ...' Jane-Frances Kelly et al., *Who lives where: Brisbane*, Grattan Institute, 2013, p. 27 and underlying data; Jane-Frances Kelly et al., *Who lives where: Perth*, Grattan Institute, 2013, p. 27 and underlying data.

Page 37, 'For people commuting on public transport ...' Jane-Frances Kelly et al., *Productive cities*, Grattan Institute, 2013, p. 27 and underlying data.

Page 37, 'Similarly, large swathes of Melbourne ...' ibid., p. 29.

Page 39, 'In most of Brisbane, the situation ...' ibid., pp. 26–7.

Page 39, 'In all of Australia's big cities ...' Jane-Frances Kelly et al., *Who lives where: Melbourne*, Grattan Institute, 2013, pp. 27–8 and underlying data.

Page 39, 'Outside the centre, by contrast ...' Jane-Frances Kelly et al., *Productive cities*, Grattan Institute, 2013, p. 28.

Page 40, 'Distance matters for employers, too.' ibid., p. 29.

Pages 40–41, 'Outside CBDs, there is also wide variation.' Jane-Frances Kelly et al., *Who lives where: Brisbane*, Grattan Institute, 2013, pp. 27–8 and underlying data; Jane-Frances Kelly et al., *Who lives where: Melbourne*, Grattan Institute, 2013, pp. 27–8 and underlying data.

Page 41, 'International academic research has confirmed these phenomena.' Patricia Melo et al., 'Agglomeration, accessibility and productivity: evidence for urbanised areas in the US', paper submitted to the Transportation Research Board, 2013, p. 17.

Page 41, 'Studies have shown that having ...' Remy Prud'homme and Chang-Woon Lee, *Size, sprawl, speed and the efficiency of cities*, paper for L'Observatoire de l'Economie et des Institutions Locales, Université de Paris XII; Alain Bertaud, *Cities as labor markets*, Marron Institute on Cities and the Urban Environment working paper no. 2, 2014, p. 24; Australian Bureau of Statistics, *Australian national accounts: national income, expenditure and product*, cat. no. 5206.0, June 2014, p. 26.

Page 42, 'Knowledge-intensive jobs typically generate ...' Grattan Institute analysis of Australian Bureau of Statistics, *Census of population and housing*, 2011; Australian Taxation Office, *Taxation statistics 2011–12*, 2014.

Page 42, 'Knowledge-intensive work doesn't only benefit ...' Enrico Moretti, *The new geography of jobs*, 2012, pp. 97–101.

Page 43, 'He had to give up his Chinese-made smartphone ...' Kim Willsher, 'Man falls just short in patriot game to be 100% French', *The Guardian*, 28 February 2014.

Pages 43–44, 'People also value the new jobs and opportunities ...' Group of Eight Australia, *International students in higher education and their role in the Australian economy*, March 2014; Reserve Bank of Australia, 'Australia's exports of education services', *RBA bulletin*, June 2008, p. 13; Department of Foreign Affairs and Trade, *Australia's top 25 exports 2013: goods and services*, 2014.

Page 44, 'The growth in international students ...' Student Housing Australia, *Company profile*, 2014, http://sha.com.au/our-company/

Page 44, 'Australia is well placed for the future ...' Grattan Institute analysis of Australian Bureau of Statistics, *Census of population and housing*, 2006–11.

CHAPTER 3 – CITIES, OPPORTUNITY AND FAIRNESS

Page 48, 'Looking at income first ...' Grattan Institute analysis of Australian Bureau of Statistics, *Census of population and housing*, 2011.

Page 49, 'In Sydney, people between twenty-five ...' Jane-Frances Kelly et al., *Productive cities*, Grattan Institute, 2013, pp. 17–18 and underlying data.

Page 49, 'The income gap between inner and outer ...' ibid., pp. 18–19.

Page 49, 'The pattern is less pronounced in Perth ...' ibid.

Page 50, 'Part of the reason outer suburban residents ...' Australian Bureau of Statistics, *Forms of employment*, cat. no. 6359.0, 2012, table 7; Grattan Institute analysis of Australian Bureau of Statistics, *Census of population and housing*, 2011; Australian Bureau of Statistics, *Employee earnings and hours*, cat. no. 6306.0, table 2; Australian Bureau of Statistics, *Australian social trends: casual employees*, cat. no. 4102.0, 2009, p. 22.

Page 50, 'Differences in wealth, or assets ...' Australian Bureau of Statistics, *Household wealth and wealth distribution*, cat. no. 6554.0, p. 18.

Page 50, 'The highest property prices are increasingly ...' Mariano Kulish, Anthony Richards and Christian Gillitzer, *Urban structure and housing prices: some evidence form Australian cities*, Reserve Bank of Australia, 2011, p. 20.

Page 50, 'Of course, access to jobs and transport ...' Jane-Frances Kelly et al., *Who lives where: Melbourne*, Grattan Institute, 2013, p. 12.

Page 51, 'A metropolitan economy ...' Jane Jacobs, *The economy of cities*, 1969.

Page 52, 'Dennis Glover's family ...' Dennis Glover, 'Working class dreams fade as jobs dry up', *The Age*, 8 February 2014.

Pages 52–53, 'Doveton was not alone.' Commonwealth Department of Infrastructure and Regional Development, *State of Australian cities 2013*, 2013, p. 142; Australian Bureau of Statistics, *Year book Australia 1988: development of manufacturing industries in Australia.*

Page 53, 'More than two million people ...' Multiple definitions of western Sydney exist. We have included the local government areas of Auburn, Bankstown, Blacktown, Blue Mountains, Camden, Campbelltown, Canterbury, Fairfield, Hawkesbury, Holroyd, Liverpool, Parramatta, Penrith, The Hills and Wollondilly. Unless otherwise stated all the statistics in this section are Grattan Institute analysis of Australian Bureau of Statistics, *Census of population and housing*, 2006 and 2011.

Pages 53–54, 'Western Sydney remains Australia's largest ...' Phillip O'Neill, 'Spatial disadvantage in the Western Sydney region', in Commonwealth Department of Infrastructure and Transport, *State of Australian cities 2013*, 2013, pp. 90–1.

Pages 54–55, 'Western Sydney has a poor match ...' Grattan Institute analysis of Australian Bureau of Statistics, *Census of population and housing*, 2006 and 2011.

Pages 55–56, 'As manufacturing has declined, governments ...' ABC online, 'Ford Australia to close Broadmeadows and Geelong plants, 1200 jobs to go', 23 May 2013; News.com.au, 'Tony Abbott announces $100m assistance package for Holden workers', 18 December 2013; Premier of South Australia, *State government releases Holden response*, media release, 21 January 2014; ABC online, 'Toyota shutdown: Victorian Premier Denis Napthine seeks federal assistance for workers', 11 February 2014.

Page 56, 'By contrast, governments feel no need ...' John McDuling, 'Optus cuts more jobs, ramps up fixed-line assault', *Australian Financial Review*, 21 March 2013; Alex McDonald, 'IBM quietly slashing Australian jobs, moving work offshore', *ABC Online*, 25 October 2013; Fran Foo, 'IBM set to slash another 500 workers', *The Australian*, 4 March 2014; Adele Ferguson, 'Job cuts boost ANZ profit', *The Sydney Morning Herald*, 30 April 2013; Peter Trute, '1200 jobs cut in a day', *The Sydney Morning Herald*, 21 February 2013.

Page 57, 'Almost all of western Sydney ...' Matt Wade and Lucy Cormack, 'Stuck in the slow lane', *The Sydney Morning Herald*, 5 April 2014.

Page 59, 'Modern Australia has many stories like the Suratwalas ...' Grattan Institute analysis of Melbourne Institute of Applied Economic and Social Research, *Household income and labour dynamics in Australia survey*, wave 11, 2013; Barbara Pocock, Natalie Skinner and Philippa Williams, *Work, life and time*, Australian Work Life Index, 2007, p. 35.

Page 59, 'Poor access to jobs is a particular problem for mothers.' Barbara Pocock, Natalie Skinner and Philippa Williams, *Time bomb: work, rest and play in Australia today*, 2012, p. 76.

Page 59, 'Many find it difficult to obtain ...' Matt Wade and Lucy Cormack, 'Stuck in the slow lane', *The Sydney Morning Herald*, 5 April 2014.

Page 60, 'The map in Figure 3.3 compares ...' Jane-Frances Kelly et al., *Productive cities*, Grattan Institute, 2013, pp. 30–1.

Page 60, 'Many mothers living far from ...' John Daley, Cassie McGannon and Leah Ginnivan, *Game-changers: economic reform priorities for Australia*, Grattan Institute, 2012, p. 38.

Page 61, 'Travel costs are a big part ...' David Eccleston, 'Why living in Sydney's outer suburbs can cost over $18k per year', *7News Online*, 9 April 2014.

Page 62, 'Between 1976 and 1991 ...' Bob Gregory and Boyd Hunter, *The macro economy and the growth of ghettos and urban poverty in Australia*, Centre for Economic Policy Research discussion paper no. 325, 1995.

Page 62, 'But by 1991, the picture was very different.' ibid.; Jane-Frances Kelly et al., *Productive cities*, Grattan Institute, 2013, pp. 33–4.

Page 62, 'Over time, this polarisation ...' See, e.g., Ana Diez, 'Investigating neighborhood and area effects on health', *American Journal of Public Health*, vol. 91, no. 11, 2001, p. 1783; John MacDonald et al., *Neighborhood effects on crime and youth violence: the role of business improvement districts in Los Angeles*, RAND technical report, 2009.

Page 62, 'Increasingly, geography is destiny.' Smart Growth America, *Measuring sprawl 2014*, 2014.

Page 63, 'Both sides of politics think that ...' John Kunkel, 'Reflections on the "Howard Project"', *IPA review*, May 2008, p. 14; Andrew Leigh, *Battler and billionaires: the story of inequality in Australia*, 2013, p. 104; Malcolm Turnbull, 'Not classy, Wayne', *Australian Financial Review*, 16 March 2012.

Page 63, 'The Committee for Sydney wrote ...' Committee for Sydney, *Sydney: adding to the dividend, ending the divide*, 2013, p. 18.

CHAPTER 4 – CITIES AND SOCIAL CONNECTION

Page 65, 'Just as cities and the economy ...' Andrew Leigh, *Disconnected*, 2010, p. 129.

Page 65, 'Household structures are also changing.' Grattan Institute analysis of Australian Bureau of Statistics, *Census of population and housing*, 1976–2011; Australian Bureau of Statistics, 'Australian households: the future' in *Australian social trends*, cat. no. 4102.0, December 2010; Ruth Weston and Lixia Qu, *Working out relationships*, Australian Institute of Family Studies: Australian family trends no. 3, 2013, p. 9; Lixia Qu and Ruth Weston, *Australian households and families*, Australian Institute of Family Studies: Australian family trends no. 4, 2013, p. 6.

Pages 65–66, 'More people are expected to live …' Australian Bureau of Statistics, *Household and family projections, Australia, 2006 to 2031*, cat. no. 3236.0, 2010.

Page 66, 'Many single-parent and single-person …' David Baker, *All the lonely people: loneliness in Australia 2001–2009*, Australia Institute, 2012, p. v.

Page 66, 'People who live by themselves …' ibid., p. 14; Adrian Franklin and Bruce Tranter, *Housing, loneliness and health,* Australian Housing and Urban Research Institute final report no. 164, 2011, pp. 7, 25.

Page 66, 'The situation can be particularly difficult …' Young Foundation, *Sinking & swimming: understanding Britain's unmet needs*, 2009.

Page 66, 'Different people obviously have different needs.' Robert Cummins et al., *The wellbeing of Australians: relationships and the Internet*, Australian Unity Wellbeing Index Survey, report 25.0, 2011; Jane-Frances Kelly et al., *Social cities*, Grattan Institute, 2012, p. 6; Julianne Holt-Lunstad, Timothy Smith and J. Bradley Layton, 'Social relationships and mortality risk: a meta-analytic review', *PLOS Medicine*, vol. 7, no. 7, 2010, p. 1.

Page 67, 'There is an ingrained idea …' Young Foundation, *Sinking & swimming: understanding Britain's unmet needs*, 2009.

Pages 67–68, 'Of course cities—their populations …' Michael Schluter and David Lee, *The R factor*, 1993, p. 9.

Page 68, 'While social media use has increased …' Donald Sacco and Mohamed Ismail, 'Social belongingness satisfaction as a function of interaction medium: face-to-face interactions facilitate greater social belong and interaction enjoyment compared to instant messaging', *Computers in Human Behaviour*, vol. 36, 2014, p. 359; Robert Cummins et al., *The wellbeing of Australians: relationships and the Internet*, Australian Unity Wellbeing Index Survey, report 25.0, 2011, p. xvii.

Pages 69–70, 'The average household size …' Graeme Hugo, 'A century of population change in Australia', in Australian Bureau of Statistics, *Yearbook 2001 Australia*, cat. no. 1301.0, 2001; Australian Bureau of Statistics, *Census of population and housing*, 2011; Productivity Commission, *Caring for older Australians*, 2011, p. 1.

Page 70, 'One contemporary example of innovation …' Jo Williams, 'Designing neighbourhoods for social interaction: the case of cohousing', *Journal of Urban Design*, vol. 10, issue 2, 2005, p. 195; John Mangan, 'Co-housing not just for hippies any more', *The Sydney Morning Herald Domain*, 10 April 2011.

Page 70, 'Cohousing gives residents opportunities for meaningful …' Jo Williams, 'Designing neighbourhoods for social interaction: the case of cohousing', *Journal of Urban Design*, vol. 10, issue 2, 2005, p. 195; Jo Williams, 'Sun, surf and sustainable housing—cohousing, the Californian experience', *International Planning Studies*, vol. 10, no. 2, 2005, p. 145.

Pages 70–71, 'Retirement villages and independent living units …' Maria Brenton, *We're in charge: cohousing communities of older people in the Netherlands—lessons for Britain*, 1998; Neshama Abraham and Kate Delagrange, 'Elder cohousing: an idea whose time has come?', *Communities*, issue 132, 2006, p. 60.

Page 71, 'Keeping a pet helps some people …' Bruce Headey, 'Health benefits and health cost savings due to pets: preliminary estimates from an Australian national survey', *Social Indicators Research*, vol. 47, no. 2, 1999, p. 237; Allen McConnel et al., 'Friends with benefits: on the positive consequences of pet ownership', *Journal of Personality & Social Psychology*, vol. 101, no. 6, 2011, p. 1243.

Page 71, 'Rental leases and strata title conditions …' WA Department of Commerce, 'Pet bonds', 2014, http://www.commerce.wa.gov.au/consumer-protection/pet-bonds

Page 73, 'The shape of our cities can …' Graham Currie and Zed Senbergs, *Exploring forced car ownership in metropolitan Melbourne*, paper for 30th Australasian Transport Research Forum, 2007, p. 21.

Page 73, 'Another study found that …' Anne Hurni, 'Marginalised groups in Western Sydney: the experience of sole parents and unemployed young people', in Graham Currie, Janet Stanley and John Stanley (eds), *No way to go: transport and social disadvantage in Australian communities*, 2007, pp. 10.1–10.11.

Pages 73–74, 'For single parents with no car …' ibid.

Page 74, 'An additional problem is access …' Jane-Frances Kelly et al., *Social cities*, Grattan Institute, 2012, p. 15.

Page 75, 'Long commutes corrode social connection …' IBM, *IBM commuter pain survey: major findings document for Australian cities*, 2011, p. 2.

Page 75, 'People who commute for long periods …' Steve Crabtree, *Wellbeing lower among workers with long commutes*, Gallup-Healthways Well-Being Index, 13 August 2010, http://www.gallup.com/poll/142142/wellbeing-lower-among-workers-long-commutes.aspx; Alois Stutzer and Bruno Frey, 'Stress that doesn't pay: the commuting paradox', *Scandinavian Journal of Economics*, vol. 110, no. 2, 2008, p. 339; John Cacioppo and William Patrick, *Loneliness: human nature and the need for social connection*, 2008.

Page 75, 'Long commutes are also bad …' Christine Hoehner et al., 'Commuting distance, cardiorespiratory fitness and metabolic risk', *American Journal of Preventative Medicine*, vol. 42, no. 6, 2012, p. 571; Erik Hansson et al., 'Relationship between commuting and health outcomes in a cross-sectional population survey in southern Sweden', *BMC Public Health*, vol. 11, 2011, p. 834.

Page 75, 'Longer commuting times also mean …' Robert Putnam, *Bowling alone: the collapse and revival of American community*, 1995.

CHAPTER 5 – HOUSING

Page 77, 'In any given year, around 100 000 people ...' Grattan Institute analysis of Australian Bureau of Statistics, *Microdata: income and housing 2011–12*, cat. no. 6541.0.30.001, 2013; Grattan Institute analysis of Australian Bureau of Statistics, *Housing occupancy and costs 2011–12*, cat. no. 4130.0, 2013; Saul Eslake, '50 years of housing failure', speech to the 122nd Annual Henry George Commemorative Dinner, 22 September 2013. Howard's remark has also been reported as 'nobody ever complains about rising house prices': Editorial, 'Housing grants should go', *The Australian*, 22 January 2014.

Pages 79–80, 'In 2011, the Grattan Institute conducted research ...' Jane-Frances Kelly, Ben Weidmann and Marcus Walsh, *The housing we'd choose*, Grattan Institute, 2011. Statistics in this section are drawn from this report unless otherwise cited.

Page 80, 'In Australia, home ownership is seen ...' Grattan Institute analysis of Australian Bureau of Statistics, *Housing occupancy and costs 2011–12*, cat. no. 4130.0, 2013.

Page 81, 'In other words, the preferences ...' Grattan Institute analysis of Australian Bureau of Statistics, *Census of population and housing*, 1976–2011.

Page 81, 'When Grattan asked the people ...' Jane-Frances Kelly, Ben Weidmann and Marcus Walsh, *The housing we'd choose*, Grattan Institute, 2011, p. 16. Rows and columns in the table may not exactly sum due to rounding.

Page 82, 'The survey was repeated in Perth ...' WA Department of Planning, *The housing we'd choose: a study for Perth and Peel*, 2013.

Page 83, 'Australia's accumulated stock of housing ...' Australian Bureau of Statistics, *Census of population and housing*, 1976 and 2011.

Page 84, 'Our research found that only ...' Jane-Frances Kelly, Ben Weidmann and Marcus Walsh, *The housing we'd choose*, Grattan Institute, 2011, p. 27.

Page 84, 'Meanwhile, in Australia's largest cities ...' ibid.

Page 85, 'Getting permission to build new housing ...' Productivity Commission, *Performance benchmarking of Australian business regulation: planning, zoning and development assessments*, 2011, p. 259.

Page 85, 'In a 2011 report, the Productivity Commission ...' ibid., pp. xxvi, xxvii, xxviii.

Page 85, 'Different rules and plans ...' ibid., pp. xxvii, xliv.

Page 85, 'Decisions about how land is used ...' ibid., pp. xxxix–xl.

Page 86, 'In many states, local residents ...' ibid., p. xxxvi; Nicole Cook et al., *Resident third party objections and appeals against planning applications: implications for higher density and social housing*, AHURI positioning paper no. 145, 2012, p. 10.

Page 86, 'Like convoluted planning and zoning arrangements ...' Elizabeth Jean Taylor, 'Do house values influence resistance to development?', *Urban Policy and Research*, vol. 31, no. 1, p. 18.

Page 86, 'After a development application ...' Nicole Cook et al., *Resident third party objections and appeals against planning applications: implications for higher density and social housing*, AHURI final report no. 197, 2012, p. 42.

Page 86, Developers report that delays getting permission ...' Chalpat Sonti, 'Housing shortage getting worse', *WA Today*, 28 April 2010.

Page 87, 'Complex rules and processes for getting permission ...' Independent Commission Against Corruption, *Anti-corruption safeguards and the NSW planning system*, 2012, p. 18.

Page 87, 'Land is the biggest contributor ...' Real Estate Institute of Western Australia, *Suburb profiles*, accessed September 2014, http://reiwa.com.au/The-WA-Market/Suburb-Profiles-Search/

Page 87, 'Land is also the biggest contributor ...' Australian Bureau of Statistics, *House price indexes: eight capital cities*, cat. no. 6416.0, September 2013, tables 1–6; Grattan Institute analysis of Australian Bureau of Statistics, *Census of population and housing*, 2011.

Page 88, 'We've seen that building housing ...' Mariano Kulish, Anthony Richards and Christian Gillitze, 'Urban structure and housing prices: some evidence from Australian cities', Reserve Bank of Australia research discussion paper, 2011; Nicole Cook et al., *Resident third party objections and appeals against planning applications: implications for higher density and social housing*, Australian Housing and Urban Research Institute final report no. 197, 2012, p. 8; Ryan Avent, *The gated city*, 2011; Council for Community and Economic Research, *Cost of living index 2013*, 2014; Edward Glaeser and Joseph Gyourko, *The impact of zoning on housing affordability*, National Bureau of Economic Research working paper no. 8835, 2002.

Page 89, 'Material and labour costs make buildings ...' Rider Levett Bucknall, *Riders Digest 2014*, 2014, p. 22.

Page 90, 'In recent years, nowhere near enough ...' Jane-Frances Kelly, Ben Weidmann and Marcus Walsh, *The housing we'd choose*, Grattan Institute, 2011, p. 27; Australian Bureau of Statistics, *Building approvals*, cat. no. 8731.0, July 2014, table 10.

Page 90, 'Until recently, greenfield development ...' Jane-Frances Kelly, Ben Weidmann and Marcus Walsh, *The housing we'd choose*, Grattan Institute, 2011, p. 27.

Page 91, 'In contrast, more homes are being built ...' Grattan Institute analysis of Australian Bureau of Statistics, *Census of population and housing*, 2001–2011; Jane-Frances Kelly, Ben Weidmann and Marcus Walsh, *The housing we'd choose*, Grattan Institute, 2011, pp. 27–8.

Page 91, 'Many commentators regard the scale ...' Marcus Spiller and Terry Rawnsley, 'Housing and urban form: a new productivity agenda', in Richard Tomlinson (ed.), *Australia's unintended cities*, 2012, p. 151.

Page 92, 'Over time, home buyers on average incomes ...' SGS Economics & Planning, 'House prices creating a divided city', *Urbecon*, vol. 1, 2011, p. 7.

Page 92, 'Consequently, in recent decades house prices ...' Anthony Richards, 'Some observations on the cost of housing in Australia', address to the Melbourne Institute Economic and Social Outlook Conference, 27 March 2008; Luci Ellis, 'Space and stability: some reflections on the housing–finance system', speech to the CITI Residential Housing Conference, 15 May 2014.

Pages 92–93, 'Another factor making it harder ...' Elizabeth Taylor and Richard Watling, *Long run patterns of housing prices in Melbourne*, Victorian Department of Planning and Community Development, 2011, p. 40.

Page 95, 'Statistics suggest young people are finding ...' Judy Yates, 'Explaining Australia's trends in home ownership', *Housing Finance International*, winter 2011, pp. 6–13; additional data provided by Yates based on Australian Bureau of Statistics, *Census of population and housing*, 2011.

Page 95, 'It isn't certain whether this decline ...' ibid.

Pages 95–96, 'Home ownership is also out of reach ...' ibid.

Page 97, 'Anne Power and Laura Lane ...' Anne Power and Laura Lane, *Housing futures: our homes and communities*, London School of Economics Centre for Analysis of Social Exclusion—report for the Federation of Master Builders, 2010, p. 20.

Page 97, 'A major contributor to increasing divides ...' Australian Bureau of Statistics, *Housing occupancy and costs 2011–12*, cat. no. 4130.0, 2013, pp.18–19; Christopher Kent, 'Recent developments in the Australian housing market', speech to the Australian Institute of Building, 14 March 2013.

Page 97, 'Some contributors to this house price growth ...' Australian Bureau of Statistics, *Australian demographic statistics*, cat. no. 3101.0, table 1; Graeme Hugo, 'A century of population change in Australia', in Australian Bureau of Statistics, *Yearbook 2001 Australia*, cat. no. 1301.0, 2001; Australian Bureau of Statistics, *Census of population and housing*, 2011.

Page 97, 'A more problematic cause of house prices ...' National Housing Supply Council, *Housing supply and affordability—key indicators 2012*, 2012, p. 23.

Pages 97–98, 'But, not enough homes are being built ...' Mark Mulligan, 'Joe Hockey denies Australia in a property bubble', *The Sydney Morning Herald*, 16 September 2014.

Page 98, 'Sometimes rising demand for Australian real estate ...' Paul Sheehan, 'Cashed-up Chinese are pricing the young out of the property market', *The Sydney Morning Herald*, 10 March 2014; Michael Janda, 'Regulator lacks resources to enforce foreign home buyer restrictions', ABC online, 31 May 2014.

Page 98, 'Reserve Bank analysis suggests ...' Reserve Bank of Australia, *Submission to the inquiry into foreign investment in residential real estate*, 2014, p. 3.

Page 98, 'One consequence of rising prices ...' Judy Yates, 'Housing in Australia in the 2000s: on the agenda too late?', in Reserve Bank of Australia, *The Australian economy in the 2000s*, 2011, p. 280.

Page 99, 'Over the last fifty years ...' Saul Eslake, '50 years of housing failure', speech to the 122nd Annual Henry George Commemorative Dinner, 22 September 2013.

Page 99, 'First-home buyer assistance has largely ...' Council of Australian Governments, *Housing supply and affordability report*, 2012, p. 26

Page 99, 'Tax concessions for property investors ...' Nicola Trotman, 'Should negative gearing be abolished', *Crikey*, 29 October 2013.

Page 99, 'Negative gearing allows investors ...' John Daley et al., *Balancing budgets: tough choices we need—supporting analysis*, Grattan Institute, 2013, pp. 20–1.

Pages 99–100, 'Tax concessions from negative gearing ...' Reserve Bank of Australia, *Submission to the Productivity Commission inquiry on first home ownership*, 2003, table 8. Affordability is measured by each country's ratio of median prices to median incomes—see Demographia, *10th annual international housing affordability survey*, 2014, p. 11. See also Michela Scatigna, Robert Szemere and Kostas Tsatsaronis, 'Residential property price statistics across the globe', *Bank of International Settlements quarterly review*, September 2014, p. 71; International Monetary Fund, *Global housing watch*, September 2014, http://www.imf.org/external/research/housing/index.htm; Saul Eslake, '50 years of housing failure', speech to the 122nd Annual Henry George Commemorative Dinner, 22 September 2013.

Page 100, 'In addition, capital gains tax rules ...' Commonwealth Treasury, *Tax expenditures statement 2013–14*, 2014, p. 12.

Page 100, 'These tax concessions are not resulting ...' Australian Bureau of Statistics, *Lending finance*, cat. no. 5671.0, July 2014, table 8.

Page 100, 'Tax concessions for housing investors ...' John Daley et al., *Balancing budgets: tough choices we need—supporting analysis*, Grattan Institute, 2013, pp. 17, 21.

Pages 100–101, 'While they stimulate very little new construction ...' 'Malcolm Edey and Luci Ellis, 'Opening remarks – inquiry into affordable housing', Reserve Bank of Australia evidence to Senate Economics References Committee, 2 October 2014; Grattan Institute analysis of Australian Bureau of Statistics, *Housing occupancy and costs 1995–96 to 2011–12*, cat. no. 4130.0, 1997–2013; Wendy Stone et al., *Long-term private rental in a changing Australian private rental sector*, Australian Housing and Urban Research Institute final report no. 209, 2013, p. 25.

Page 101, 'These tax concessions ...' David Murray et al., *Financial system inquiry—final report*, 2014, p. 278.

Page 103, 'Households renting their home represent ...' Wendy Stone et al., *Long-term private rental in a changing Australian private rental sector*, Australian Housing and Urban Research Institute final report no. 209, 2013, p. 22; Aida Caldera-Sánchez and Dan Andrews, *To move or not to move: what drives residential mobility rates in the OECD?*, 2011, p. 21.

Page 104, 'The result is that renters move much more frequently ...' Kath Scanlon and Ben Kochan (eds), *Towards a sustainable private rented sector: The lessons from other countries*, 2011; Kath Hulse, Vivienne Milligan and Hazel Easthope, *Secure occupancy in rental housing: conceptual foundations and comparative perspectives, Australian Housing and Urban Research Instititute final report no. 170,* 2011, pp. 127–8, 131–2, 154–6.

Page 105, 'Renters also often report …' Rent.com.au, 'What renters want', 18 July 2011, http://www.rent.com.au/articles/what-renters-want.

Pages 107–108, 'The experience of Lauren Beaumont …' Jonathan Kearns, 'The outlook for dwelling investment', Address to the Australian Business Economists' lunchtime briefing, 13 November 2012; National Housing Supply Council, *Housing supply and affordability issues 2012–13,* 2013, p. 7.

Page 108, 'In light of such a shortage …' Anthony Richards, 'Some observations on the cost of housing in Australia', *Reserve Bank of Australia bulletin,* April 2008, p. 28; National Housing Supply Council, *Housing supply and affordability issues 2012–13,* 2013, p. 7.

Page 108, 'Lower-income renters' affordability problems …' National Housing Supply Council, *Housing supply and affordability—key indicators 2012,* 2012, p. 47.

Page 108, 'Consequently, many households on lower incomes …' Anthony Richards, 'Some Observations on the Cost of Housing in Australia', *Reserve Bank of Australia bulletin,* April 2008, p. 28. Lower-income households are defined as those in the bottom two income quintiles. See also National Housing Supply Council, *Housing supply and affordability—key indicators 2012,* 2012, pp. 42–3; Council of Australian Governments Reform Council, *Affordable housing 2010–11,* 2012, pp. 8, 11.

Page 108, 'Some have to make big sacrifices and compromises …' Terry Burke et al., *Experiencing the housing affordability problem,* Australian Financial Review Housing Congress, 2007, pp. 40, 74.

Page 108, 'Moreover, lower-income renters …' See, e.g., Terry Burke et al., 'Transport disadvantage and low-income rental housing', Australian Housing and Urban Research Institute positioning paper no. 157, 2014, p. 15.

Pages 108-109, 'In Sydney and Melbourne especially …' Housing NSW, *Rent and sales report: time series of median weekly rents 1990 to 2014,* 2014.

Page 109, 'The shrinking supply of public housing …' Australian Bureau of Statistics, *Housing occupancy and costs 2011–12,* cat. no. 4130.0, 2013, p. 21; Carol Nader, 'Crisis in public housing', *The Age,* 31 January 2011.

Page 109, 'Governments once played a major role …' Saul Eslake, '50 years of housing failure', speech to the 122nd Annual Henry George Commemorative Dinner, 22 September 2013.

CHAPTER 6 – TRANSPORT

Pages 112–113, 'Our largest cities were settled …' Graeme Davison, *Car wars: how the car won our hearts and conquered our cities,* 2004, p. 74.

Page 113, 'Debates about transport tend to be polarised …' City of Yarra, 2014, http://trainsnottollroads.com.au/

Pages 113–114, 'Commuting times are increasing …' Grattan Institute analysis of Melbourne Institute of Applied Economic and Social Research, *Household income and labour dynamics in Australia survey*, wave 11, 2013.

Page 114, 'People living in large cities' outer suburbs …' Bureau of Infrastructure, Transport and Regional Economics, *Population growth, jobs growth and commuting flows—a comparison of Australia's four largest cities*, 2013, p. 132.

Page 114, 'Longer commutes are particularly tough …' Grattan Institute analysis of Melbourne Institute of Applied Economic and Social Research, *Household income and labour dynamics in Australia survey*, wave 11, 2013.

Page 115, 'In Wyndham, Melton and Cardinia …' Victorian Auditor-General, *Developing transport infrastructure and services for population growth areas*, 2013, p. 13; Commonwealth Department of Infrastructure and Transport, *State of Australian cities 2012*, 2012, p. 91; NSW Bureau of Transport Statistics, *2011–12 Household travel survey summary report*, 2013, p. 22.

Pages 115–116, 'City centres are where economic opportunity …' Aisha Dow, 'Wyndham council's race to the CBD shows cyclists are on a winner', *The Age*, 3 April 2014.

Page 116, 'Other modes of transport …' ibid.; Bureau of Infrastructure Transport and Resource Economics, *Population growth, jobs growth and commuting flows—a comparison of Australia's four largest cities*, 2013, p. xiii.

Page 116, 'But too many of these journeys …' TomTom, *Australia and New Zealand traffic index*, 2014, pp. 4, 13.

Pages 116–117, 'Traffic congestion is getting worse.' Rosie Squires, 'Morning peak a slow, four-hour slog', *Daily Telegraph*, 20 February 2011; NSW Roads and Maritime Services, *Key roads performance reports*, 2012–2013; Vicroads, *Traffic monitor 2012–13*, 2014, pp. 7–9, 19–20, 23.

Page 117, 'The costs of congestion …' Bureau of Infrastructure Transport and Regional Economics, *Estimating urban traffic and congestion cost trends for Australian cities*, 2007; Commonwealth Department of Infrastructure and Transport, *State of Australian cities 2013*, 2013, p. 275.

Page 118, 'There is only so much road space …' VicRoads, *Traffic monitor 2012–13*, 2014, pp. 3, 14–15.

Page 118, 'An increasing number of seemingly discretionary …' Analysis of Victorian 1978–79 Melbourne home interview travel survey and 2007–08 Victorian integrated survey of travel and activity in Craig McGeogh, *30 years of travel in Melbourne: 1978/79 and 2007/08*, paper for the Australasian Transport Research Forum, 2010, pp. 9, 17; New South Wales Bureau of Transport Statistics, *Household travel survey 2011–12*, 2013, p. 40.

Page 118, 'Congestion caused by a finite amount …' Bureau of Infrastructure Transport and Regional Economics, *Australian infrastructure statistics yearbook 2013*, 2013, Table T 3.3i; Vicroads, *Traffic monitor 2012–13*, 2014, p. 24; Commonwealth Department of Infrastructure and Transport, *State of Australian cities 2011*, 2011, p. 63.

Pages 118–119, 'Bottlenecks can also stem ...' Vicroads, *Traffic monitor 2012–13*, 2014, p. 18.

Page 119, 'Level crossings where train lines ...' Victorian Government, *Cranbourne-Pakenham rail corridor project*, 2014, p. 1.

Page 119, 'Good or bad road management ...' Victorian Auditor-General, *Using ICT to improve traffic management*, 2014, p. 27.

Page 119, 'Roads connect lots of people ...' David Cosgrove, 'Long-term patterns of Australian public transport use', *Australian Transport Research Forum 2011 proceedings*, 2011, p. 13.

Pages 119–120, Cars continue to be the main form ...' See, e.g., Bureau of Infrastructure Transport and Resource Economics, *Population growth, jobs growth and commuting flows—a comparison of Australia's four largest cities*, 2013.

Page 120, 'Cars are especially important ...' Grattan Institute analysis of Australian Bureau of Statistics, *Census of population and housing*, 2011.

Page 120, 'Since 2005, the 40-kilometre-long M7 ...' Ernst and Young, *The economic contribution of Sydney's toll roads to NSW and Australia*, 2008, pp.37–9.

Pages 120–121, 'In response, the government built CityLink.' Imran Muhammad, Nicholas Low and Leigh Glover, *Mega projects in transport and development: background in Australian case studies: City Link motorway expansion*, Australasian Centre for the Governance and Management of Urban Transport, 2006; Allen Consulting Group, John Cox and Centre for Policy Studies, *The economic impact of Melbourne City Link*, consultancy report to the Melbourne City Link Authority, 1996, p. i.

Page 121, 'New roads also fill up fast.' Gilles Duranton and Matthew Turner, 'The fundamental law of road congestion: evidence from US cities', *American Economic Review*, vol. 101, no. 6, 2011, p. 38; Adam Carey, 'East West Link buys time, but won't solve traffic woes, says authority', *The Age*, 28 March 2014; Victorian Government, *2014–15 Budget overview*, p. 8; Linking Melbourne Authority, *East West Link comprehensive impact statement: chapter seven—transport*, 2013, p. 17.

Page 121, 'Driving makes enormous sense for individuals ...' Ed Glaeser, *Triumph of the city: how our greatest invention makes us richer, smarter, greener, healthier and happier*, 2011.

Pages 121–122, 'Public transport can carry many more ...' Peter Martinovich, 'The integration of rail transit and land use in Western Australia', Engineers Australia conference on railway engineering, 2008; NSW Roads and Maritime Services, *Buses*, http://www.rms.nsw.gov.au/usingroads/buses/index.html.

Page 122, 'Public transport is especially useful ...' David Cosgrove, 'Long-term patterns of Australian public transport use', *Australian Transport Research Forum 2011 proceedings*, 2011, p. 12; Australian Bureau of Statistics, *Census of population and housing—method of travel to work, 1976–2011, Australian capital cities*, quoted in Paul Mees and Lucy Groenhart, *Transport policy at the crossroads: travel to work in Australian cities 1976–2011*, 2012, p. 10; Paul Mees and Lucy Groenhart, *Transport policy at the crossroads: travel to work in Australian cities 1976–2011*, 2012, p. 15.

Page 122, 'By enabling large numbers of people ...' Grattan Institute analysis of Australian Bureau of Statistics, *Census of population and housing*, 2011; New South Wales Government, *Sydney city centre access strategy*, 2013, pp. 10–11.

Page 122, 'Each person taking public transport ...' Christopher McCahill and Norman Garrick, 'Automobile use and land consumption: empirical evidence from 12 cities', *Urban Design International*, vol. 17, no. 3, 2012, p. 221.

Page 123, 'A recent report for the Victorian government ...' SGS Economics and Planning, *Long run economic and land use impacts of major infrastructure projects*, 2012, p. 90.

Page 123, 'Increased public transport use ...' Transport for NSW, *NSW long term transport master plan*, 2012, p. 93; Queensland Government, *Inner city rail capacity study*, 2008.

Page 124, 'Public transport usually costs passengers ...' See, e.g., Jian Wang, *Commuter costs and potential savings: public transport versus car commuting in Australia*, 2013.

Page 124, 'Public transport also helps enable people ...' Grattan Institute analysis of Australian Bureau of Statistics, *Census of population and housing 2011*.

Pages 125–126, 'Access is the first barrier many people face ...' Victorian Auditor-General, *Developing transport infrastructure and services for population growth areas*, 2013, pp. 16–17.

Page 126, 'A recent newspaper report ...' Jacob Saulwick, 'For many, public transport is now a private hell', *The Sydney Morning Herald*, 12 November 2012; NSW Department of Planning and Infrastructure, *2010/11 Metropolitan Development Program report: residential forecasts 2010/11–2019/20*, 2011, p. 11.

Page 126, 'In many parts of Australia's cities ...' Grattan Institute analysis of Kurt Iveson and Laurence Troy, 'Mind the gap in our public transport system', media release, chart and accompanying data, 12 November 2012, http://sydney.edu.au/news/84.html?newsstoryid=10504; Chris Loader and John Stanley, 'Growing bus patronage and addressing transport disadvantage—the Melbourne experience', *Transport Policy*, vol. 16, 2009, p. 109; Victorian Auditor-General, *Developing transport infrastructure and services for population growth areas*, 2013, p. 19.

Page 126, 'Once the bus or train arrives ...' NSW Bureau of Transport Statistics, *2011–12 Household travel survey summary report*, 2013, p. 19.

Page 127, 'Congestion slows down many bus services ...' Nicole Hasham, 'Military Road plan: Sydney's northern beaches look to be major beneficiaries of state budget transport proposals', *The Sydney Morning Herald*, 11 June 2014; Nicole Hasham and Leesha McKenny, 'North Sydney cautious about plans to fix Military Road traffic', *The Sydney Morning Herald*, 12 June 2014;

Graham Currie, 'Research perspectives on the merits of light rail vs bus', presentation to Bureau of Infrastructure, Transport and Resource Economics Colloquium, 2009, p. 21.

Page 127, 'Buses further from city centres ...' Victorian Auditor-General, *Developing transport infrastructure and services for population growth areas*, 2013, p. 20; Rhonda Daniels and Corinne Mulley, *Explaining walking distance to public transport: the dominance of public transport supply*, paper for World Symposium on Transport and Land Use Research, 2011, p. 18.

Page 127, 'It is perhaps not surprising ...' Chris Loader and John Stanley, 'Growing bus patronage and addressing transport disadvantage—the Melbourne experience', *Transport Policy*, vol. 16, 2009, p. 107; Peter Newman, *The Perth rail transformation*, Light Rail Conference, 2012, p. 2; Australian Bureau of Statistics, *Census of population and housing—method of travel to work, 1976–2011, Australian capital cities*, quoted in Paul Mees and Lucy Groenhart, *Transport policy at the crossroads: travel to work in Australian cities 1976–2011*, 2012, p. 10.

Page 127, 'The introduction of dedicated busways ...' Australian Bureau of Statistics, *Census of population and housing—method of travel to work, 1976–2011, Australian capital cities*, quoted in Paul Mees and Lucy Groenhart, *Transport policy at the crossroads: travel to work in Australian cities 1976–2011*, 2012, p. 4.

CHAPTER 7 – WHY OUR CITIES STAY BROKEN

Page 130, 'The Commonwealth government is far removed ...' News.com.au, 'Voters want Federal Government response to housing affordability', 15 July 2013; Committee for Sydney, *Sydney: adding to the dividend, ending the divide—2014 update*, 2014, p. 6.

Page 131, 'Yet state governments have tight budgets.' See, e.g., *The World Today*, radio program, ABC Local Radio, 'Bracks needs votes in Melbourne, regions', 4 November 2002.

Pages 131–132, 'The City of Brisbane is a partial exception.' Brendan Gleeson, Jago Dodson and Marcus Spiller, 'Governance, metropolitan planning and city-building: the case for reform', in Richard Tomlinson (ed.), *Australia's unintended cities*, 2012, p. 128.

Page 132, 'The rules set out three zones ...' Victorian Department of Transport, Planning and Local Infrastructure, *Reformed residential zones*, Advisory note no. 50, 2013, p. 2.

Pages 132–133, 'The rules were sensible in theory.' Victorian Minister for Planning, *Reformed planning zones to protect Glen Eira*, media release, 5 August 2013; Clay Lucas, 'High-rise bans in Melbourne's richest suburbs', *The Age*, 16 June 2014; Greg Gliddon and Dana McCauley, 'Boroondara and Port Phillip get mixed results from State Government on planning zones', *Progress Leader*, 18 June 2014.

Page 133, 'The Government's own demographic projections ...' Alan Davies, 'Does this strategic plan really spurn sprawl', *The Urbanist*, 4 June 2014; Victorian Department of Transport, Planning and Local Infrastructure, *Victoria in future 2014: population and household projections to 2051*, 2014.

Page 133, 'Local parochialism can also compromise ...' Victorian Auditor-General's Office, *Managing traffic congestion*, 2013, p. 48.

Pages 133–134, 'However, the inner-city councils ...' Parliament of Victoria Library, *The 2010 Victorian state election*, research paper no. 1, 2011, p. 6.

Page 134, 'Since 1981, Auburn's population has grown ...' Jane-Frances Kelly et al., *Tomorrow's suburbs: building flexible neighbourhoods*, Grattan Institute, 2012, p. 13.

Page 137, 'In a large 2010 survey of residents ...' Productivity Commission, *Performance benchmarking of Australian business regulation: planning, zoning and development assessments*, 2011, p. xxxvii.

Page 137, 'There is a big mismatch between ...' ibid.

Page 138, 'In the lead-up to the 2010 election ...' Victorian Liberal Nationals Coalition, *The Victorian Liberal Nationals Coalition plan for planning*, 2010, p. 11.

Pages 138–139, 'Similarly, when authorities in Portland ...' David Rusk, 'Growth management: the core regional issue' in Bruce Katz (ed), *Reflections on regionalism*, 2000, p. 99; Martha Bianco, 'Robert Moses and Lewis Mumford: competing paradigms of growth in Portland, Oregon', *Planning Perspectives*, vol. 16, no. 2, 2001, p. 99; Jane-Frances Kelly, *Cities: who decides?*, Grattan Institute, 2010, p. 38.

Page 139, 'People in big Australian cities ...' Kym McHugh, 'Public must be involved in planning', *The Advertiser*, 15 March 2013.

Page 141, 'But people benefiting financially ...' Australian Taxation Office, *Taxation statistics 2011–12*, 2014, table 1.

Page 141, 'Three overlapping groups of people benefit ...' SGS Economics and Planning, *Long run economic and land use impacts of major infrastructure projects*, 2012, p. 85.

Pages 141–142, 'The second group benefiting from improved transport ...' Philip Lowe, 'Productivity and infrastructure', speech to the IARIW-UNSW conference on productivity measurement, drivers and trends, 26 November 2013.

Pages 142–143, 'Second, users of public transport only contribute ...' Commonwealth Department of Infrastructure and Transport, *State of Australian cities 2012*, 2012, p. 95; Chris Hale, *Evolving futures for Australian and international passenger rail*, paper for Australian Transport Research Forum, 2011, p. 11; Transport and Tourism Forum, *Meeting the funding challenges of public transport*, 2010, p. 24.

Pages 143–144, 'Today's economy is very different ...' Lisa Herbert, 'Local farmers may not benefit from inland rail line', *ABC Rural online*, 10 March 2014; Adam Carey and Josh Gordon, 'Abbott warns Victorian Libs: no money for urban rail', *The Age*, 4 April 2013.

Page 144, 'Official statistics and data …' See, for instance, United States Bureau of Economic Analysis, *News release: GDP by metropolitan area, advance 2013, and revised 2001–12*, 16 September 2014, from www.bea.gov/newsreleases/regional/gdp_metro/gdp_metro_newsrelease.htm; Eurostat 'European statistics on regions and cities', 2014, from epp.eurostat.ec.europa.eu/portal/page/portal/product_details/publication?p_product_code=KS-02-13-692

Page 145, 'Even worse than failing to understand …' *Sunday Herald Sun*, 'Premier John Brumby admits that Labor has let commuters down', 31 October 2010; ABC Local Radio, 'Vic campaign mastermind says Labor was out of date', *PM*, 15 December 2010, transcript at http://www.abc.net.au/pm/content/2010/s3094222.htm; Ashley Gardiner, 'Vicious backlash in south-eastern suburbs', *Herald Sun*, 29 November 2010; Clay Lucas and Jason Dowling, 'Smoke and mirrors', *The Age*, 6 October 2011.

Page 145, 'Sometimes politicians abdicate responsibility …' Tom Dusevic, 'The second coming of Bob Carr', *The Australian*, 21 April 2012; Peter Harris, 'Infrastructure for an ageing Australia', speech to the Committee for the Economic Development of Australia conference, 9 May 2014, p. 7.

Pages 145–146, 'In the decade after Carr's comment …' Committee for Sydney, *Sydney: adding to the dividend, ending the divide*, 2013, pp. 2, 11.

Page 146, 'First, a common cry is that …' *The Australian*, 'Supply reason for house price surge', 17 September 2014.

Pages 146–147, 'Second, the difficulties of managing large …' Courtney Trenwith, 'Calls for more WA cities', *WA Today*, 15 February 2012; Paul Howes, 'Building new cities in the west', speech to Australia-Israel Chamber of Commerce CEO luncheon, 6 August 2010.

Page 147, 'New cities do better when they …' World Bank, *World development report*, 2009, p. 145.

Pages 147–148, 'Job creation schemes in areas …' John Daley and Annette Lancy, *Investing in regions: making a difference*, Grattan Institute, 2011, p. 24; Productivity Commission, *Trade and assistance review 2010–11*, 2012 pp. 86–7.

Page 148, 'Governments are also frequently called on …' Bernard Salt, 'Welcome to the metropolis', *The Australian*, 17 March 2012.

Page 148, 'But relocating government offices …' Farrah Tomazin and Matthew Murphy, 'TAC offers staff sweeteners for Geelong move', *The Age*, 11 April 2006; Victorian Transport Accident Commission, *Annual report*, 2009, p. 12.

Page 148, 'It can also be incredibly expensive …' Farrah Tomazin and Matthew Murphy, 'TAC offers staff sweeteners for Geelong move', *The Age*, 11 April 2006; Stephen Ward, *The decentralisation of core government services*, Urban Development Institute of Australia, 2007.

Page 149, 'Far too many governments announce grand …' New South Wales Department of Planning, *Metropolitan development program: annual reports*, 2006–07 to 2011–12; see also Committee for Sydney, *Sydney: adding to the dividend, ending the divide*, 2013, p. 11.

Page 149, 'Promises to build transport infrastructure ...' 'New underground planned for Sydney's West', *Network: The Railways of Australia Quarterly*, vol. 27, no. 4, October 1990; NSW Government, *Action for transport 2010: Sydney rail projects*, media release, 23 November 1998; NSW Government, *Iemma government locks in future city rail corridors*, media release, 18 February 2006; NSW Government, *Metropolitan transport plan*, 2010; Sarah Collerton, 'Gillard's $2b rail promise for RSL forum', *ABC online*, 11 August 2010.

Pages 149–150, 'Victorian governments have produced some impressive ...' Victorian Auditor-General, *Developing transport infrastructure and services for population growth areas*, 2013, pp. 23–4; Public Transport Victoria, *Network development plan—metropolitan rail*, 2012, p. 8.

Page 150, 'Major projects aren't the only ...' Adam Carey, 'Epping hell: residents "betrayed" by promises', *The Age*, 15 December 2011.

Pages 150–151, 'If our infrastructure planning systems ...' Peter Harris, 'Infrastructure for an ageing Australia', speech to the Committee for the Economic Development of Australia conference, 9 May 2014.

Page 151, 'Yet the same Coalition policy document ...' Liberal–National Coalition Parties, *The Coalition's policy to deliver the infrastructure for the 21st century*, 2013, p. 4; Infrastructure Australia, *Infrastructure priority list update—December 2013*, 2013, p. 1.

Page 151, 'Separately, the then Opposition leader ...' Adam Carey and Josh Gordon, 'Abbott warns Victorian Libs: no money for urban rail', *The Age*, 4 April 2013.

Page 151, 'Big projects are expensive ...' Productivity Commission, *Public infrastructure*, 2014, pp. 26–9.

Pages 151–152, 'Examples of cost overruns ...' John Daley, Cassie McGannon and Amelie Hunter, *Budget pressures on Australian governments 2014 edition*, Grattan Institute, 2014, p. 48.

CHAPTER 8 – HOW WE CAN FIX OUR CITIES

Page 154, 'In 2010, the Grattan Institute ...' Jane-Frances Kelly, *Cities: who decides?*, Grattan Institute, 2010, p. 7.

Page 157, 'And a significant proportion of the population ...' David Rusk, 'Growth management: the core regional issue' in Bruce Katz (ed), *Reflections on regionalism*, 2000; Martha Bianco, 'Robert Moses and Lewis Mumford: competing paradigms of growth in Portland, Oregon', *Planning Perspectives*, vol. 16, no. 2, 2001, p. 95; Jane-Frances Kelly, *Cities: who decides?*, Grattan Institute, 2010, p. 38.

Page 163, 'Some state governments are using ...' Jane-Frances Kelly, Peter Breadon and Julian Reichl, *Getting the housing we want*, Grattan Institute, 2011, p. 25; Peter Newton et al., *Towards a new development model for housing regeneration in greyfield residential precincts*, Australian Housing and Urban Research Institute final report no. 171, 2011.

Page 164, 'Another beneficial side effect of a simpler ...' Independent Commission Against Corruption, *Anti-corruption safeguards and the NSW planning system*, 2012.

Page 166, 'Change should be introduced gradually ...' Tax Institute, 'Negative gearing—should we move towards the United Kingdom system?', *ConTax*, September 2012, p. 2.

Page 166, 'Some in the real estate ...' Nicola Trotman, 'Should negative gearing be abolished?', *Crikey*, 29 October 2013; Australian Bureau of Statistics, *Lending finance*, cat. no. 5671.0, July 2014, table 8; Jonathan Kearns, 'The outlook for dwelling investment', Address to the Australian Business Economists' lunchtime briefing, 13 November 2012; National Housing Supply Council, *Housing supply and affordability issues 2012–13*, p. 7; SQM Research, *Vacancy rates*, media release, 19 August 2014.

Pages 166–167, 'The second claim is that restricting ...' Saul Eslake, '50 years of housing failure', speech to the 122nd Annual Henry George Commemorative Dinner, 22 September 2013; Australian Bureau of Statistics, *Lending finance*, cat. no. 5671.0, July 2014, table 8.

Pages 167–168, 'The Irish experience shows that changes ...' Ireland Central Statistics Office, *Census of the population of Ireland*, 2002, 2006, 2011.

Page 168, 'For people on Rent Assistance ...' Ken Henry et al., *Australia's future tax system: report to the treasurer*, 2009, pp. 610–11.

Page 168, 'It is hard to see the situation ...' Saul Eslake, '50 years of housing failure', speech to the 122nd Annual Henry George Commemorative Dinner, 22 September 2013.

Page 169, 'Making much better use ...' Infrastructure Australia, 'Transport funding, financing and investment—addressing the infrastructure deficit', presentation to Committee for Economic Development of Australia, undated, p. 10; Rod Eddington, *The case for action: advice to government*, report of the Eddington transport study, 2006.

Page 169, 'Reducing bottlenecks helps to ensure ...' Transport for NSW, *Sydney clearways strategy: keeping Sydney moving*, 2013.

Pages 169–170, 'Dedicated bus (and tram) lanes ...' Victorian Auditor-General's Office, *Using ICT to improve traffic management*, 2014, p. 19; Bruno Lancelot, *The future of trams in Melbourne*, Yarra Trams presentation, 27 May 2010.

Page 170, 'Better traffic-management systems ...' John Wright, Charles Karl and James Luk, *Traffic management systems for Australian urban freeways*, report for Council of Australian Governments review of urban congestion trends, impacts and solutions, 2006, p. 11.

Page 171, 'Even so, targeted, incremental improvements ...' Public Transport Victoria, *Metropolitan train peak passenger loads—May 2014*, 2014, pp. 2–3, 10–11, 26–7.

Page 172, 'In fact, many Australian industries ...' Australian Competition and Consumer Commission, *Regulatory experts tackle tough questions on efficient infrastructure*, media release, 7 August 2014.

Page 172, 'To be effective, a congestion charge ...' National Roads and Motorists' Association, 'Did you know a 5% decrease in trips during school holidays increases travel speeds by 50%', NRMA blog, 29 January 2014; Jacob Saulwick and Andrew Stevenson, 'How do you spell the end of school holidays? Gridlock', *The Sydney Morning Herald*, 16 July 2012; Vicroads, *Traffic monitor 2012–13*, 2014, p. 23.

Page 173, 'There are several ways to test ...' ACIL Tasman, *Pricing congestion in Sydney*, discussion paper prepared for Infrastructure NSW, p. 16.

Page 173, 'Whatever the arrangement, it must be designed ...' John Daley, Cassie McGannon and Leah Ginnivan, *Game-changers: economic reform priorities for Australia – supporting analysis*, Grattan Institute, 2012, p. 30.

Page 174, 'Peak and off-peak pricing ...' Melissa Webb, Simon Gaymer and Peter Stuchbery, *Opportunities for managing peak train travel demand: a Melbourne pilot study*, paper for the Australian Transport Research Forum, 2010, p. 18; Ashley Gardiner, 'Passengers give free morning travel the flick', *Herald Sun*, 14 June 2011.

Page 174, 'Ensuring outer areas have adequate connections ...' Simon Johanson, '5800 more people, still no facilities', *The Age*, 9 February 2012.

Page 175, 'Bus patronage has grown substantially ...' Public Transport Victoria, *Smartbus*, accessed September 2014, http://ptv.vic.gov.au/projects/buses/smartbus/; Public Transport Victoria, *Market intelligence fact sheet*, 17 May 2012; Public Transport Victoria, *Bus patronage 2008–09 to 2011–12*, 2013.

Page 176, 'Public protests and a change of government ...' Bureau of Infrastructure Transport and Regional Economics, *Understanding Australia's urban railways*, report 131, 2012, pp. 51, 55; Committee for Perth, *'What we thought would kill us'—case study 2: the evolution of Perth's passenger rail*, 2011, p. 3; Imran Muhammad, Nicholas Low and Leigh Glover, *Mega projects in transport and development: background in Australian case studies – Perth urban railway*, Australasian Centre for the Governance and Management of Urban Transport, 2006; WA Public Transport Authority, *Transperth patronage*, 2014, http://www.pta.wa.gov.au/NewsandMedia/TransperthPatronage/tabid/218/Default.aspx.

Page 176, 'Perth's railways still lag behind ...' NSW Bureau of Transport Statistics, *Rail journeys*, electronic publication no. E2014–02, 2014; Australian Bureau of Statistics, *Census of population and housing*, 2006 and 2011; Bureau of Infrastructure Transport and Regional Economics, *Understanding Australia's urban railways*, report 131, 2012, p. 52.

Page 177, 'The system's design responds well ...' Commonwealth Department of Infrastructure and Transport, *State of Australian cities 2012*, 2012, p. 97.

Page 177, Frequent services throughout the day ...' Bureau of Infrastructure Transport and Regional Economics, *Understanding Australia's urban railways*, report 131, 2012, pp. 52, 56; Paul Mees and Lucy Groenhart, *Transport policy at the crossroads: travel to work in Australian cities 1976–2011*, 2012, p. 24.

Page 178, 'More dispersed housing in middle and outer ...' Bureau of Infrastructure
    Transport and Regional Economics, *Understanding Australia's urban rail-
    ways*, report 131, 2012, p. 54.
Page 178, 'The Committee for Perth, a local coalition ...' Committee for Perth,
    *'What we thought would kill us'—case study 2: the evolution of Perth's pas-
    senger rail*, 2011, p. 14.
Page 178, 'Another argument for not expanding ...' Tony Abbott, *Battlelines*, 2009,
    pp. 173–4; Commonwealth Department of Infrastructure and Transport,
    2012, *State of Australian cities 2012*, 2012, p. 95.
Page 179, 'Nor is it good enough for experts ...' United Kingdom Department for
    Transport, *Transport analysis guidelines: unit A2.1—wider impacts*, 2014.

Index